MW00578809

Discipleship
Handbook

A Resource for
Seventh-day Adventist
Church Members

ISBN: 978-0-9963136-0-5

Preparation of the
Discipleship Handbook

Background. For many years, the Michigan Conference has sought to develop a culture of active soul-winning and discipleship. In 2010, then Personal Ministries Director Royce Snyman and Conference Evangelist Steve Vail directed a pilot program focused on local church training and discipleship. Out of that effort, and with direction and support from the Michigan Conference officers and Executive Committee, the Training Center Church (TCC) Committee was formed. This committee develops resources to aid local churches in becoming training centers for dedicated Christian workers.

Preparation. Jim Howard served as the chair of the committee and principal author, with Kameron DeVasher, Mark Howard and Staci Schefka also contributing to the original manuscript. The TCC Committee, consisting of the aforementioned authors, Jeff Akenberger, Gene Hall, Tom Hubbard, and Justin Ringstaff, performed the principal editing.

Copy Editing and Design. Hélène Thomas served as the principal copy editor, along with valuable contributions from Emilie DeVasher and Sonya Howard. Kenton Rogers created the cover and layout design, and Stephanie Howard coordinated the printing.

Many administrators, department directors, pastors, and lay people provided helpful counsel and support. To each one, we offer our sincere appreciation.

About the *Discipleship Handbook*

"The practical and succinct nature of this *Discipleship Handbook*, with its corresponding *Mentor's Guide*, will be a tremendous blessing to new and older members alike. What a delight to see the Michigan Conference, through its Training Center Church Committee, focus on developing resources such as this handbook that affirm and educate church members in the Seventh-day Adventist faith while also mobilizing them for personal evangelistic outreach. This is what the Bible and the Spirit of Prophecy instruct and encourage.

"Under the leading of the Holy Spirit, this important *Discipleship Handbook* and accompanying *Mentor's Guide*, adding to the many wonderful resources produced by the church, will help fulfill God's great commission to 'Go … and make disciples' (Matthew 28:19). What a privilege to be part of this great commission and final loud cry to the world, sharing the everlasting gospel in the context of the three angels' messages of Revelation 14. This handbook puts into action the marvelous counsel from the Spirit of Prophecy, 'The work of God in this earth can never be finished until the men and women comprising our church membership rally to the work and unite their efforts with those ministers and church officers' (*Testimonies for the Church*, vol. 9, p. 117). Jesus is coming soon! So lift that banner high and tell of the One who has given us salvation and who will soon return to take us home! Maranatha!"

— Ted N. C. Wilson, President,
General Conference of Seventh-day Adventists

"One of the greatest needs in Seventh-day Adventist evangelism today is nurturing new converts. The Great Commission is to 'make disciples'—not merely to baptize. Without a well thought through, intentional strategy of discipleship, new converts will often be spiritually weak or leave the church altogether. The *Discipleship Handbook* is a practical guide for new converts. It shares how they can grow in Christ and provides an understanding of the life and culture of the Seventh-day Adventist Church. This ready reference guide for new converts provides the biblical foundation for them to be strong in the faith themselves and also Spirit-filled witnesses for Christ. I highly recommend it for pastors and evangelists and plan to provide it to the newly baptized converts in our evangelistic meetings."

— Mark Finley, International Evangelist

"Continuing to grow in faith is the privilege of all believers. The *Discipleship Handbook* will encourage your growth as a disciple of Christ, connecting you with the powerful principles of God's Word and leading you deeper into a fulfilling relationship with Jesus."

— John Bradshaw, Speaker/Director, It Is Written

"This *Discipleship Handbook* and its companion *Mentor's Guide* are powerful new tools for the gospel commission of "making disciples." They are very balanced, and extremely practical, and I hope they become widely available around the world church to help leaders and members carry out the Lord's commission."

— Jerry Page, Ministerial Secretary,
    General Conference of Seventh-day Adventists

"I have never read anything better on discipleship than this *Discipleship Handbook*. Its organization, completeness, faithfulness to the Bible, and clarity are remarkable. But its best jewel is its content. Nothing important to be a good Seventh-day Adventist disciple is missing. Every Adventist should read and practice its content. Personal spiritual growth and the growth of the church in membership would be a permanent reality. God will bless everyone who practices its teachings."

— Mario Veloso, Former Associate Secretary,
General Conference of Seventh-day Adventists

"The valuable information and practical instruction given in this *Discipleship Handbook* will prepare the church to engage in the joyful experience of making disciples who make other disciples. As you read this new resource, my hope is that the conviction of the Holy Spirit will burn in your heart and mind, leading you to become a living link in the great chain of disciples described in Matthew 28:19-20. Following our Lord's command, we can reach the world with the message of the gospel, grow in grace, and one day enjoy the hope of heaven that today vibrates in our hearts!"

— Guillermo Biaggi, Vice-President,
General Conference of Seventh-day Adventists

"Few books present in such a clear, practical, and well-rounded way what it really means to take the Great Commission to the world, as this *Discipleship Handbook,* with its companion *Mentor's Guide.* If you want to understand the mission of the church, and true discipleship, you need to read this book."

> — Robert Costa, Associate Ministerial Secretary,
> World Evangelism & Church Growth Coordinator,
> General Conference of Seventh-day Adventists

"With the passing of time, Christian denominations tend to secularize and institutionalize, losing much of their original identity and missionary passion. The *Discipleship Handbook* can be extremely useful in transforming old and new believers into active missionaries of the Adventist message. This book should be required reading for every Seventh-day Adventist who would like to see the preaching of the everlasting gospel accomplished in this generation."

> — Alberto R. Timm, Associate Director,
> Ellen G. White Estate, Inc.

"This *Discipleship Handbook* will be very useful to confirm new believers in the truth. It does not replace the usual Bible studies that prepare people for baptism, but it is rather a wonderful complement. I sincerely hope that it will be used in all of our churches. I am sure that it will bring results for eternal life."

> — Carlos A. Steger, Dean of Theology,
> River Plate University, Argentina

Table of Contents

Section 5 - **Christian Lifestyle**

Section 6 - **Cycle of Evangelism**

Appendices

Introduction

There is no higher calling than to be a disciple of Jesus Christ. Nothing compares to knowing and following the Savior of the world. To know Him is to love Him, and to follow Him is a wonderful adventure. Still, the discipleship journey is full of pitfalls and snares that threaten to lead us away from the narrow path that leads to heaven. If the devil had his way, every Christian would be lulled to spiritual slumber or led into forbidden paths that would steal the heart away from God. Therefore, it is not enough to merely become a baptized Christian. It is imperative that we continue to grow into active and mature disciples of Christ.

The *Discipleship Handbook* will benefit anyone seeking such an experience with Jesus. Its primary use is in conjunction with the accompanying *Mentor's Guide* as part of a 6-month discipleship process for Seventh-day Adventist church members. The 26 chapters in this handbook correspond with 26 weekly meetings between member and mentor. Over these 26 weeks, indispensable spiritual habits will be formed. Without these vital components of the Christian life, we are in danger of having a form of godliness without the power (see 2 Timothy 3:5). The *Discipleship Handbook,* when approached with a sincere heart, is a tool that can keep the heart burning with love for Christ and the life active in ministry to others. To aid in this development is the purpose of the *Discipleship Handbook.*

Section 1

Discipleship

1

To Be Like Jesus

"A disciple is not above his teacher, but everyone who is perfectly trained will be like his teacher" (Luke 6:40). Here in one short statement is outlined the object of the Christian life. The goal of every true disciple is to be like Jesus.

When Jesus called the disciples He said, "Follow Me;" not merely "Follow My teachings," but "Follow Me." We cannot truly follow His instruction apart from Him. A review of the earthly ministry of Jesus reveals that His disciples were with Him nearly everywhere He went. They learned to pray by listening to Jesus pray. They learned the importance of Scripture by seeing how Jesus depended on the Scriptures. They learned to love by seeing love in action in the life and ministry of Jesus. Jesus said, "By this all will know that you are My disciples, if you have love for one another" (John 13:35). In other words, "When people see you acting like Me, they will know you are My disciples."

Discipleship is the process of becoming like Jesus by spending time with Jesus. Discipleship classes alone won't do it. Religious forms won't do it. The personal relationship between disciple and Teacher is the heart of discipleship.

The Cost of Discipleship

While our relationship with Jesus brings us great joy, some of Christ's strongest statements emphasize the cost of following Him and of being His disciple. "If anyone desires to come after Me, let him deny himself, and take up his cross, and follow Me. For whoever desires to save his life will lose it, but whoever loses his life for My sake will find it" (Matthew 16:24-25). "Whoever of you does not forsake all that he has cannot be My disciple" (Luke 14:33).

According to Jesus, discipleship involves self-denial and sacrifice. It is not for those seeking popularity or selfish pursuits. Jesus said that the gate is narrow and the way difficult for those who follow Him (see Matthew 7:14). He reminds us, "If the world hates you, you know that it hated Me before it hated you" (John 15:18). The true disciple will face opposition for standing out from the crowd.

Compelling Love

With such a cost, why would we want to follow Jesus? Quite simply, because we love Him! We surrender all to follow Jesus because we have found the "pearl of great price" (Matthew 13:46). We have had our hearts changed by the unconditional love of a crucified Savior. "For the love of Christ compels us" (2 Corinthians 5:14). "We love Him because He first loved us" (1 John 4:19). The book *Steps to Christ* reminds us that "when love springs up in the heart" it makes every burden light. "Duty becomes a delight, and sacrifice a pleasure" (*Steps to Christ,* p. 59). Rather than following Jesus out of fear of loss or hope of gain, genuine Christians do so willingly and joyfully out of love for the One who, as Paul so beautifully stated, "loved me, and gave Himself for me" (Galatians 2:20). This great love far exceeds the attractions of this world.

When Jesus asked if the cost of discipleship was too high, Peter answered for every disciple down through the ages when he said, "To whom shall we go? You have the words of eternal life" (John 6:68). And so He does. For He has promised that "there is no one who has left house or brothers or sisters or father or mother or wife or children or lands, for My sake and the gospel's, who shall not receive a hundredfold now in this time

> "The love of Christ compels us."

… and in the age to come, eternal life" (Mark 10:29-30). The benefits of following Jesus far outweigh the cost; not merely because of golden streets or immortal bodies, but because of the unsurpassed peace and joy found in fellowship with Christ. As the Lord assured Abraham, so He now assures us, "I am … your exceedingly great reward" (Genesis 15:1).

Surrounded by the Spirit

Jesus taught that the "first and great commandment" of the law was found in Deuteronomy 6:5, "You shall love the Lord your God with all your heart, with all your soul, and with all your strength." Immediately after this instruction in Deuteronomy, we find the secret to a victorious Christian life: "And these words which I command you today shall be in your heart. You shall teach them diligently to your children, and shall talk of them when you sit in your house, when you walk by the way, when you lie down, and when you rise up. … You shall write them on the doorposts of your house and on your gates" (Deuteronomy 6:6-9). It was not enough to avoid the idolatry and worldliness of the surrounding nations. God's people were also to guard their hearts by surrounding themselves with the law of God.

Following Jesus in true discipleship requires more than just removing that which is sinful. It must also include adding to our lives that which is spiritual. "For to be carnally minded is death, but to be spiritually minded is life and peace" (Romans 8:6). "Set your mind on things above, not on things on the earth" (Colossians 3:2). We can never be like Jesus if our time is spent focusing on the things of the world. Just as the disciples were with Jesus nearly all the time, we must surround ourselves with spiritual rather than earthly influences. We must add to our lives non-negotiable spiritual activities that will keep our minds set on "things above." Because our sinful natures are so weak, disciples of Christ will carry these out by *faith*—even when they don't *feel* like it. Establishing these consistent spiritual habits is a vital secret to spiritual power.

Practical Application

Below is a list of eight spiritual habits that are essential for the disciple of Christ:

1. Daily personal prayer
2. Daily personal study of the Bible
3. Daily morning and evening family worship
4. Weekly Sabbath school attendance
5. Weekly church attendance
6. Weekly prayer meeting or mid-week small group Bible study attendance
7. Regular personal witnessing
8. Regular involvement in local church ministry

"Where your treasure is, there your heart will be also" (Luke 12:34). If you invest time with Jesus, His people, and His work, your heart will be intertwined with His heart. Then, and only then, can the goal of discipleship be realized—to be like Jesus. As you continue in this *Discipleship Handbook,* you will learn many important things about the Christian life. But above all else, you will establish essential spiritual habits that will transform your life and guard your soul.

Take time to evaluate the list on the previous page. What obstacles do you face in establishing these as regular habits? What re-arranging might you need to do to your schedule? What do you need to remove from your life in order to add these spiritual components of prayer, study, fellowship, and ministry that also characterized the life of Jesus?

Section 2

Devotional Life

2

Spirit and Life

J esus didn't just know the Scriptures; He depended on them. He spoke of them, not merely as something beneficial, but as something vital to life itself. When weariness and hunger plagued Him in the wilderness and the devil enshrouded Him in clouds of perplexity and temptation, Jesus did not consult His feelings. He did not consult His reason, or His knowledge, or His heart. There was only one thing He knew He could trust. And so He answered the devil not with His own words or thoughts, but with the words of Scripture—"It is written … It is written … It is written" (Matthew 4:4, 7, 10). The Scriptures were more than motivational or inspirational to Jesus. They were His lifeline. "It is written, 'Man shall not live by bread alone, but by every word that proceeds from the mouth of God'" (Matthew 4:4).

When Jesus was pushed to the brink, He found victory by relying upon the divine inspiration of God's Word. So it is with us. We must have a power and wisdom greater than ourselves to navigate the storms and temptations of daily life. This power and wisdom can be found only in God's Word, the written revelation of "Christ the power of God and the wisdom of God" (1 Corinthians 1:24).

The Source of Spiritual Life and Power

"Unless you eat the flesh of the Son of Man and drink His blood, you have no life in you" (John 6:53). This mysterious statement was a turning point in the ministry of Jesus. Soon after speaking these words, many of His disciples "went back and walked with Him no more" (John 6:66). What did Jesus mean by saying that we must "eat the flesh of the Son of Man and drink His blood?" These words were not to be taken literally, but spiritually, as Jesus later explained, "The words that I speak to you are spirit, and they are life" (John 6:63).

The Word of God is the Christian's source of life and power. Jesus was saying that without regularly feeding on His Word,

Daily Bible reading and prayer is referred to as the "devotional life" because we must be devoted to it.

"you have no life in you." The Bible gives valuable information about history, vital instruction regarding salvation and the Christian life, warnings about the future, and a knowledge of the character of God. But even this broad description falls short of the primary function of the Word of God for the disciple of Christ. What is that function? To give life—spiritual life. Without "eating" the Word of God, we have no spiritual life in us.

Consider the following Bible texts, noting the allusions to the spiritual life found in the Word: "The words I speak to you are spirit, and they are *life*" (John 6:63); "For the word of God is *living* and powerful" (Hebrews 4:12); "Man shall not *live* by bread alone, but by every word that proceeds from the mouth of God" (Deuteronomy 8:3; Matthew 4:4); "Having been *born* again … through the word of God" (1 Peter 1:23). These texts reveal that the Bible is more than a guide for living; it creates spiritual life itself. There is creative power in God's Word.

When God said, "Let there be light," there was light. "He spoke and it was done, He commanded and it stood fast" (Psalm 33:9). In the same way, reading God's Word can create a love for spiritual things where before there was none. We are "born again … through the word" (1 Peter 1:23). And just as we receive new life from the Word, we must be kept spiritually alive by the same Word. "As you therefore have received Christ Jesus the Lord, so walk in Him" (Colossians 2:6). "If you continue in My word, then you are truly disciples of Mine" (John 8:31 NASB). We must continue to drink the "pure milk of the word" so that we may "grow thereby" (1 Peter 2:2).

The Devotional Life

Because we need the Bible to maintain spiritual life, we cannot safely pick up or leave off the reading of it on a whim. We must make daily Bible reading a spiritual habit in our lives. If we at first fail to understand or feel blessed by reading the Bible, we should not be discouraged. If by faith we remain consistent, God will in time fulfill His promise, "The entrance of Your words gives light; it gives understanding to the simple" (Psalm 119:130). Daily Bible reading, along with daily personal prayer, is referred to as the "devotional life" because we must be devoted to it. It takes a commitment. It is not optional for the Christian because without it our eternal destiny is on shaky ground. We may go to church, be kind to others, and give to the poor, but without regular time in God's Word there will be a decay of personal spiritual life. Temptation will overpower us and deception will find us to be easy targets. *The Great Controversy,* page 519, says it this way, "Satan well knows that all whom he can lead to neglect prayer and the searching of the Scriptures, will be overcome by his attacks. Therefore he invents every possible device to engross the mind."

Practical Application

The Bible teaches that "all Scripture is God-breathed" (2 Timothy 3:16 NIV). Just as God breathed into Adam to give him life, so when we read "God-breathed" Scripture every morning it gives spiritual life to the soul. This is why the Bible and the Spirit of Prophecy (the writings of Ellen G. White) are best for our daily devotional reading. These books were written under the special inspiration of the Holy Spirit. Other books may be read at other times with great benefit, but while these books may be *inspiring,* the books we read for our daily devotional time should be *inspired.* We should read what we know to be the voice of God.

In the back of this *Discipleship Handbook* is a Bible and Spirit of Prophecy reading plan that will walk you through the entire Bible at a steady pace. Make a commitment to spend at least 30 minutes a day in prayer and study. When we make the devotional life a priority in our lives, we find that His words "are spirit, and they are life."

After His resurrection, Jesus explained the Scriptures to two disciples along the road to Emmaus. They later said, "Did not our heart burn within us while He talked with us on the road, and while He opened the Scriptures to us?" (Luke 24:32). What a privilege is ours! We can pray for the Holy Spirit each morning before reading the Bible. Then Jesus will open the Scriptures to us just as He did to His disciples, and our hearts will burn within us. Today, Jesus invites you to hold this precious communion with Him through the living Word of God.

Principles for Effective Bible Study

Ephesians 6:17 – "The sword of the Spirit" is "the word of God." Always compare counsel you receive from others, or impressions you receive in your own mind, with the Bible. If an idea doesn't agree with the Bible, don't believe it. "The Spirit and the Word agree" (*Faith and Works,* p. 88).

1 Corinthians 2:14 – Spiritual things are spiritually discerned. Pray and ask for the Holy Spirit before studying the Bible.

1 Corinthians 2:13 – Compare "spiritual things with spiritual." Let the Scriptures interpret themselves by comparing different passages of Scripture.

Isaiah 28:10 – "Precept must be upon precept." Read all that there is on a subject and base your beliefs on the conclusion that contains the greatest weight of evidence.

2 Timothy 4:3-4 – "The time will come when they will not endure sound doctrine." Guard against disregarding the Bible when it doesn't agree with your habits or lifestyle.

2 Timothy 3:16 – "All Scripture is given by inspiration of God." Trust the whole Bible. Don't pick and choose.

John 7:17 – "If anyone wills to do His will" he will know the truth. Be willing to obey truth as it is revealed.

A Method for Personal Bible Study

1. Follow a daily reading plan, so you will always have something to read (see Appendix A).

2. As you read, ask yourself questions to help you focus on the text and discover practical lessons for your life. Here are some questions you could ask:

    ### What?

    -   What does the passage say?
    -   What does the passage tell me about Jesus or God?
    -   What does the passage tell me about the help that God gives?

    ### So What?

    -   Why is the passage important or relevant?
    -   Is the passage convicting me of a sin that God wants me to confess?

    ### Now What?

    -   Is this passage describing some change that God wants me to make in my life?
    -   Is there an example here that I am to follow?
    -   Is there a promise in this passage that I can claim?

3. Write in a notebook at least one lesson God taught you from your reading, and how you will apply it to your life.

4. Conclude with prayer, talking to God about what you learned and asking Him to help you live it out.

5. Meditate on those verses during the day and share what you learned with someone else.

3

The Testimony of Jesus

Long before the Bible was written, God communicated to humanity through prophets (see Luke 1:70). Both the Hebrew and Greek words translated "prophet" mean "spokesperson" (compare also Exodus 4:16 with Exodus 7:1). A prophet is not merely one who foretells the future, but a spokesperson for God. Though the entrance of sin had brought separation between God and man, God in His mercy sent these holy men and women to be His voice and communicate His will (see Isaiah 59:2; 2 Peter 1:21).

During both Old and New Testament times, prophets actively provided warnings, reproof, counsel and instruction from God. For many of these prophets we have no written record of their messages—prophets like Ahijah, Iddo, Isaiah's wife, and Philip's four daughters (see 2 Chronicles 9:29; Isaiah 8:3; Acts 21:9). Still, they provided authoritative and much needed counsel to God's people at critical periods in their history. Other prophets did leave behind a record of their messages, which Jesus called the "Scriptures of the prophets" (Matthew 26:56), and Paul referred to as the "prophetic Scriptures" (Romans 16:26). The

Bible we have today is simply a collection of prophetic writings from the days of Moses to the time of the early church.

The Prophetic Gift Continues

Many believe that once the books of the Bible were written there was no longer a need for prophets. They immediately reject anyone who claims the gift of prophecy in modern times. However, long after the Bible was written, God's people would continue to need the instruction, warnings, and comfort provided by the prophetic gift. This is why, in the midst of a list of spiritual gifts that would be needed in the church to the end of time, Paul includes the gift of prophecy (see Ephesians 4:11; also Romans 12:3-8; 1 Corinthians 12:4-11). These gifts, which also include evangelists, pastors, and teachers, were given "till we all come to the unity of the faith and of the knowledge of the Son of God, to a perfect man, to the measure of the stature of the fullness of Christ" (Ephesians 4:12-13). The gift of prophecy, like the gifts of evangelism or teaching, is still available to the church because we have yet to fully come to "the unity of the faith" or to "the measure of the stature of the fullness of Christ."

Still other evidences are given in the Scriptures that the gift of prophecy would continue after Bible times. One of these can be found in Joel 2:28-31, where God promises that "your sons and your daughters shall prophesy" when the Holy Spirit is poured out "before the coming of the great and awesome day of the Lord." This passage reveals that some will "dream dreams" and "see visions" just before the second coming of Christ. Perhaps the greatest biblical evidence for the prophetic gift in modern times, however, is found in the book of Revelation and the characteristics of God's end-time church.

The Gift of Prophecy in the Remnant Church

In Revelation 12:17, John writes, "The dragon was enraged with the woman, and he went to make war with the rest of her offspring, who keep the commandments of God and have the testimony of Jesus Christ." A woman represents a church in Bible prophecy (see Jeremiah 6:2; 2 Corinthians 11:2). The "rest of her offspring" ("remnant of her seed" in the King James Version) refers to God's faithful church at the end of time. This church is described as keeping the commandments of God, which would include the seventh-day Sabbath, and having "the testimony of Jesus Christ." Later in Revelation, we learn that "the testimony of Jesus is the spirit of prophecy" (Revelation 19:10) and that those who have the testimony of Jesus are "the prophets" (Revelation 22:9). Prophets, serving as messengers for God, do not give their own testimony, but "the testimony of Jesus."

Revelation 12:17 predicts that the last-day church will have unique characteristics. This church will keep all of the commandments, including the Sabbath, and it will also have the prophetic gift to guide it. The Seventh-day Adventist Church affirms that the ministry of Ellen G. White is a direct fulfillment of this last-day gift of prophecy.

The twin characteristics of the last-day church are here brought to view: the *commandments* of God and the *testimony* of Jesus. Another way to say this is the *law* and the *prophets*. These are not new to the student of the Bible. Throughout history, these two means of instruction have been used by God to guide His people (see Psalm 78:5; Isaiah 8:16, 20). However, when the people of God persisted in rebellion against His law and rejected the testimony given by the prophets who were sent to them (see

Nehemiah 9:26), He stopped giving them prophetic visions and dreams (see Lamentations 2:9).

This is precisely what happened early in the history of the Christian church. After the death of the apostles, compromise crept into the church until it eventually substituted the first day of the week, Sunday, for the seventh-day Sabbath of God's law. Daniel 7:25 prophesied that this would happen, declaring that the medieval church would "intend to change times and law." In Daniel 8, this was symbolized by a little horn who would "cast truth down to the ground" (Daniel 8:12). During this time, while the truth of the Sabbath was cast to the ground and disregarded, there was no prophet given to guide the now unfaithful church. When "the Law is no more," then "her prophets find no vision from the Lord" (Lamentations 2:9).

Eventually, both the law and the prophets would be restored. In answer to the question of "how long" the apostasy would continue, the Bible predicted that it would be for "two thousand three hundred days" (Daniel 8:13-14). Just as prophesied, the cleansing of the heavenly sanctuary began in 1844. This event marked the end of the 2,300-day prophetic time period and pointed God's people back to the Ark of the Covenant, the law of God, and the seventh-day Sabbath.

> *The law and the prophets were again working together.*

After many centuries, the truth of the Sabbath was finally being restored. What twin witness would God restore along with the Sabbath truth? The gift of prophecy! In exact fulfillment of the 2,300-day prophecy, God not only restored the truth of His law that was cast down, but He also restored the gift of prophecy when He gave Ellen White her first prophetic vision in December of 1844. The law and the prophets were again working together.

Ellen White herself writes, "The law of God and the Spirit of Prophecy go hand in hand to guide and counsel the church, and whenever the church has recognized this by obeying His law, the spirit of prophecy has been sent to guide her in the way of truth. … As the third angel's message arose in the world, which is to reveal the law of God to the church in its fullness and power, the prophetic gift was also immediately restored. This gift has acted a very prominent part in the development and carrying forward of this message" (*Loma Linda Messages,* p. 33).

Tests of a Prophet

The Bible instructs, "Do not quench the Spirit. Do not despise prophecies. Test all things; hold fast what is good" (1 Thessalonians 5:19-21). We are not to believe everyone who claims to be a prophet, but to "test all things." The reason for testing any claim to the prophetic gift is made clear by Jesus when He warns, "Beware of false prophets, who come to you in sheep's clothing, but inwardly they are ravenous wolves" (Matthew 7:15).

There are several biblical tests that may be used to determine if a claim to the prophetic gift is genuine. Seventh-day Adventists believe that Ellen White passes these biblical tests. Consider the following:

Must confess Jesus Christ (see 1 John 4:1-3). Ellen White's writings consistently reveal Christ as the central theme.

Must agree with the law and the prophets (see Isaiah 8:20; 1 Corinthians 14:32). In contrast with the mainstream religious teaching of her day, Ellen White taught faithfulness to the entirety of God's law and consistently pointed to the Bible as the final rule of faith and practice. "The Lord desires you to study your Bibles. He has not given any additional light to take the place of His Word. This light is to bring confused minds to His Word" (*Selected Messages,* book 3, p. 29).

Predictions must come to pass (see Deuteronomy 18:22; Jeremiah 28:9). Ellen White's predictions have been, and continue to be fulfilled. For example, she described a vision of the Civil War three months before the war began, the San Francisco earthquake of 1906 two days before it struck, and the unity that is presently forming between Protestantism and Catholicism.

Life and influence must be consistent with biblical teaching (see Matthew 7:20). The fruit of Ellen White's life and teachings harmonized with Scripture, and her writings have led multitudes to a genuine conversion to Christ.

Receives supernatural visions or dreams (see Numbers 12:6). During her 70 years of ministry, Ellen White received from God approximately 2,000 visions and dreams. While in vision, she experienced the same supernatural physical characteristics as Bible prophets, such as ceasing to breathe and receiving supernatural strength (see Daniel 10:17-19).

The Bible and the Bible Only

"But if we study the Bible," one might ask, "why do we need to study anything else? Isn't the Bible all we need?" While this question gives an appearance of faithfulness to Scripture, it actually denies it. For it is the Bible itself that reveals the law and the prophets working in tandem throughout history. It is the Bible itself that urges us to test present-day claims to the prophetic gift and accept those that are genuine. And it is the Bible itself that tells us that the gift of prophecy would be a characteristic of the last-day church. In other words, we read the writings of a modern prophet *because the Bible tells us to do so.*

A modern prophet is not, however, a substitute for the Bible. The same Spirit who inspires modern prophets inspired the prophets of old. "Since it was the Spirit of God that inspired the Bible, it is impossible that the teaching of the Spirit should ever be contrary to that of the word. The Spirit was not given— nor can it ever be bestowed—to supersede the Bible" (*The Great Controversy,* p. vii).

It is a sad reality that God's people have been notorious for claiming to follow His Word while living in direct violation to its plainest teachings. The primary role of God's prophets in every age was to point His people back to His Word as the standard of faith and practice. Their purpose was not to *take the place of* the Bible, but to *exalt* the Bible. In *Early Writings,* p. 78, Ellen White writes, "I recommend to you, dear reader, the Word of God as the rule of your faith and practice. By that Word we are to be judged. God has, in that Word, promised to give visions in the 'last days'; not for a new rule of faith, but for the comfort of His people, and to correct those who err from Bible truth."

> *We read the writings of a modern prophet because the Bible tells us to do so.*

Spiritual Discernment for Perilous Times

The apostle Paul describes the period immediately preceding the second coming of Christ as "perilous times" (2 Timothy 3:1). Of these times, Jesus warned that "even the elect" (Matthew 24:24) could be deceived, as Satan works "with all power, signs and lying wonders" (2 Thessalonians 2:9). "All the depths of satanic skill and subtlety acquired … will be brought to bear against God's people in the final conflict" (*The Great Controversy,* p. ix). In order to meet this crisis, God has given us a special manifestation of the gift of prophecy in the ministry of Ellen G. White.

We must remember that without the ministry of the Holy Spirit we can never arrive at a right understanding of truth (see 1 Corinthians 2:14). It is the Holy Spirit whom Jesus promised would guide us into all truth (see John 16:13). One of the primary ways He does this is through the gift of prophecy. To be guided by the Spirit, we must be willing to heed the counsel of the prophets whom the Spirit inspires.

At a time when Satan's deceptions are at their height, when every wind of doctrine is blowing, and we live in an atmosphere of theological confusion, God has given His people a discerning and authoritative voice to unite us on the truths of His Word. The fundamental beliefs of the Seventh-day Adventist Church affirm our conviction that this voice can be heard in the writings of Ellen G. White.

Practical Application

As mentioned in our last chapter, there are many inspirational books that can be read with benefit. But we should not be content to read only *inspirational* books when we could be reading *inspired* books. The writings of Ellen White are a product of divine inspiration. They have been specially given by God to His church in these last days to prepare us for the second coming of Christ. They expose the enemy's deceptive snares and establish the reader in the truths of Scripture. Yet, "many are going directly contrary to the light which God has given to His people, because they do not read the books which contain the light and knowledge in cautions, reproofs, and warnings" (*Testimonies for the Church,* vol. 5, p. 681).

Recommit to spending at least 30 minutes a day in prayer and study, using the Bible and Spirit of Prophecy reading plan in the back of this handbook. Read the writings of Ellen G. White alongside your Bible, and discover for yourself how they illuminate your understanding of the Bible, establish you in the truth, and deepen your walk with God.

"Believe in the Lord your God, and you shall be established; believe His prophets, and you shall prosper" (2 Chronicles 20:20).

4

Secret Prayer

For all the publicity given to prayer in Christianity today, most Christians still don't pray all that much. Prayer is something we know we *should* do, but seldom *actually* do. Not that we don't pray before meals, or during church, or for a moment here and there. But for many, the art of secret prayer evades us. We struggle to know how to pray and wonder if it is actually helping when we do. The good news is, we are not alone. The disciples struggled with prayer, too. In Luke 11, we read about the disciples asking Jesus how to pray. The book *Christ's Object Lessons,* p. 140, gives this vivid description: "Christ's disciples were much impressed by His prayers and by His habit of communion with God. One day after a short absence from their Lord, they found Him absorbed in supplication. Seeming unconscious of their presence, He continued praying aloud. The hearts of the disciples were deeply moved. As He ceased praying, they exclaimed, 'Lord, teach us to pray.'"

The Model Prayer

In response to the disciples' request, Jesus gave us the model prayer (see Luke 11:2-4). And while Christians throughout history have repeated the Lord's Prayer, so beautiful in its simplicity, its purpose was not limited to a word for word recitation. It also taught important aspects of personal prayer:

Our Father in heaven. We are invited to address God using a title that expresses His love and affection for us.

Hallowed be Your name. Approach God with reverence.

Your kingdom come. Be ready to say goodbye to this world.

Your will be done. Determine to obey God's will.

Give us this day our daily bread. Express gratitude and acknowledge total dependence upon God.

Forgive us our sins. Confess specific sins and exercise faith in the sacrifice of Christ for your forgiveness.

We also forgive. Let go of bitterness, jealousy, hatred, and pride.

Do not lead us into temptation. Acknowledge your weaknesses, and seek purity by avoiding temptation.

Deliver us from the evil one. Cry out for victory over sin.

If we believe that the Lord's Prayer merely gives us the exact words to pray, we will miss out on the relationship with God that is built through open communication. "Prayer is the opening of the heart to God as to a friend" (*Steps to Christ*, p. 93).

Practical Lessons on Secret Prayer

In addition to the Lord's Prayer, Jesus taught many other practical lessons on prayer by precept and example:

Pray in a solitary place every morning. Jesus not only taught the importance of alone time with God, He lived it. "Now in the morning, having risen a long while before daylight, He went out and departed to a solitary place; and there He prayed" (Mark 1:35). It is best to pray before the day begins and in a place where you can be alone and without distraction. We should do this every day. "Neglect the exercise of prayer, or engage in prayer spasmodically, now and then, as seems convenient, and you lose your hold on God" (*Prayer*, p. 12).

Kneel, if physically able, during secret prayer. "He knelt down and prayed" (Luke 22:41). Praying on your knees more deeply impresses your own heart with humility before God.

Pray out loud. "Christ's disciples … found Him absorbed in supplication. Seeming unconscious of their presence, He continued praying aloud" (*Christ's Object Lessons*, p. 140). Praying out loud, even if just a whisper, strengthens your faith and helps prevent the mind from wandering during prayer.

Pray earnestly. "Being in agony, He prayed more earnestly" (Luke 22:44). We cannot assume that the Lord will answer casual or mechanical prayers. Ellen White admonishes, "Our languid, half-hearted prayers will not bring us returns from heaven. Oh, we need to press our petitions! … Be in earnest in the matter" (*Prayer*, p. 75). We have the assurance, "The effective, fervent prayer of a righteous man avails much" (James 5:16).

Pray persistently. "Keep on asking and it will be given you; keep on seeking and you will find; keep on knocking and the door will be opened to you" (Matthew 7:7 AMP). Commenting on this verse, Ellen White wrote, "God does not say, Ask once, and you shall receive. … Unwearyingly persist in prayer" (*Prayer*, p. 71). Persistence in prayer is not to appease or persuade God, but to prepare our own hearts for an answer. Earnest, persevering prayer *will change your heart.*

Pray in faith. When we pray, we should believe that God hears and answers our prayers according to His wisdom. "Therefore I say to you, whatever things you ask when you pray, believe that you receive them, and you will have them" (Mark 11:24). By faith, we may present before God the promises of His Word. "Every promise in the word of God furnishes us with subject matter for prayer" (*Thoughts from the Mount of Blessing*, p. 133).

Pray for purity of soul. "With earnest, fervent prayer plead for purity of soul" (*Prayer*, p. 13). We may be able to change outward behavior through strong willpower, but only communion with God can purify the thoughts and motives of the heart.

Pray for the Holy Spirit. Pray that the Lord will convert your soul anew every day. Ask specifically for the Holy Spirit. "As never before we must pray for the Holy Spirit to be more abundantly bestowed upon us" (*Gospel Workers,* p. 288). You may claim the promise of Jesus, "If you … know how to give good gifts to your children, how much more will your heavenly Father give the Holy Spirit to those who ask Him!" (Luke 11:13). In addition to power for daily living, the Holy Spirit will also lay upon our hearts the things for which we need to pray.

> We must dedicate time for prayer in order to experience the power of prayer.

"Likewise the Spirit also helps in our weaknesses. For we do not know what we should pray for as we ought" (Romans 8:26).

Pray for others. Jesus told Peter, "I have prayed for you, that your faith should not fail" (Luke 22:32). We should pray that health and salvation be given to our families, friends, church members and leaders, and others with whom we share God's Word. Note the confidence with which Paul could write to the believers in Rome, "For God is my witness … that without ceasing I make mention of you always in my prayers" (Romans 1:9).

Take time to pray. "Having risen a long while before daylight … He prayed" (Mark 1:35). We must dedicate ample time for prayer in order to experience the life-changing power of prayer. There are no shortcuts. "A worker cannot gain success while he hurries through his prayers and rushes away to look after something that he fears may be neglected or forgotten" (*Testimonies for the Church,* vol. 7, p. 243). Taking more time in prayer can help us to get beyond mere repetition and become more earnest in pouring out our hearts to God.

Work out your prayers. We are not only to pray, but to live as though we expect God to answer our prayers. "Work out your own prayers, and you will find that you are co-operating with Christ" (*The Signs of the Times,* November 6, 1901). Jesus' life was spent between the mountain and the multitude; between prayer and ministry to others. "He who does nothing but pray will soon cease to pray, or his prayers will become a formal routine. When men … cease to work earnestly for the Master … they lose the subject matter of prayer, and have no incentive to devotion" (*Steps to Christ,* p. 101).

Pray even when you don't feel like it. Jesus taught that "men always ought to pray and not lose heart" (Luke 18:1). It is a fatal mistake to be irregular in prayer; to pray only when we feel close to God or when we sense a special need. On the contrary, "When we feel that we have sinned and cannot pray, it is then the time to pray" (*Prayer,* p. 298). A consistent prayer life doesn't come naturally. It requires faith, time, and commitment. If we lose heart and become inconsistent in our prayers, we open the door for the enemy to come in. "The darkness of the evil one encloses those who neglect to pray" (*Steps to Christ,* p. 94). With stakes this high, we cannot afford to neglect secret prayer.

Practical Application

Chapters two and three of this handbook challenged you to spend at least 30 minutes each day in devotional time with God. Now make a commitment that at least 15 minutes of that time will be spent in personal prayer, applying the practical lessons described in this chapter. Also, develop a prayer list consisting of the names of individuals you want to remember in prayer each day and keep that list with your Bible.

Communion with God is a necessity and a privilege. Although it requires effort and discipline, it comes with a precious promise: "He who dwells in the secret place of the Most High shall abide under the shadow of the Almighty" (Psalm 91:1).

5

By Beholding

The power of the devotional life is that we become like Jesus as we spend time with Jesus. "We all, with unveiled face, beholding as in a mirror the glory of the Lord, are being transformed into the same image from glory to glory, just as by the Spirit of the Lord" (2 Corinthians 3:18). We become like that which we behold. If we behold the glory of the Lord—His character—we will be "transformed into the same image."

To behold, however, requires more than a passing glance. Hurried prayers and a rushed reading of the Bible, performed merely as a task on our to-do list, will fall short of producing the transformation that comes by beholding. The purpose of our devotional life is not merely to satisfy a requirement of God, or to learn interesting stories in the Bible. Rather, the purpose is to change our hearts and lives so that our character reflects the character of Jesus. We need more than *information*; we need *transformation!*

> *We need more than information; we need transformation!*

The Influence of a Christ-like Character

A Christ-like character will give power to the message we preach. "If we would … be kind and courteous and tenderhearted and pitiful, there would be one hundred conversions to the truth where now there is only one" (*Welfare Ministry,* p. 86). Far too many Christians are actually a hindrance to the gospel because, while they profess to believe in Jesus, they act nothing like Him. Rather than being kind and courteous, they are cold, indifferent, or argumentative. Such behavior will repel others rather than attract. "No one has ever been reclaimed from a wrong position by censure and reproach; but many have thus been driven from Christ and led to seal their hearts against conviction" (*Thoughts from the Mount of Blessing,* p. 128).

How much better to display a Christ-like character! Sympathy, humility, and love should be evident in all our interactions with others. We are told that "Jesus did not suppress one word of truth, but He uttered it always in love. He exercised the greatest tact and thoughtful, kind attention … with the people. He was never rude, never needlessly spoke a severe word, never gave needless pain to a sensitive soul" (*Steps to Christ,* p. 12).

> *If the truth we profess does not make us like Jesus, it will lose its appeal no matter how logical it may be.*

While we need kindness, gentleness and patience, we must also not neglect the active virtues of courage, energy and perseverance. Jesus was never idle in the work of salvation. Driven by love, He was active and fervent. He lived a life of strict integrity, purity, and faithfulness to the truth. While He had the gentleness of a lamb, He also had the moral courage of a lion. He did not shrink from speaking truth even when it was unpopular, but "He uttered it always in love."

If the truth we profess does not make us like Jesus, it will lose its appeal no matter how logical it may be. On the other hand, "The revelation of Christ in your own character will have a transforming power upon all with whom you come in contact" (*Thoughts from the Mount of Blessing,* p. 128).

Strength for the Struggle

The goal of character transformation can only be accomplished "by the Spirit of the Lord" (2 Corinthians 3:18). Herein lies the importance of the devotional life. Communion with God brings the Holy Spirit into our experience and gives us power to resist the temptations of the enemy. "When the enemy comes in like a flood, the Spirit of the Lord will lift up a standard against him" (Isaiah 59:19). Oh, how much we need the Spirit of God! Only then will the fruit of the Spirit—"love, joy, peace, longsuffering, kindness, goodness, faithfulness, gentleness, self-control" (Galatians 5:22-23)—be seen in our lives and characters.

While the Holy Spirit will work in us "both to will and to do for His good pleasure" (Philippians 2:13), it must be understood that transformation of character is not an effortless experience. "A noble, all-round character is not inherited. It does not come to us by accident. ... It is formed by hard, stern battles with self" (*Christ's Object Lessons,* p. 331). "Not even God can make our characters noble or our lives useful, unless we become co-workers with Him. Those who decline the struggle lose the strength and joy of victory" (*The Ministry of Healing,* p. 487). With the aid of the Holy Spirit, we *can* find victory in the battle with self; but we must not decline the struggle.

Thoughts and Feelings

Character is not merely defined by our behavior, but "the thoughts and feelings combined make up the moral character" (*Testimonies for the Church*, vol. 5, p. 310). In order for our lives to be truly pleasing to God, we must seek purity of thought as well as action. As David wrote, "You desire truth in the inward parts" (Psalm 51:6). True character development will involve Spirit-led efforts to redirect our thoughts before they go down forbidden paths. "Your imagination was not given you to be allowed to run riot and have its own way without any effort at restraint or discipline" (*Testimonies for the Church*, vol. 5, p. 310).

Just because we do not act upon wrong thoughts does not make them acceptable to God. Jesus taught that to "be angry" (Matthew 5:22) with our brother can put us in danger of judgment. And to "look at a woman to lust after her" (Matthew 5:28) is adultery of the heart. If we indulge in these, or other sinful thoughts, they will eventually destroy us. For this reason, Jesus makes this seemingly radical statement: "If your right eye causes you to sin, pluck it out and cast it from you; for it is more profitable for you that one of your members perish, than for your whole body to be cast into hell" (Matthew 5:29).

While we are not to take these words of Jesus literally, they do advocate going to great lengths to guard against sinful tendencies. If department store fliers fill your thoughts with covetousness, throw them away. If social media makes you jealous or envious of the lives of others, delete your account. If TV or Internet leads you to dabble in immoral content, cancel your service. But remember that to starve the sinful nature is only half the battle. We must also feed the spiritual nature by daily communion with God in order to find victory over sinful thoughts. It is by beholding that we become changed. Therefore, the apostle Paul counsels, "Set your mind on things above, not on things on the earth" (Colossians 3:2). "For those who live according to the flesh set their minds on the things of the flesh, but those who live according to the Spirit, the things of the Spirit" (Romans 8:5).

Practical Application

In your devotional time this week, be honest with God. Say with the Psalmist, "Search me, O God, and know my heart; try me, and know my anxieties; and see if there is any wicked way in me, and lead me in the way everlasting" (Psalm 139:23-24). Surrender anything that would hinder your relationship with the Lord. "In giving ourselves to God, we must necessarily give up all that would separate us from Him" (*Steps to Christ,* p. 44).

As you pray and study each day, respond to the convictions of the Holy Spirit. "Be doers of the word, and not hearers only" (James 1:22). If you read His promises to forgive *you,* accept that forgiveness and respond by forgiving *others.* If you read of His kindness and compassion, respond by humbly changing your own attitude and actions. If you read that covetousness is idolatry, get rid of any idol that is robbing your own affections from God. Every day in your time with God, the Holy Spirit will show you ways to better reflect the life and character of Jesus. Follow wherever He leads.

Remember, however, that the work of character development, also termed sanctification, "is not the work of a moment, an hour, a day, but of a lifetime" (*The Acts of the Apostles,* p. 560). Do not be discouraged if you continue to see imperfections in your character. This is actually evidence that the Spirit is working in your life. "The closer you come to Jesus, the more faulty you will appear in your own eyes. ... This is evidence that Satan's delusions have lost their power; that the vivifying influence of the Spirit of God is arousing you" (*Steps to Christ*, p. 64).

To know Jesus and to develop a Christ-like character is not only the goal of discipleship, but of our preparation for heaven; and the only way to become like Jesus is to spend time with Jesus. By beholding His glory we are changed from "glory to glory"—from one degree of Christ-like character development to the next. One day, we will reflect Him fully. "Beloved, now we are children of God; and it has not yet been revealed what we shall be, but we know that when He is revealed, we shall be like Him, for we shall see Him as He is" (1 John 3:2). What a wonderful promise!

6

The Family Altar

"For this reason I bow my knees to the Father of our Lord Jesus Christ, from whom the whole family in heaven and earth is named" (Ephesians 3:14-15). As Christians, we are part of "the whole family in heaven and earth"—a family that includes boys, girls, men, women, heavenly angels, and the Father, Son, and Holy Spirit. What an incredible thought! The church is to be God's family on earth, waiting for the day when we will be reunited with our family in heaven. God, our Father, has built the entire universe on the concept of a loving family.

Ever since sin entered the world, however, the devil has been out to destroy our families. As a result, it is hard to know what a Christian home should even look like anymore. Not that we don't appreciate our parents and the homes in which we grew up, but in today's generation the dysfunctional

> *We must bring Christ into our families.*

family has become more the norm than the exception. There is only one way for us to experience the joy and peace of heaven in our homes. We must bring Christ into our families.

Union With Christ

"The cause of division and discord in families and in the church is separation from Christ. To come near to Christ is to come near to one another. The secret of true unity in the church and in the family is not diplomacy, not management, not a superhuman effort to overcome difficulties—though there will be much of this to do—but union with Christ" (*The Adventist Home,* p. 179).

As the members of the family draw near to Christ through personal communion with God, they will also draw near to one another. Only a union with Christ can give us the humility and grace that we need in order to live in harmony with other imperfect people! With this union, we may experience an atmosphere of love and harmony in the home.

Family Devotions

In addition to personal devotional time, one of the best ways to restore a union with Christ in our families is to cultivate the important habit of family devotions. In this we have the Patriarch Abraham as an example. "For I have known him, in order that he may command his children and his household after him, that they keep the way of the Lord, to do righteousness and justice" (Genesis 18:19). These are the words of approval given by the Lord Himself concerning the family leadership of His servant Abraham.

As he and his family journeyed from place to place, Abraham did not neglect to build an altar to the Lord wherever he pitched his tent (see Genesis 12:7-8; 13:18). At this altar Abraham and his family would worship the Lord together twice each day. "His was a life of prayer. Wherever he pitched his tent, close beside it was set up his altar, calling all within his encampment to the morning and evening sacrifice" (*Patriarchs and Prophets,* p. 128).

Just as the morning and evening sacrifices were offered in Old Testament times, so a short and interesting time of family worship should bless our homes every morning and evening. "If ever there was a time when every house should be a house of prayer, it is now. Fathers and mothers should often lift up their hearts to God in humble supplication for themselves and their children. Let the father, as priest of the household, lay upon the altar of God the morning and evening sacrifice, while the wife and children unite in prayer and praise. In such a household Jesus will love to tarry" (*Patriarchs and Prophets,* p. 144).

> *As the members of the family draw near to Christ, they will also draw near to one another.*

"In too many households prayer is neglected. Parents feel that they have no time for morning and evening worship. They cannot spare a few moments to be spent in thanksgiving to God for His abundant mercies … They have no time to offer prayer for divine help and guidance and for the abiding presence of Jesus in the household. They go forth to labor as the ox or the horse goes, without one thought of God or heaven" (*Patriarchs and Prophets,* p. 143).

Family worship is as important to the family as personal devotions are to the individual. The time of family worship is an opportunity to express gratitude for blessings received, and to impress each member of the family with the need to "seek first the kingdom of God and His righteousness" (Matthew 6:33).

Regular family worship invites holy angels to guard the home, creates a spiritual atmosphere, and binds the family together. The following counsel, taken from pages 519-521 of the book *Child Guidance,* will help to guide you in the establishment of family worship in your home:

Fixed times for worship. "In every family there should be a fixed time for morning and evening worship."

In the morning and around the sunset hour. "In every family let prayer ascend to heaven both in the morning and at the cool sunset hour. … Morning and evening the heavenly universe take notice of every praying household."

Father, or mother in his absence, to lead. "Before leaving the house for labor, all the family should be called together; and the father, or the mother in the father's absence, should plead fervently with God to keep them through the day."

Secure the protection of angels. "Come in humility, with a heart full of tenderness, and with a sense of the temptations and dangers before yourselves and your children; by faith bind them upon the altar, entreating for them the care of the Lord. Ministering angels will guard children who are thus dedicated to God."

Keep it short and interesting. "Let the seasons of family worship be short and spirited. Do not let your children or any member of your family dread them because of their tediousness or lack of interest. When a long chapter is read and explained and a long prayer offered, this precious service becomes wearisome, and it is a relief when it is over."

Components of family worship. "Let the father select a portion of Scripture that is interesting and easily understood; a few verses will be sufficient to furnish a lesson which may be studied and practiced through the day. Questions may be asked, a few earnest, interesting remarks made, or [an] incident, short and to the point, may be brought in by way of illustration. At least a few verses of spirited song may be sung, and the prayer offered should be short and pointed. The one who leads in prayer should not pray about everything, but should express his needs in simple words and praise God with thanksgiving."

Not to be governed by circumstances. "Family worship should not be governed by circumstances. You are not to pray occasionally and, when you have a large day's work to do, neglect it. In thus doing you lead your children to look upon prayer as of no special consequence."

Not to neglect due to enjoying company. "In our efforts for the comfort and happiness of guests, let us not overlook our obligations to God. The hour of prayer should not be neglected for any consideration. Do not talk and amuse yourselves till all are too weary to enjoy the season of devotion. At an early hour of the evening, when we can pray unhurriedly and understandingly, we should present our supplications and raise our voices in happy, grateful praise. … Let all who visit Christians see that the hour of prayer is the most precious, the most sacred, and the happiest hour of the day."

Practical Application

This week, begin the practice of morning and evening family worship in your home. If you are single, you can apply the practical instruction found in this chapter when you have guests in your home. If you are married without children, you can enjoy family worship between husband and wife. Regardless of your circumstances, make a commitment to establish morning and evening family worship as a spiritual habit in your life. Here is a sample outline for family worship, including ideas for your devotional reading:

1. Opening Prayer (1-2 minutes)
2. Devotional Reading (5-7 minutes)
   - Read a story or passage from the Bible
   - Read an age-appropriate, continuous spiritual story
   - Read a Spirit of Prophecy or other devotional book
   - Read children's Sabbath School lesson and rehearse weekly memory verse
3. Sing a hymn or spiritual song (3 minutes)
4. Closing prayer (2 minutes)

You may also want to consider the following resources that have benefited children and families for many years:

- *My Bible Friends*—4 vol. set by Etta Degering for ages 1-8
- *The Bible Story*—10 vol. set by Arthur Maxwell for ages 8-adult
- *Sing for Joy—Worship Songs for Primaries*
- *He Is Our Song—The Music Collection for Youth*

Other family worship resources may be obtained at: www. adventistbookcenter.com.

"Choose for yourselves this day whom you will serve. ... But as for me and my house, we will serve the Lord" (Joshua 24:15).

Section 3

Personal Witnessing

7

Our Mission

The Seventh-day Adventist Church is sometimes referred to by its members as a "prophetic movement." Those who have attended a prophecy seminar held by Seventh-day Adventists may assume this means that our church is active in teaching Bible prophecy. But the term "prophetic movement" means much more. It is not primarily a reference to how the church teaches prophecy, but to the fact that the church was born out of prophecy! The Bible itself predicted the rise of the Seventh-day Adventist Church. It outlines our history. It gives our identity. The Bible itself mandates the mission of every Seventh-day Adventist.

The Sealing of Daniel

To understand the prophetic rise of the Seventh-day Adventist Church, we begin with the closing chapter of the book of Daniel. Daniel is told to "seal the book" until "the time of the end" (Daniel 12:4). In other words, the prophetic writings of the book of Daniel were to be "sealed," or not fully understood, until a period referred to as "the time of the end." As Daniel listens to two holy beings in conversation with one another, he learns how long it will be until the "time of the end." The answer is given with vivid imagery, "Then I heard the man clothed in linen … when he held up his right hand and his left hand to heaven, and swore by Him who lives forever, that it shall be for a time, times, and half a time" (Daniel 12:7). Students of Bible prophecy know that this period represents the time of papal persecution that began in 538 A.D. It started with the beginning of the civil reign of the papacy and ended in 1798 A.D., exactly 1,260 years later. The book of Daniel would be sealed until 1798 A.D., when the "time of the end" would begin.

The Opening of Daniel

The companion prophecy to Daniel 12 is Revelation 10. Daniel 12 taught us that the end-time prophecies of Daniel would be "sealed" until 1798 A.D. Revelation 10 shows us what happens after 1798 A.D., when the book of Daniel would be more fully understood. In Revelation 10:1-2, a messenger from heaven is introduced who has a "little book open in His hand." This open book is none other than the book of Daniel that had previously been sealed. There are other connecting links between the two chapters. The heavenly messenger of Daniel 12 is called the "man clothed in linen." He is described in Daniel 10:6 as having a "face like the appearance of lightning" and "feet like burnished bronze." The messenger of Revelation 10:1 has a "face like the sun, and his feet like pillars of fire." The messenger of Daniel 12 "held up his right hand and his left hand to heaven, and swore by Him who lives forever."

> *A new understanding opened to God's people as they studied the book of Daniel.*

SECTION 3 - PERSONAL WITNESSING

The messenger of Revelation 10 "raised up his hand to heaven and swore by Him who lives forever." The messenger of Daniel 12 announced that Daniel's prophecies would be sealed until "the time of the end," or 1798 A.D. The messenger of Revelation 10 stood at the beginning of "the time of the end" to announce that the book was now open.

The Advent Movement

In the early 1800's, shortly after the opening of the "little book" in 1798 A.D., God's people began to make sense of the prophecies of Daniel like never before. The prophecy of Daniel 8:14, predicting when the "sanctuary shall be cleansed," was at the heart of this discovery. This cleansing was to occur at the end of 2,300 prophetic days, or 2,300 literal years (see Ezekiel 4:4-6). Through earnest study of the Bible, a Baptist farmer named William Miller made a startling discovery. At about the same time as other Bible students around the world, Miller saw that the 2300-day prophecy of Daniel 8 shared the same starting point as the 70-week prophecy of Daniel 9. The starting point for the 70 weeks, the decree of Artaxerxes to "restore and build Jerusalem," was already known to be 457 B.C. Using this as the starting point for the prophecy of Daniel 8, Miller and thousands of others concluded that the cleansing of the sanctuary would occur 2,300 years later on October 22, 1844.

While their prophetic timeline was accurate, they did make one critical mistake. In common with the belief of the time, they understood the sanctuary to represent the earth. The cleansing of the sanctuary, then, was interpreted to mean that Jesus would cleanse the earth by fire at His second coming. Thousands, convinced that Jesus was soon to come, joined the Great Second Advent Movement.

Sweet Then Bitter

A new understanding, albeit with one significant error, had opened up to God's people as they studied the book of Daniel. This is exactly as God's Word had prophesied. Daniel 12, along with Revelation 10, predicted that after 1798 A.D. there would be an opening, or new understanding, of the book of Daniel. The Advent Movement of the early to mid-1800's was a direct fulfillment of that prophecy.

The fulfillment of Revelation 10 becomes even more specific in its representation of this movement. The apostle John is asked to take the open book from the heavenly messenger's hand and eat it. "Then I took the little book out of the angel's hand and ate it, and it was as sweet as honey in my mouth" (verse 10). The eating of the book represents deep study and wholehearted belief in Daniel's prophecies. Thousands were thrilled with the thought that they would soon see Jesus coming in the clouds of heaven! It was truly "as sweet as honey" in their mouths. "But when I had eaten it, my stomach became bitter" (verse 10). Inspiration could not have painted a more accurate depiction of the bitter disappointment that came over those Advent believers when Jesus did not come as expected. In proportion to the sweetness of their expectation was the bitterness of their disappointment. Overnight, thousands abandoned the movement.

You Must Prophesy Again

After using the illustration of the sweet-then-bitter book to describe what would come to be known as the Great Disappointment, Revelation 10 turns to the future. A clear mandate is given to those who experienced the disappointment but did not abandon their faith. "You must prophesy again" (verse 11). There was more truth to be shared before Jesus would come. The scope of their mission was to embrace the whole world—"peoples, nations, tongues, and kings" (verse 11).

Four chapters later, we find the message that was to become the heart of their mission. In Revelation 14, the church is symbolized by three angels proclaiming messages to "every nation, tribe, tongue, and people" in preparation for the return of Jesus. The world-wide message of Revelation 14:6-14 was to become God's final message to a dying world. It was to become the message of the Seventh-day Adventist Church:

"The Everlasting Gospel." Salvation has been made possible through the life, death, and resurrection of Jesus Christ. Whosoever will may be saved by grace through faith.

"Fear God and give glory to Him." This is an appeal to commit our lives to God and prepare for the coming of Jesus.

"The hour of His judgment has come." Just after the disappointment, it was discovered that 1844 marked the beginning of a heavenly judgment. The Adventist Church continues to believe and proclaim that "His judgment has come."

"Worship Him who made heaven and earth." This is a direct reference to the fourth commandment. The final message must include a call to keep God's commandments, including the Sabbath.

"Babylon is fallen." Babylon and her daughters symbolize religious systems that teach errors about the Bible. God's church at the end of time would restore the truth that was "cast ... to the ground" (Daniel 8:12). This includes correcting views on salvation, death, hell, the second coming, and more. When truth is restored, Babylon falls.

"If anyone worships the beast ... and receives his mark ... he himself shall also drink of the wine of the wrath of God." God's people must warn the world against following tradition over God's law. This is God's last offer of mercy. Those who choose to follow tradition are contrasted with the saints in verse 12 who "keep the commandments of God and the faith of Jesus."

In Matthew 24:14, Jesus said, "This gospel of the kingdom will be preached in all the world as a witness to all the nations, and then the end will come." This prophecy is repeated and enlarged in Revelation 14. After beautifully describing the complete gospel message of the Seventh-day Adventist Church going to the whole world, Revelation 14:14-16 describes Jesus coming in the clouds at His second coming.

Practical Application

As a loving Shepherd, our Savior has been leading His people. For our affirmation, He has left a record of our history in the very pages of Bible prophecy. A deeper discovery of Daniel's prophecies was predicted in the Bible. The joyful expectation of Christ's return and the Great Disappointment that followed were both predicted in the Bible. The discovery that judgment had already begun was predicted in the Bible. The re-discovery of the seventh-day Sabbath along with many other Bible truths was predicted in the Bible. The restoration of the gift of prophecy to His commandment-keeping church was predicted in the Bible, as was the worldwide nature of our work. We are truly a prophetic movement. God has inscribed our history in the sacred pages of the Bible so that we can know with assurance that He is still leading us today.

But multitudes do not have any assurance, and are unprepared to meet Jesus when He comes. Therefore, we have a divine mandate to share our message with the world. "You *must* prophesy again" was the command of Revelation 10. Not might, or should, or could. We must. "The world is to be warned by the proclamation of this message. If we blanket it, if we hide our light under a bushel … we are answerable to God for our failure to warn the world" (*Manuscript Releases,* vol. 19, p. 41).

The mission of the Seventh-day Adventist Church is to make disciples of all people, communicating the everlasting gospel in the context of the three angels' messages of Revelation 14:6-12, leading them to accept Jesus as personal Savior and unite with His remnant Church, discipling them to serve Him as Lord, and preparing them for His soon return.

This is the mission of the Seventh-day Adventist Church.

This is *your* mission.

8

Called to Witness

Witnessing is not a spiritual gift. Perhaps nothing has had a more crippling effect upon the mission of the church than the idea that sharing Bible truth with others is the job of the paid clergy, or of only a few "gifted" lay people. The call to share God's Word is given to every disciple of Christ. When calling His first disciples, Jesus made this promise, "Follow Me, and I will make you become fishers of men" (Mark 1:17). If we have chosen to become His disciples, then we have chosen to become fishers of men. The book *Christian Service,* p. 68, aptly states, "The dissemination of the truth of God is not confined to a few ordained ministers. The truth is to be scattered by all who claim to be disciples of Christ."

Sharing the Joy of Salvation

In John 4:10-14, Jesus offered "living water" to a woman of Samaria. In all who would drink it, He said that this water would become "a fountain of water springing up into everlasting life." When we drink the waters of salvation we become a life-giving "fountain of water," sharing the gospel of salvation with others.

"No sooner is one converted than there is born within him a desire to make known to others what a precious friend he has found in Jesus. The saving and sanctifying truth cannot be shut up in his heart" (*The Desire of Ages*, p. 141).

David expressed the same truth in Psalm 51:12-13 when he wrote, "Restore to me the joy of Your salvation. ... Then I will teach transgressors Your ways, and sinners shall be converted to You." It is the overwhelming joy of salvation that leads us to tell others about the truth that has changed our own lives.

You Shall Be Witnesses

Jesus told His disciples that when the power of the Holy Spirit would come upon them, they would become His witnesses (see Acts 1:8). In a court of law, witnesses must be credible in order to be taken seriously. It is important that they have a reputation for being honest, benevolent, and kind. But if they never actually open their mouths to testify on the witness stand, their noble characters won't be of much help! So it is with us. Living godly lives is an important witness in itself, but in order for others to be saved by the gospel we must eventually share it. "Let the redeemed of the Lord say so" (Psalm 107:2).

Witnesses tell what they have personally experienced; what they have seen and heard. While the disciples were able to literally see and hear Jesus, we see Him today through the pages of the Bible. To witness today, then, must include sharing with others the Bible truths that have gripped our own hearts!

Jesus commanded His own disciples to "preach the gospel" (Mark 16:15), which was later illustrated by an angel flying in the midst of heaven "having the everlasting gospel to preach" (Revelation 14:6). To "preach the gospel" refers not merely to preaching from behind a pulpit, but to proclaiming God's Word to others, whether publicly or personally. In the early church, it was not only the apostles, but also the church members who "went everywhere preaching the word" (Acts 8:4). The biblical model of church includes every member actively sharing the truth which they have "seen and heard" (Acts 4:20; 22:15) in God's Word.

Yet many Christians still conclude that witnessing is for "the other guy." Lack of experience, poor memory, an introverted personality, or fear of failure are often given as reasons why "witnessing just isn't my gift." We often forget that it wasn't natural or easy for the disciples to share the gospel either. These were mainly fishermen, not seminary graduates. The reason they prayed "that with all boldness" (Acts 4:29) they might speak His Word, was that they wrestled with fear just like we do! Had they not been willing to come out of their comfort zone, the church would not be here today, and we would never have known the saving truth of the gospel. Witnessing is not reserved for eloquent scholars with outgoing personalities. It is the sacred calling of every disciple.

Moved With Compassion

In order to overcome our objections to witnessing, we need motivation; the kind of motivation exemplified by the missionary heart of Jesus. "But when He saw the multitudes, He was moved with compassion for them, because they were weary and scattered, like sheep having no shepherd" (Matthew 9:36). The compassion of Jesus "moved" Him to labor for lost souls and caused Him to mourn the fact that they had no one to lead them. "The harvest truly is plentiful, but the laborers are few. Therefore pray the Lord of the harvest to send out laborers into His harvest" (Matthew 9:37-38).

Today, Jesus is still looking for genuine disciples who will be moved with compassion to labor for those "having no shepherd." To have no shepherd means that they need someone to lead them into the truth. The book *Christian Service,* p. 69, refers to this "burden of leading souls into the truth" as a responsibility that the Lord has placed upon every church member. If we are Christians, then the burden of Christ has become our burden. Jesus paid too much, and the value of a soul is too high, to allow inconvenience, reputation, or fear to prevent us from giving our best to lead souls into the truth.

This same missionary spirit has compelled the faithful of all ages to share God's Word. Paul considered himself "a debtor both to Greeks and to barbarians, both to wise and to unwise" (Romans 1:14). Jeremiah couldn't shake the compelling duty to share God's Word, but said, "His word was in my heart like a burning fire shut up in my bones; I was weary of holding it back, and I could not" (Jeremiah 20:9). When Peter and John were severely threatened to stop preaching the gospel, they replied, "Whether it is right in the sight of God to listen to you more than to God, you judge. For we cannot but speak the things which we have seen and heard" (Acts 4:20).

> *"If the cause in which we are engaged means anything, it means everything."*

Some causes are simply greater than our fears. The cause of God—the salvation of souls—is just such a cause. As Adventist pioneer Stephen Haskell once said, "If the cause in which we are engaged means anything, it means everything" (James R. Nix, compiler, *The Spirit of Sacrifice and Commitment,* 2000, p. 129).

Vital Benefits

As we labor for the salvation of others, God uses this experience in the salvation of our own souls. This is why soul-winning labor is a necessary part of our preparation for heaven. Consider these incredible benefits that can be gained in no other way:

Joy of seeing souls saved. "In order to enter into His joy—the joy of seeing souls redeemed by His sacrifice—we must participate in His labors for their redemption" (*The Desire of Ages,* p. 142).

Development of spirituality and devotion. "Those who are most actively employed in doing with interested fidelity their work to win souls to Jesus Christ, are the best developed in spirituality and devotion" (*Evangelism,* p. 356).

Increased knowledge of the truth. "The more one tries to explain the word of God to others, with a love for souls, the plainer it becomes to himself. The more we use our knowledge and exercise our powers, the more knowledge and power we shall have" (*Christ's Object Lessons,* p. 354).

Strength to resist evil. "Strength to resist evil is best gained by aggressive service" (*The Acts of the Apostles,* p. 105).

Development of Christ-like character. "In order for us to develop a character like Christ's, we must share in His work" (*The Desire of Ages,* p. 142).

Fitness for heaven. "Those who reject the privilege of fellowship with Christ in service, reject the only training that imparts a fitness for participation with Him in glory" (*Education,* p. 264).

Growth in Spirituality. "Let ministers teach church members that in order to grow in spirituality, they must carry the burden that the Lord has laid upon them—the burden of leading souls into the truth" *(Christian Service,* p. 69).

Is it any wonder that Satan is trying with all his power to keep us from sharing God's Word? He hopes not only to keep others in darkness, but to prevent our own souls from being saved. "Satan is now seeking to hold God's people in a state of inactivity, to keep them from acting their part in spreading the truth, that they may at last be weighed in the balance and found wanting" (*Christian Service,* p. 37).

Practical Application

While we should serve our church and community in various ways, no ministry is a substitute for personal witnessing. This week, incorporate into your lifestyle one or more of these simple and effective methods of sharing the truth:

- Share your testimony of what God has done for you.
- Distribute truth-filled tracts and literature.
- Distribute DVDs on Bible prophecy.
- Study a weekly series of Bible lessons with someone.
- Host a weekly small group Bible study or DVD viewing in your home.

When sharing truth with others, we should remember the words of Jesus in John 16:12, "I still have many things to say to you, but you cannot bear them now." Handing someone every piece of literature you own, or engaging in a marathon Bible study may seem like a good idea at the time, but to do so can result in spiritual overload for the poor soul you're trying to reach. As a general rule, share Bible truth at a steady pace, one major topic at a time. And before sharing potentially sensitive topics, it is best to study areas that will likely meet with agreement, and which will establish confidence in the Bible as the authority for your beliefs.

In laboring for the salvation of others, we are never alone. "We are to be laborers together with the heavenly angels in presenting Jesus to the world. With almost impatient eagerness the angels wait for our co-operation. … And when we give ourselves to Christ in wholehearted devotion, angels rejoice that they may speak through our voices to reveal God's love" (*The Desire of Ages,* p. 297). Not only are we co-laborers with the angels, but by sharing the burden of Christ for lost souls we will find a fellowship with our Savior that can be experienced in no other way. His reassuring promise is especially given to all those who carry the gospel to the world, "I am with you always, even to the end of the age" (Matthew 28:20).

Section 4

Church Life

63

9

Sacred Assemblies

The Bible refers to the church as "the body of Christ" (1 Corinthians 12:27). This symbol helps us to understand the vital importance of being united with our church family. Likening church members to different parts of a physical body, the apostle Paul writes that "the eye cannot say to the hand, 'I have no need of you'; nor again the head to the feet, 'I have no need of you'" (1 Corinthians 12:21). Said simply, we need one another! The church needs every one of its members and every member needs the church. It is spiritually fatal for any Christian to attempt to live a life independent from the life of the church.

"Another obligation, too often lightly regarded ... is the obligation of church relationship. Very close and sacred is the relation between Christ and His church—He the bridegroom, and the church the bride; He the head, and the church the body. Connection with Christ, then, involves connection with His church. The church is organized for service; and in a life of service to Christ, connection with the church is one of the first steps. Loyalty to Christ demands the faithful performance of church duties" (*Education*, p. 268).

The Ministry of Attendance

One of the simplest "church duties," and yet one of the most neglected, is attending church functions. It is impossible to be truly connected with any person or organization without spending time together. When a man and woman begin to spend significant time together in pursuit of each other's affections, we often say that they are beginning to get *involved*. So it is with the church. To be *involved* in the church does not begin with leading departments, sitting on church boards, or taking up platform duties on Sabbath morning. It begins with the simple and natural habit of regularly attending the functions of the church out of a love for Christ, His Word, and His people.

This voluntary sacrifice of personal time not only clearly conveys an interest in the cause of God, but it also increases that interest, providing necessary preparation for any line of service. Our lives become bound up in the life of the church; our affections and interests become one with the church. Only then can the beautiful experience described by the apostle Paul truly become a reality, "If one member suffers, all the members suffer with it; or if one member is honored, all the members rejoice with it" (1 Corinthians 12:26).

The apostle Paul looks beyond the personal benefits of attending church functions when he counsels, "And let us consider one another in order to stir up love and good works, not forsaking the assembling of ourselves together, as is the manner of some, but exhorting one another, and so much the more as you see the Day approaching" (Hebrews 10:24-25).

It is not merely for our own spiritual growth that we should join in "the assembling of ourselves together," but we are admonished to "consider one another." It is incredibly discouraging when only a small percentage of members attend church functions. Those who do attend are tempted to wonder if it is really worth it when so few appear to see any value in the church and its mission. On the other hand, regular attendance tends to "stir up love and good works," encouraging others to keep pressing on and living for Christ. The apostle Paul concludes that this is all the more important as we "see the Day" of Christ's coming "approaching."

Many simply do not grasp that the very life of the church is dependent upon the consistent attendance of its members. We must remember that we are not to be merely consumers, choosing only to attend when we sense the need for a personal blessing or when the scheduled speaker appeals to us. When we become baptized members, we accept the responsibility of being producers—seeking to regularly bless and strengthen *others* in the church.

The importance of attendance is so great, it may rightly be called the "ministry of attendance." Develop the habit of regularly attending church functions and you will forever be an invaluable blessing to your local church. Even if others begin to lag in their attendance, it should only increase your commitment. "With your heart softened by the love of Jesus, go to the meeting, feeling that you are personally responsible for its success. If but few attend, you should feel under double responsibility" (*Pastoral Ministry*, p. 184).

> *The importance of attendance is so great, it may rightly be called the "ministry of attendance."*

There are three weekly, sacred services that should become part of the life of every Seventh-day Adventist: Sabbath school, the Sabbath worship service, and prayer meeting or mid-week small group Bible study.

Sabbath School

Every Seventh-day Adventist church has a time of Bible study, immediately before or after the worship service, known as Sabbath school. There are four goals for the Sabbath school:

1. Study of Scripture
2. Fellowship
3. Community outreach
4. World mission emphasis

This time of study and fellowship, accompanied by mission stories and opportunities for service, is essential to the life of the church. Every church member should be a member of a Sabbath school class.

Still, some members choose to skip Sabbath school and attend only the preaching service. Common reasons for this include a fear of interacting with others, a desire for more sleep or preparation time in the morning, or a lack of perceived value in Sabbath school. We should allow none of these reasons, however, to keep us away from Sabbath school. First, God wants us to interact with fellow Christians, not only for our joint encouragement here, but because we'll be dwelling together throughout eternity! Second, God can help us to get to bed earlier in order to have ample time for sleep and Sabbath morning preparations. And finally, if we fail to see value in Sabbath school, we can ask God for ways to make it more interesting ourselves, feeling that we are "personally responsible for its success." We should let nothing prevent us from gaining and giving a blessing at Sabbath school.

Sabbath Worship Service

The divine worship hour should be the high point of every week for the Christian. Describing the life of Jesus, Luke wrote, "And as His custom was, He went into the synagogue on the Sabbath day, and stood up to read" (Luke 4:16). It was Jesus' custom, or regular habit, to attend worship service every Sabbath. In the Old Testament book of Leviticus, the Sabbath was described as a day of "holy convocation" (Leviticus 23:3), or a sacred assembly. We are not keeping the Sabbath in the fullness for which it was intended if we only worship God alone at home. There is time for solitude, but the Sabbath is also a time for corporate worship. Even in the new earth, the Lord tells us through the prophet Isaiah that from one Sabbath to another, "all flesh shall come to worship before Me" (Isaiah 66:23).

Of course this does not mean that we are never allowed to spend a Sabbath in solitude; but weekly church attendance should be our custom. Even while traveling we may keep our weekly habit strong by attending a nearby Seventh-day Adventist church. This is a great way to get to know fellow believers.

As a rule, we should not hop from church to church each Sabbath, looking for the most interesting program, but we should invest ourselves in the local church where our membership resides. We "are to be producers as well as consumers" (*The Acts of the Apostles*, p. 353). Investing in your own local church will ensure that your sympathies and efforts will be productive of good.

Prayer Meeting or Mid-Week Bible Study

One more area of attendance that should be considered a weekly habit for the disciple of Christ is the prayer meeting or mid-week service. Most churches hold such a service, if not a small group Bible study, to provide a needful spiritual boost to its members. Those who do not regularly attend spiritual functions outside of Sabbath services place themselves at greater risk of temptation. Prayer and the study of God's Word are the source of our strength, and joining together for this purpose during the week is vital to our spiritual growth.

So essential is prayer meeting to the church that Ellen White wrote, "A prayer meeting will always tell the true interest of the church members in spiritual and eternal things. The prayer meeting is as the pulse to the body; it denotes the true spiritual condition of the church" (*Pastoral Ministry,* p. 183).

If attendance at prayer meeting indicates the true spiritual condition of the church, then it must also reflect the truth about our own spiritual condition. "Those who are really seeking for communion with God will be seen in the prayer meeting, faithful to do their duty, and earnest and anxious to reap all the benefits they can gain. They will improve every opportunity of placing themselves where they can receive the rays of light from heaven" (*In Heavenly Places,* p. 91).

Practical Application

If you are not already doing so, begin this week to establish a habit of weekly attendance at the *sacred assemblies* of the Sabbath school, church worship service, and prayer meeting or mid-week Bible study. While it is important to be involved in many other church functions, regularity in these three weekly services will form the foundation of your life in the church until Jesus comes. Your faithfulness in attendance will prove to be a blessing, not only for you, but for countless other souls.

"Where your treasure is, there your heart will be also" (Luke 12:34). Do not wait until you *feel* like attending church functions. *Choose* to invest your time in the services and meetings of the local church, and God will use your ministry of attendance to give you a greater love for Him, His cause, and His people.

10

Sacred Ceremonies

I n our discipleship journey, we share with our local church family many moments of both joy and sadness. "If one member suffers, all the members suffer with it; or if one member is honored, all the members rejoice with it" (1 Corinthians 12:26). Sacred ceremonies and ordinances provide opportunities for spiritual reflection and acknowledge our dependence upon God at important junctures in our lives. Within the Seventh-day Adventist Church, important ceremonies and ordinances include baptisms, communion services, child dedications, ordinations, anointings of the sick, funerals, and weddings.

Baptism

Jesus said in Mark 16:16, "He who believes and is baptized will be saved." Here Christ commands all who profess faith in Him to be baptized. We are "buried with Him through baptism into death" (Romans 6:4). Baptism symbolizes dying to our old, sinful ways and being resurrected into a new life of obedience to Christ. In light of this, the only biblical mode of baptism is full immersion in water.

The baptismal service is one of the greatest highlights in the life of the church and serves as the doorway into church membership. Candidates carefully study the biblical beliefs and practices of the Seventh-day Adventist Church prior to baptism. This ensures that they are ready for this public commitment to Christ and for membership in His body—the church (see 1 Corinthians 12:13). Children are not baptized until they are able to comprehend the spiritual significance of this important step.

In some cases, individuals who were already baptized by immersion while in another denomination are accepted into Seventh-day Adventist Church membership on what is called "Profession of Faith." The only difference between a baptismal service and one in which someone is received into membership by Profession of Faith, is that the former includes the actual immersion of the candidate under water.

The baptismal service typically begins when the pastor or elder reads aloud from the *Seventh-day Adventist Church Manual* the 13 baptismal vows summarizing the beliefs of the church. In the presence of the congregation, the candidate, or group of candidates, positively affirms these vows. This is sometimes followed by a brief personal testimony from the candidate(s). An official vote is then taken from the congregation to accept the candidate into local church membership upon being baptized.

In addition to the actual lowering of the candidate into the water, baptismal services may also include congregational singing, gifts for the newly baptized, and a time for congratulations and fellowship afterward. New members are given a baptismal certificate at the conclusion of the service.

Baptisms are performed in church baptisteries, lakes, pools, or anywhere else where sufficient water is present for full immersion. While often occurring in the local church during Sabbath morning worship services, they may be held at many other times and in various settings.

Communion

The Lord's Supper, or communion service, was instituted by Jesus Himself (see 1 Corinthians 11:23-26). Partaking of unleavened bread and the pure juice of the grape as symbols of Christ's body and blood, we remember His sacrifice and the promise of forgiveness that it provides. The communion service is truly the gospel in symbols, and it is a solemn but joyous service of the church.

Before the communion service, Adventists follow the example of Jesus in the upper room by participating in what is called the Ordinance of Humility, or foot-washing service (see John 13:1-17). This service provides a symbolic washing away of sin, and serves as a welcome new start for the Christian who has made mistakes but has not necessarily so turned from God's will that re-baptism is necessary.

For the foot-washing, men and women go to separate rooms with the exception of occasions when provision has been made for families. In the rooms where the ordinance is to be held, deacons

> *"If you know these things, blessed are you if you do them."*

and deaconesses have prepared towels and wash basins for the service. Each member finds a partner to share in the ordinance. They pray together, wash one another's feet, and often sing a hymn along with others in the room. It is a time of humility, heart-searching, and even reconciliation if needed. This service prepares the heart to rejoice in the forgiveness of Christ as reflected in the Lord's Supper that follows.

Adventists practice open communion, meaning that Christians of any denomination are welcome to participate in this sacred ordinance. Because the communion service is a believer's ordinance, children are encouraged not to participate until after they are baptized and can appreciate its spiritual significance.

As a general rule, Seventh-day Adventist churches schedule communion once a quarter, making it important not to miss this special service. Feelings of unworthiness have been known to keep some away, but it is precisely because we *are* unworthy that the foot-washing and communion services are so needed. The inclination to merely *observe* at church services rather than *participate* is also not a good reason to skip out when communion is scheduled. It was Jesus who instructed us to partake of the Lord's Supper, and it was Jesus who said, "If you know these things, blessed are you if you do them" (John 13:17).

Child Dedication

Though Adventists do not baptize infants, we do follow the biblical practice of dedicating children to the Lord. Mary and Joseph dedicated Jesus in the Temple (see Luke 2:22), Hannah dedicated young Samuel to the Lord (see 1 Samuel 1:27-28), and Jesus Himself took little children "up in His arms, laid His hands on them, and blessed them" (Mark 10:16). The dedication service is usually conducted during the Sabbath worship service and may be conducted by the pastor or local church elder. This brief service has the following key elements:

- Thanks to God for the gift of new life.
- Parents make a covenant with God to raise the child in the nurture and admonition of the Lord (see Ephesians 6:4).
- The congregation makes a commitment to support the parents.
- Prayer is offered for a special blessing on the life of the child.

Though child dedication services have no age limit, children above the age of one or two years old are seldom dedicated, leading the service to be commonly referred to as a "baby" dedication. The service begins with parents, and sometimes other family members, being invited to come before the congregation for the dedication. A few remarks are then given by the one officiating, concluding with the parents agreeing to covenant with God in the raising of the child. Following this, a prayer for the help and blessing of God is offered while the one officiating either holds the child, or places a hand upon his or her head. At the conclusion of the service, a special certificate is given to the parents to commemorate the event.

Ordination

While all Christians are called by God to offer spiritual service to the church and community, the New Testament indicates that some servant leaders should be set apart by the laying on of hands for a particular line of service. These include gospel ministers, local elders, and deacons.

Ministers, or pastors, are ordained only after a period of internship in active service to give evidence of their calling. After approximately four or five years of active service, a review process is conducted to determine whether the candidate will be approved for ordination by the local conference and union conference executive committees. Upon approval, the ordination service for pastors is often conducted at the annual local conference camp meeting. The ceremony includes the laying on of hands by conference leaders and other ordained pastors, and a special ordination prayer. Once ordained, Seventh-day Adventist pastors are recognized by the church worldwide as being authorized to function in all rites and ceremonies and to organize churches.

Local church elders and deacons are also publicly ordained, usually during the Sabbath morning worship service. Deaconesses may also be included in this service. Previously ordained local elders are invited to kneel around those being ordained and to lay their hands on them as an ordained minister prays. Local elders and deacons may not participate in administering the ordinances of the church until they are ordained.

Anointing of the Sick

In James 5:14-15, we are instructed, "Is anyone among you sick? Let him call for the elders of the church, and let them pray over him, anointing him with oil in the name of the Lord. And the prayer of faith will save the sick, and the Lord will raise him up. And if he has committed sins, he will be forgiven." Based on this instruction, Seventh-day Adventist church members confronted by serious illness or injury may ask for the elders of the church to conduct an anointing service on their behalf. If someone is too ill to personally make a request, friends or family may ask for the service.

Anointing addresses not only the need for physical healing, but for forgiveness as well. It is a time of sober reflection, self-examination, and surrender that brings peace to the one who casts all of his or her cares upon God. The chapter "Prayer for the Sick," in the book *The Ministry of Healing* by Ellen G. White, is recommended reading to help the one being anointed prepare spiritually for the service. Anointing is not a last rite for the dying, but an exercise of faith in Christ's power to heal the living. The oil used in the service, rather than having mystical powers, is a symbol of the healing power of the Holy Spirit. The anointing and prayer service is conducted in faith and in humble submission to God's will, though it may not always include immediate physical healing.

The anointing service is usually officiated by a pastor, with the assistance of local elders, though in some cases a local elder may lead out. Family, friends, or other church members may also be invited. The service includes preliminary remarks on the purpose and circumstances of the anointing, the reading of Scripture, and encouraging words spoken by those attending. Finally, the attendees gather around the one being anointed and a time of prayer follows in which some or all of the attendees offer a brief prayer. After all others have prayed, the officiating pastor or elder prays and places oil on the forehead of the one being anointed, symbolizing the healing touch of the Holy Spirit. The anointing service, rather than being designed for mass audiences or healing services, is intensely personal, addressing the specific needs of one person.

Funeral

Seventh-day Adventist funerals are similar in most respects to those conducted by other Christians. One significant difference is that loved ones are comforted by the promise of the resurrection rather than a false assurance that the deceased is enjoying the pleasures of heaven (see 1 Thessalonians 4:16-18). Death is an unconscious sleep in which we await the resurrection at the second coming of Christ (see Psalm 13:3; Ecclesiastes 9:5-6). The Bible does not teach that the dead have already ascended to heaven (see Acts 2:34).

People commonly ask whether the practice of cremation is allowed by the Bible. We find no biblically-prescribed method of caring for the body of the deceased so long as proper respect is given. The concern over how God will resurrect those who have been cremated could also apply to those who have been buried, since their bodies eventually return to dust. God is not dependent upon the exact raw materials of this earthly body when resurrecting the dead in Christ.

Seventh-day Adventists do not believe that expensive arrangements are necessary to honor the deceased. Instead, their funerals are characterized by simplicity and respect. They are often preceded, either earlier the same day or in the days prior to the funeral, by a time of family visitation and viewing of the deceased.

The funeral service itself is usually conducted in a funeral home or local church. It may consist of prayer, Scripture readings, a eulogy or life sketch, a time for friends and family to share memories of the deceased, musical selections, and a short sermon. A brief graveside service often follows the funeral. Then, if requested by the family, a funeral luncheon is sometimes provided by the deaconesses of the church.

Wedding

It was God who ordained marriage as a sacred union between a man and a woman. Weddings, then, are to be joyous and spiritual occasions in which a lifelong covenant is made before God and witnesses. Before conducting a wedding ceremony, couples are usually given premarital counseling to help prepare

> *The number one Guest whom we should seek to please is the Lord Jesus Christ.*

them for the experiences of married life. Based on the biblical principle that a couple should be equally yoked, Seventh-day Adventist ministers are strongly encouraged to only officiate at the marriage ceremonies of those who share the same religious faith (see 2 Corinthians 6:14).

Local Seventh-day Adventist churches are often available for weddings, but fees and official church policies vary. Church members are encouraged to consider the following in order to secure God's blessing on their wedding:

- Schedule the wedding, rehearsal, and reception for a different time than Sabbath if activities are being planned that may be incompatible with those sacred hours. To avoid significant personal preparation, church decorating and cleanup, or employing photographers and other services on the Sabbath, many Seventh-day Adventist weddings are held on Sundays.
- Dress in harmony with biblical principles of modesty.
- Avoid worldly music and dancing.
- Refrain from providing alcohol, caffeinated beverages, or unclean meats.

- Be careful not to spend so lavishly, in an effort to keep up with modern wedding practices, that significant debt is incurred.

The number one Guest whom we should seek to please at every wedding, is the Lord Jesus Christ. It is He who joins husband and wife in marriage and provides the blessing they seek. Seventh-day Adventist weddings should bear witness to our family and friends that Jesus has first place in our lives.

Practical Application

Over the course of your life as a Seventh-day Adventist, you will likely see or participate in many if not all of the sacred ceremonies mentioned in this chapter. If you are a church member, you have already been baptized. Now you should have a better understanding of other ordinances and ceremonies that you will attend in your local church or conference. These sacred events are important moments, not only in our lives individually, but in the life of the church.

11

God of Order

From the miraculous inner workings of the human body to the harmonious interdependence seen throughout the vast universe, it may be clearly seen that "God is a God of order" (*Patriarchs and Prophets,* p. 376). Whenever we waste valuable time looking for something we failed to put away properly, or work on a project led by someone with no real direction or plan, we are reminded of the importance of organization for both efficiency and peace of mind. "For God is not the author of confusion but of peace" (1 Corinthians 14:33). Everything that God directs is organized. "Everything connected with heaven is in perfect order; subjection and thorough discipline mark the movements of the angelic host" (*Patriarchs and Prophets,* p. 376).

The Church in the Wilderness

When God desired to communicate His character through ancient Israel, He began by organizing His people. Clear assignments were given in great detail so that all could clearly understand their responsibilities. God was the sovereign leader,

Moses the visible leader, seventy elders of the tribes assisted Moses, priests and Levites were given specific assignments in the ministry of the sanctuary, chiefs or princes ruled over the tribes, and under these were captains over thousands, over hundreds, over fifties, and over tens. Specific details were given for the building of the tabernacle and all its furnishings (see Exodus 25-40). Details were given for the various offerings and services of the tabernacle (see Leviticus 1-7). A specific place was assigned for each tribe to camp around the tabernacle and a specific order was given for each tribe to set up and break camp (see Numbers 2). The families of the three sons of Levi were each given separate responsibilities for the care and transport of specific furnishings of the tabernacle (see Numbers 3). Specific trumpet signals were given by the priests to indicate every movement of the congregation (see Numbers 10).

> *The organization of Israel was awe-inspiring.*

The organization of Israel was awe-inspiring. Consider the following description of the wayward prophet Balaam as he looked upon the Israelite camp. "As Balaam looked upon the encampment of Israel he beheld with astonishment the evidence of their prosperity. They had been represented to him as a rude, disorganized multitude, infesting the country in roving bands that were a pest and terror to the surrounding nations; but their appearance was the reverse of all this. He saw the vast extent and perfect arrangement of their camp, everything bearing the marks of thorough discipline and order" (*Patriarchs and Prophets,* p. 447).

The New Testament Church

Just as ancient Israel was organized by God, so "the church … was organized for service" (*The Acts of the Apostles*, p. 9). First, Jesus appointed twelve apostles whom He trained to be leaders in His cause (see Mark 3:14). Seven deacons were later chosen to handle specific needs of the growing church (see Acts 6:1-6). This early step toward church organization was followed by the direct blessing of God. "Then the word of God spread, and the number of the disciples multiplied greatly in Jerusalem" (Acts 6:7). As churches began to spring up in different places from the spreading of the gospel, they also "appointed elders in every church" (Acts 14:23; see also Titus 1:5) to oversee and lead out in the ministry of local congregations.

The early church experienced astounding growth from the beginning, with thousands of individual members being added to the body of Christ. "Those who gladly received his word were baptized; and that day about three thousand souls were added to them" (Acts 2:41). "And the Lord added to the church daily those who were being saved" (Acts 2:47). Every baptism resulted in another member being "added" to the church body. "For by one Spirit we were all baptized into one body" (1 Corinthians 12:13).

There are some who shun being part of an organization. They claim to be members of the "invisible" body of Christ, while seeing no need of becoming a member of a local congregation. But this is inconsistent with God's Word. The very word "body," used to describe the church, indicates the need for a close inter-action and interdependence with other believers. Furthermore, if new converts were not clearly identified as members of the early church, there would have been no need for elders, or overseers, because there would have been no one to oversee! Instead, the Bible shows that newly baptized believers were integrated into a local congregation with a clear system of organization. Each local church provided the support, oversight and guidance that these new members needed.

"As an important factor in the spiritual growth of the new converts the apostles were careful to surround them with the safeguards of gospel order. … This was in harmony with the gospel plan of uniting in one body all believers in Christ" (*The Acts of the Apostles,* p. 185).

Organization and Unity

One of the great blessings of organizing the early church was that it helped maintain unity throughout the body of believers. In one instance, a doctrinal difficulty arose over the necessity of circumcision. Rather than each individual church following its own conviction on the matter, thereby risking a schism in the body, the apostles and elders came together in Jerusalem to pray, study, and come to a united decision based on Scripture (see Acts 15). As the Holy Spirit gave wisdom to various representatives of the church, the council arrived at a correct understanding of God's Word on the matter. Messengers then delivered the outcome of the Jerusalem Council to each individual church so that all could follow the collective decision. Unity was thus maintained among the believers. While Christ is the head of the church, He worked through human leaders and representatives to maintain harmony and biblical unity throughout the body.

Seventh-day Adventist Organization

Many early Advent believers feared that church organization would inevitably lead to corruption. However, the Bible's testimony on the matter, and prophetic guidance given through Ellen G. White, led to a thorough organization of the Seventh-day Adventist Church. As to the reasons for this organization, we read, "As our numbers increased it was evident that without some form of organization there would be great confusion, and the work would not be carried forward successfully. To provide for the support of the ministry, for carrying the work in new fields, for protecting both the churches and the ministry from unworthy members, for holding church property, for the publication of the truth through the press, and for many other objects, organization was indispensable"(*Last Day Events,* p. 46).

> *While Christ is the head of the church, He works through human leaders and representatives.*

Today, in harmony with the biblical model, the Seventh-day Adventist Church is organized with a representative form of church government. This means authority in the church is a delegated authority, ultimately derived from the membership of local churches. Executive responsibility is given to representative bodies and officers to govern the church. The four main levels of organization in the church are as follows:

1. General Conference
2. Union Conferences
3. Local Conferences
4. Local Churches

The General Conference of Seventh-day Adventists oversees the worldwide work of the church. Every five years, delegates from around the world come to official General Conference sessions (similar to the Jerusalem Council in Acts 15) where reports are presented, the world church president and other leaders are elected, changes in the *Seventh-day Adventist Church Manual* (the official guidebook for church policies) are voted upon, and other church business is conducted. Between these quinquennial sessions, the Executive Committee of the General Conference organization administers the church. This Committee meets twice yearly at what are called Spring Meeting and Annual Council, or as needed between times.

For purposes of efficiency, the General Conference is organized into thirteen world divisions, each with its own president, other officers, and executive committee. These divisions are not separate levels of organization, but serve as regional offices to more effectively meet the needs of the various languages and geographical areas of the world church. The thirteen world divisions and two attached fields are:

1. East-Central Africa Division (ECD)
2. Euro-Asia Division (ESD)
3. Inter-American Division (IAD)
4. Inter-European Division (EUD)
5. North American Division (NAD)
6. Northern Asia-Pacific Division (NSD)
7. Southern Africa-Indian Ocean Division (SID)
8. South American Division (SAD)
9. South Pacific Division (SPD)
10. Southern Asia Division (SUD)
11. Southern Asia-Pacific Division (SSD)
12. Trans-European Division (TED)

13. West-Central Africa Division (WAD)
14. Israel Field
15. Middle East and North Africa Union

The second main level of church organization is the union conference, or union field/mission, of which there are more than 100 around the world. In North America there are nine union conferences, each covering four or more states or provinces in its territory. Unions hold legal title to church-owned institutions that serve the entire union (such as colleges) and also publish news magazines for their constituent members.

The third main level of organization within the church is the local conference, or local field/mission. Local conference territories may include one or more states or provinces. There are over 600 such conferences around the world and over 50 of these are in the North American Division. Local conferences employ the pastors, teachers, evangelists, Bible workers, and administrators who work in the conference territory. Conferences also own and operate Seventh-day Adventist academies (high schools) and youth camps. They oversee the work of Seventh-day Adventist elementary schools in their territory and hold title, through their legal corporation, to the churches and schools in the conference. Conferences also sponsor annual camp meetings featuring seminars, inspirational preaching, outstanding music, and a major focus on evangelism.

The fourth, and perhaps most important, level of organization is the local church. This is where the majority of front line ministry happens, and where individual church membership is held. The Seventh-day Adventist Church currently consists of over 19 million members worldwide, and continues to grow at a rate of approximately 3,000 new members a day.

Every year or two, local congregations nominate and elect new officers. Their duties and qualifications for church office, as well as the process for their nomination, are all outlined in the *Church Manual.* Among these officers are the local elders who assist the pastor in the leadership of the church. Deacons and deaconesses are elected to oversee ministry to those in need, assist with church ordinances, and care for the physical church building. Officers for the Sabbath School are also chosen, as well as leaders for various church departments such as personal ministries, community services, health ministries, family ministries, women's ministries, men's ministries, youth ministries, Pathfinder and Adventurer Clubs, communications, treasury, religious liberty, and music ministry.

Key church officers are designated in the *Church Manual* as members of the church board, which is the primary committee of the local church. The most important function of the church board is planning the evangelization of the outreach territory of the church. The board generally meets only once a month, making it important for church board members to attend each month if at all possible. Though only board members may vote on agenda items, other church members are often welcome to attend and observe. If the church operates a school, a separate board usually oversees its business and activities.

At least once a year, a business meeting is called in which all church members in regular standing are entitled to vote. The business meeting is the governing body and highest authority of the local church. Periodically, when there is little or no need for discussion, items requiring a vote by the local church body may be brought forward using a minimum of time during the Sabbath worship service.

If an item in need of a vote is presented on Sabbath morning, it is often presented on two different Sabbaths in the form of a first and second reading. The first reading informs the church of an item requiring a vote, and gives members time to consider the matter or discuss it with leadership before the vote is taken on a subsequent Sabbath, at the time of the second reading. Items requiring a majority vote from the entire church include the election of church officers, changes in individual membership status, church disciplinary action, annual church budgets, and major expenses or evangelistic initiatives.

Practical Application

This week, obtain a list of church officers and ministries for your own local church. As you review the list, consider where the Lord may be leading you to get involved. Discuss with a mentor, elder, or pastor, areas where you may begin to serve within your local church.

In addition, ask an elder or your pastor if you may attend an upcoming church board meeting to better understand how the church operates. Also ask when your local church's business meetings are held, and make a commitment to always attend these important church-wide sessions. Go to these meetings in humility and ask God how you can become an even greater benefit to your local church.

12

Only One Thing to Fear

In chapter 7, "Our Mission," we looked at the prophetic rise and mission of the Seventh-day Adventist Church. We reviewed how our history as a denomination was preceded by the urgent proclamation of the soon return of Jesus through the preaching of William Miller and many others. When Jesus did not return on October 22, 1844, the Advent believers (those who believed from the 2300-day prophecy of Daniel 8:14 that Jesus would return on that day) experienced what became known as the Great Disappointment. Out of that disappointment, however, the Seventh-day Adventist Church was soon born. This chapter will review in more detail the key events and developments that led to the biblical foundation and ultimate formation of the Seventh-day Adventist Church.

Why is it important to understand how God has led in our church's history? As Ellen White so aptly states, it is because it would cost us too much should we ever forget. "In reviewing our past history, having traveled over every step of advance to our present standing, I can say, Praise God! As I see what God has wrought, I am filled with astonishment and with confidence in

Christ as Leader. We have nothing to fear for the future, except as we shall forget the way the Lord has led us, and his teaching in our past history" (*Selected Messages,* book 3, p. 162).

We have nothing to fear, *except* as we forget. Let us, then, take time to remember how God has led, and His teaching in our past history.

After the Disappointment

On October 23, the morning after the Great Disappointment, Hiram Edson, an Advent believer living in Port Gibson, New York, met with other believers in his barn to seek God for direction. He would later write, "We continued in earnest prayer until the witness of the Spirit was given that our prayer was accepted and that light should be given" and "our disappointment be explained." (C. Mervyn Maxwell, *Tell It to the World,* 1976, p. 49).

Later that morning Edson set out, along with a friend, to visit and encourage some of their Adventist neighbors. Of his experience while passing through a grain field, Edson writes, "I was stopped about midway of the field. Heaven seemed open to my view, and I saw distinctly and clearly that instead of our High Priest coming out of the most holy place of the heavenly sanctuary to this earth … He, for the first time, entered on that day into the second apartment of that sanctuary, and that He had a work to perform in the most holy place before coming to the earth. … And my mind was directed to the tenth chapter of Revelation" (*The Review and Herald,* June 23, 1921, p. 5).

> *We have nothing to fear, except as we forget.*

The Lord had answered their morning prayer for an explanation of the disappointment. They could now see that they had passed through the sweet then bitter experience described in Revelation 10, and that the sanctuary to be cleansed was not the earth, but the sanctuary in heaven (see Hebrews 8:1-2, 5). Jesus had entered the Most Holy Place of heaven's sanctuary for His final work as our High Priest!

Two months later, in December of 1844, 17-year-old Ellen Harmon, later to be known as Ellen White, received her first vision while praying with a small group of ladies. She writes, "While I was praying at the family altar, the Holy Ghost fell upon me, and I seemed to be rising higher and higher, far above the dark world. I turned to look for the Advent people in the world, but could not find them, when a voice said to me, 'Look again, and look a little higher.' At this I raised my eyes, and saw a straight and narrow path, cast up high above the world. On this path the Advent people were traveling to the city, which was at the farther end of the path. They had a bright light set up behind them at the beginning of the path, which an angel told me was the midnight cry. This light shone all along the path and gave light for their feet so that they might not stumble. If they kept their eyes fixed on Jesus, who was just before them, leading them to the city, they were safe. But soon some grew weary, and said the city was a great way off, and they expected to have entered it before. Then Jesus would encourage them by raising His glorious right arm, and from His arm came a light which waved over the Advent band, and they shouted, 'Alleluia!'" (*Early Writings*, p. 14).

This vision was a great assurance to the small band of Advent believers. It revealed not only that God's hand was in the Advent Movement, but that He would guide them safely home if they kept their eyes on Jesus. This was the beginning of Ellen Harmon's ministry as a messenger of the Lord, in which she shared with the Adventist believers what God revealed to her in visions or dreams. She at first shrunk from this task because her health was poor, and she feared the opposition she might receive, but God promised to sustain her. James White, a twenty-three-year-old Adventist preacher, soon began laboring together with Ellen, and in August of 1846 they were married.

Becoming Established in the Sanctuary

Back in Port Gibson, Hiram Edson, O. R. L. Crosier, and F. B. Hahn were earnestly studying their Bibles to better understand the light given to Edson while he was walking in the grain field. They studied the 2300-day prophecy in the light of the sanctuary and its services, the Day of Atonement, and the work of Jesus as High Priest. Through these studies, it became increasingly clear that on October 22, 1844, Jesus began a work of cleansing that would prepare God's people for His return.

Crosier published their findings in the *Day-Star Extra* and sent it out to Adventist believers across the East Coast. When Ellen White received one of these papers she was thrilled that God had revealed to them the very things He had been showing her! The doctrine of the sanctuary was established as one of the landmarks of our faith.

A Complete System of Truth

Discovering the meaning of the cleansing of the sanctuary (see Daniel 8:14) was the key by which a beautiful chain of truth was revealed to the early Adventists. Subjects such as the judgment, the law of God, the Sabbath, and later the state of man in death, were each brought to light through a proper understanding of Christ's work in the heavenly sanctuary.

Ellen White explains, "The subject of the sanctuary was the key which unlocked the mystery of the disappointment of 1844. It opened to view a complete system of truth, connected and harmonious, showing that God's hand had directed the great advent movement and revealing present duty as it brought to light the position and work of His people" (*The Great Controversy,* p. 423).

Discovering the Sabbath

Early in the year 1844, in Washington, New Hampshire, Adventist preacher Frederick Wheeler decided to visit some of his parishioners. He stopped at the home of Rachel Oaks, a Seventh-day Baptist widow who had been attending services at his church. She spoke to him about his sermon the previous Sunday where he had said we must observe all of the Ten Commandments. She asked him why then he was breaking the fourth commandment. This led to a Bible study on the Sabbath. Elder Wheeler accepted the Sabbath, becoming the first Sabbath-keeping Adventist minister in North America. He shared the truth about the Sabbath with Freewill Baptist minister Thomas M. Preble, who then wrote and published an article entitled, *Tract Showing That the Seventh Day Should be Observed as the Sabbath.* A copy of this article made it to Fairhaven, Massachusetts, and to the home of an Advent believer named Joseph Bates.

Born in 1792, Joseph Bates, a retired sea captain, was much older than most of the early Adventist pioneers. He had given away all of his fortune to proclaim the soon return of

Jesus prior to 1844. Upon reading Preble's tract, Bates rode on horseback to Washington, New Hampshire to meet with Elder Wheeler. The two men studied the Sabbath doctrine throughout the night.

Convinced that Saturday is the Bible Sabbath, Bates returned home determined to share this truth with others. Upon reading the article on the sanctuary written by Crosier, and being convinced of its truthfulness, he traveled to upstate New York and shared the Sabbath truth with Edson, Crosier, and the others there. They all accepted it. Bates soon wrote his famous tract, *The Seventh Day Sabbath: A Perpetual Sign,* which was read and studied by the newly married James and Ellen White. They too began to keep the Sabbath.

Some six months later, on April 3, 1847, Ellen White was given a vision of the law of God in the heavenly sanctuary, with a halo of light around the fourth commandment. This brought a clearer understanding of the importance of the Sabbath doctrine, and affirmed the young Adventists in their biblical understandings.

The doctrine of the cleansing of the heavenly sanctuary had brought to view the Ark of the Covenant in the Most Holy Place. The light shining from that ark was opening to the view of these Advent believers the beautiful truth of the law of God and the seventh-day Sabbath.

The Third Angel's Message

The significance of the seventh-day Sabbath became more and more apparent as the early Adventists gained a deeper understanding of Bible prophecy. "Because the mark of the beast is placed on those who do not keep the commandments, the early

Adventists began to see that the seal of God is for those who do keep them—who keep all of them, including the Sabbath. They discovered, in fact, that the seal of God *is* the Sabbath, properly observed through faith in Jesus. And this interpretation of theirs was confirmed through extensive Bible study and by one or more visions given to Ellen White" (C. Mervyn Maxwell, *Tell It to the World,* 1976, pp. 92-93).

As the pioneer Adventists discovered that the seal of God referred to the seventh-day Sabbath, they also came to realize that the mark of the beast was to be the counterfeit Sabbath of the papacy—Sunday. These early Adventists now understood that God had revealed to them the light concerning the Sabbath and the mark of the beast so that they could proclaim a final message of warning and mercy. They were to give the third angel's message of Revelation 14:9-12 to the whole world!

Sabbath Conferences

In 1848, a series of "Sabbath conferences" were held. Adventist believers who had embraced the Sabbath, the sanctuary, and the spirit of prophecy, came from all over New England and spent days praying and studying the Scriptures together. The increased doctrinal clarity gained from these meetings helped to establish the biblical foundations of what would later become the Seventh-day Adventist Church. During this time, God again used the gift of prophecy to help guide His people, giving Ellen White one or two visions at each of the conferences.

The visions, however, were not a substitute for Bible study. Ellen White wrote of the experience: "Often we remained together until late at night, and sometimes through the entire night, praying for light and studying the Word. ... When they came to the point in their study where they said, 'We can do nothing more,' the Spirit of the Lord would come upon me, I would be taken off in vision, and a clear explanation of the passages we had been studying would be given me, with instruction as to how we were to labor and teach effectively. Thus light was given that helped us to understand the scriptures in regard to Christ, His mission, and His priesthood. A line of truth extending from that time to the time when we shall enter the city of God, was made plain to me, and I gave to others the instruction that the Lord had given me."

She went on to explain: "During this whole time I could not understand the reasoning of the brethren. My mind was locked, as it were, and I could not comprehend the meaning of the scriptures we were studying. ... I was in this condition of mind until all the principal points of our faith were made clear to our minds, in harmony with the Word of God. The brethren knew that when not in vision, I could not understand these matters, and they accepted as light direct from heaven the revelations given" (*Selected Messages*, book 1, pp. 206-207). God designed that the doctrinal pillars of our faith be rooted in the study of Scripture before affirming and further clarifying them through visions given to Ellen White.

> *God designed that the doctrinal pillars of our faith be rooted in the study of Scripture.*

Since those early days of deep Bible study, various efforts have been made to alter the doctrinal foundation of the Seventh-day Adventist Church. Regarding such attempts, Ellen White cautions, "What influence is it that would lead men at this stage of our history to work in an underhanded, powerful way to tear down the foundation of our faith—the foundation that was laid at the beginning of our work by prayerful study of the Word and by revelation? Upon this foundation we have been building for the past fifty years" (*Selected Messages,* book 1, p. 207).

The Publishing Work

For the third angel's message to be given with a "loud voice" to the entire world, a regular publication would be necessary. In November of 1848, God gave Ellen White a message for her husband. She told him, "You must begin to print a little paper and send it out to the people. Let it be small at first; but as the people read, they will send you means with which to print, and it will be a success from the first. From this small beginning it was shown to me to be like streams of light that went clear round the world" (*Life Sketches of Ellen G. White,* p. 125).

This was the beginning of what would become *The Advent Review and Sabbath Herald* (today the *Adventist Review*), the general paper of the Seventh-day Adventist Church. The publishing work began in Rochester, New York, where a dedicated group of young people in their 20s worked on the paper. Among them was Uriah Smith, who became the editor at the age of 23. Smith held this position with but few interruptions for 50 years. Also involved was J. N. Andrews, after whom Andrews University is named. A deep Bible student, Andrews was also a writer, a traveling preacher, and later our first official overseas missionary.

The *Adventist Review* was born in a time of great personal sacrifice, financial struggle, long, tedious hours of work, and sadness—as several office workers succumbed to tuberculosis. In spite of the difficult conditions, the small group of believers continued to publish the paper. This publication served as the primary means of educating and uniting the believers who would later form the membership of the Seventh-day Adventist Church.

Formal Organization

In 1852, Joseph Bates traveled west in hopes of sharing the sanctuary message and Sabbath truth with others. God led him to Battle Creek, Michigan, where he inquired for "the most honest man in town." Directed to the home of David Hewitt, he began to share the prophecies of Daniel and Revelation. Being the honest man that he was, David Hewitt embraced these Bible teachings and became the first Sabbath-keeping Adventist in Battle Creek.

A few years later, the believers in Michigan invited James and Ellen White to move from Rochester to Battle Creek. In November of 1855, the Review and Herald Publishing Association, along with the hand press, was moved to a newly erected office building in Battle Creek. All of this was made possible by liberal donations from the Advent believers.

The need for organizational unity and division of responsibility became increasingly apparent, as the number of Sabbath-keeping Adventists multiplied. In response to published invitations, ministers from five states met at Battle Creek, Michigan, to attend a "General Conference" from September 28 to October 1, 1860. Here James White urged the formation of an organization that could legally own the publishing house.

In order to hold property, the new organization was required to choose a name. Some were opposed to having a name, feeling that by doing so Adventists would become "just another denomination." Or even worse, some feared we would become part of "Babylon." Eventually, the delegates agreed that a name was necessary. David Hewitt suggested the name "Seventh-day Adventist," and it was adopted. About this decision, Ellen White writes, "The name Seventh-day Adventist, carries the true features of our faith in front, and will convict the inquiring mind" (*Testimonies for the Church,* vol. 1, p. 224).

The following year, 1861, the Michigan Conference of Seventh-day Adventists was organized. In 1863, the General Conference was organized with 3,500 members. John Byington was asked to serve as the first president. The years that followed saw the establishment of Battle Creek College and the Battle Creek Sanitarium, the beginnings of our worldwide education and health work.

Practical Application

When we trace the history of the Seventh-day Adventist Church, we can clearly see God's hand guiding this young movement and placing it on a firm foundation of Scripture. The early Adventist pioneers were determined to obey the truth and share it with others. Their dedication should motivate us to the same level of commitment and sacrifice.

Remember, "We have nothing to fear for the future, except as we shall forget the way the Lord has led us, and His teaching in our past history" (*Life Sketches of Ellen G. White,* p. 196). Choose a book or video that will help you to continue learning about the history of the Seventh-day Adventist Church. As you see God's hand in the past, you will be inspired to trust His leadership in the church and in your own life today. May we never forget!

13

Tell It to the World

J esus promised, "This gospel of the kingdom will be preached in all the world as a witness to all the nations, and then the end will come" (Matthew 24:14). While Christians have long understood that the gospel must be proclaimed to the entire world, we discover in the book of Revelation that there is a unique and distinct context in which that gospel must be shared before Jesus will return.

Revelation 14 and the Everlasting Gospel

In the prophecy of Revelation 14:6, the everlasting gospel is being preached to the whole world just as Matthew said it would be. In verse 14, we see the expected result—"One like the Son of Man" coming to the earth on a cloud—a representation of the second coming of Christ and the end of the world. Matthew had said that the gospel must go to the whole world before the end, but between Revelation 14:6 (gospel to the world) and Revelation 14:14 (the end) we learn that there are distinct and essential components to the end-time message that will usher in the coming of Christ:

The hour of His judgment has come (Revelation 14:7). This judgment began in 1844 when Christ entered the Most Holy Place to cleanse the heavenly sanctuary (see Daniel 8:14).

Worship Him who made heaven and earth, the sea and springs of water (Revelation 14:7). A reference to the fourth commandment (Exodus 20:8-11) and the importance of keeping the seventh-day Sabbath.

Babylon is fallen (Revelation 14:8). Popular false teachings on topics such as death, hell, and the secret rapture must be exposed, the truth restored, and an invitation given to genuine Christians unknowingly holding to the errors of spiritual Babylon to "come out of her, my people" (Revelation 18:4).

Do not worship the beast or receive his mark (Revelation 14:9-11). A final warning not to obey the laws of men when they contradict the law of God.

Keep the commandments of God and the faith of Jesus (Revelation 14:12). The commandments of God are to be obeyed by faith (see Romans 3:31). Law and grace, faith and works, are not opposed to one another.

From these unique details, we are struck with a sobering reality. The message of Revelation 14 that will bring about the end is none other than that which is proclaimed by the Seventh-day Adventist Church. We cannot depend upon the missionary efforts of other denominations that are not sharing these essential truths. We must carry this message to the entire world.

Note how Ellen White drew the same conclusion directly from Revelation 14: "In a special sense Seventh-day Adventists have been set in the world as watchmen and light-bearers. To them has been entrusted the last warning for a perishing world.

On them is shining wonderful light from the Word of God. They have been given a work of the most solemn import—the proclamation of the first, second, and third angels' messages. There is no other work of so great importance. They are to allow nothing else to absorb their attention" (*Evangelism,* p. 119).

Again, from the same author: "The usual subjects on which the ministers of nearly all other denominations dwell will not move them. We must proclaim our God-given message to them. The world is to be warned by the proclamation of this message. If we blanket it, if we hide our light under a bushel, if we so circumscribe ourselves that we cannot reach the people, we are answerable to God for our failure to warn the world" (*Manuscript Releases,* vol. 19, p. 41).

Missionary Movement

In light of the sacred trust given to us, the Seventh-day Adventist Church is driven by a special burden to take the three angels' messages to the entire world. As Adventists, we commonly refer to our denomination as a "movement," a name that aptly describes our work as one that cannot afford to grow stagnant. It must be aggressively advanced in our own neighborhoods and towns, and to the ends of the earth.

This strong conviction has led the Seventh-day Adventist Church to actively preach, teach and evangelize around the world. It has also led to the development of various lines of ministry. Publishing, health, humanitarian

> *We must carry this message to the entire world.*

service, education, foreign missions, and media development represent just a few of the many ministries that aid in fulfilling the special mission of the Seventh-day Adventist Church.

Publishing

Since the early years of its history, the Seventh-day Adventist Church has seen special significance in the publishing work. Though the work had small beginnings, Ellen White was shown in vision that these publications would become "like streams of light that went clear round the world" (*Life Sketches of Ellen G. White*, p. 125).

Ellen White's early prediction proved to be an accurate description of this important work. Church publications such as *The Advent Review and Sabbath Herald*, today known as the *Adventist Review*, would eventually circle the globe, along with many other church papers. In addition, the Tract and Missionary Society was developed in the early years of the Adventist Church, serving as the springboard for literature outreach by church members. Thousands of missionary tracts, magazines, and books carrying Bible truth are still printed every year for distribution by Seventh-day Adventists as an essential form of evangelism.

Referring to the importance of this work, Ellen White penned, "More than one thousand will soon be converted in one day, most of whom will trace their first convictions to the reading of our publications" (*Evangelism*, p. 693). For this reason, Seventh-day Adventist Church members are urged to regularly share truth-filled literature. "The truth must not be muffled now. Plain statements must be made. Unvarnished truth must be spoken, in leaflets and pamphlets, and these must be scattered like the leaves of autumn" (*Christian Service*, p. 147).

In addition to tracts and literature, a plan for giving Bible readings, today commonly called Bible studies, also began in 1883. These simple lessons, written in question-and-answer format so that a Bible text answers each question, provided a simple but effective way for church members to share their faith with others. Ellen White was shown a vision of a coming reformation in which she saw hundreds and thousands of Seventh-day Adventists sharing the truth in this way. Today the church produces multiple sets of Bible study lesson guides, beautifully designed and full of essential biblical truths. Members are strongly encouraged to regularly study these lessons with anyone who may be searching for truth.

Other forms of publishing work that have been important to our history, and continue to be active today, include literature evangelism (selling books from house-to-house), correspondence Bible schools, and bookstores called Adventist Book Centers.

Health

On June 5, 1863, Ellen White was given a vision on various aspects of health to communicate to the church. This was the beginning of a healing ministry that would become one of the greatest blessings that the Seventh-day Adventist Church would give to the world.

In 1866, the Western Health Reform Institute, later known as the Battle Creek Sanitarium, began its operations. This world-renowned health resort was led for many years by the first Seventh-day Adventist physician, Dr. John Harvey Kellogg. Here Dr. Kellogg and his staff provided treatment using natural remedies and taught how to prevent disease through a healthy lifestyle.

Adventists promote a lifestyle that includes a vegetarian diet, regular exercise, water, sunlight, rest, fresh air, trust in God, and abstinence from addictive substances such as alcohol, tobacco, and caffeine. Studies have shown that those who follow this plan for optimum health live nearly ten years longer than the rest of the population, and experience improved quality of life, even in their later years.

God instructed Ellen White that this prescription for a healthy life was, to the three angels' messages, what the right arm is to the body. While the message of health should not be given pre-eminence over the everlasting gospel and the three angels' messages, it should also not be separated from it. Just as the healing ministry of Jesus led to spiritual healing, helping people find physical health today is still a means of opening the door of the heart to the gospel. "When properly conducted, the health work is an entering wedge, making a way for other truths to reach the heart" (*Colporteur Ministry,* p. 131).

Today, health education continues to be a vital part of the church's mission. The Seventh-day Adventist Church operates nearly 200 hospitals and sanitariums, and approximately 300 clinics, as well as providing health education through lifestyle centers, printed publications, vegetarian cooking classes, smoking cessation seminars, and many other health events.

Community Service and Humanitarian Aid

Jesus clearly taught the importance of caring for those in need. "Assuredly, I say to you, inasmuch as you did it to one of the least of these My brethren, you did it to Me" (Matthew 25:40). In harmony with the teachings and spirit of Jesus, the Seventh-day Adventist Church has developed broad and extensive ministries that offer compassionate service to others.

In Acts 9:36, a woman named Tabitha, or Dorcas, is extolled for her life of service, "This woman was full of good works and charitable deeds which she did." With a desire to emulate her example, the Seventh-day Adventist Church officially recognized the Dorcas Society as its organized community outreach program in 1874. After many years of development, this work is now organized into Adventist Community Services (ACS) in North America, and the Adventist Development and Relief Agency (ADRA) internationally.

ACS consists of more than 1,100 centers run by local Adventist churches. These centers provide services that may include giving food and clothing to those in need, disaster response, tutoring and mentoring programs, elder care, community development, and urban ministries.

ADRA is the worldwide humanitarian aid agency of the Seventh-day Adventist Church. Organized for the specific purposes of individual and community development and international disaster relief, ADRA ministers to the needs of people without regard to race, gender, and political or religious affiliation. ADRA has a presence in more than 120 countries and operates in six main areas of service: providing food and water, establishing livelihoods, promoting health, responding to emergencies, supporting families, and protecting the vulnerable.

Education

Seventh-day Adventists view education, in its broadest sense, as a means of restoring the image of God in humanity. "To restore in man the image of his Maker, to bring him back to the perfection in which he was created, to promote the development of body, mind, and soul, that the divine purpose in his creation might be realized—this was to be the work of redemption. This is the object of education, the great object of life" (*Education,* p. 15).

This philosophy of education, derived from the Bible and the writings of Ellen White, extends beyond mere preparation for an earthly career. "True education means more than the pursual of a certain course of study. It means more than a preparation for the life that now is. ... It prepares the student for the joy of service in this world and for the higher joy of wider service in the world to come" (*Education,* p. 13).

While the first and primary source of education is the home, the Seventh-day Adventist Church has also developed an educational system with the following important characteristics:

The Bible our primary textbook. "The Holy Scriptures are the perfect standard of truth, and as such should be given the highest place in education" (*Education,* p. 17). Students are taught that the Bible is the Word of God and should be the trustworthy authority in their lives. They are taught the fundamental teachings of the Bible, and the duty and privilege of sharing the truth with others.

Physical training. Practical training and physical labor are vital components to a well-rounded education. Academics, while important, should not be emphasized to the exclusion of physical labor. Such labor is necessary to build character and to prepare students for practical usefulness in life.

Developing thinkers. Rather than relying on rote memorization, students are taught to use their God-given mental powers to think and to act in harmony with God's will. "It is the work of true education to develop this power, to train the youth to be thinkers, and not mere reflectors of other men's thought" (*Education,* p. 17).

Training missionaries. As part of the spiritual development of the students, true education will teach the importance of working for the salvation of others. It will prepare students to share the everlasting gospel in the context of the three angels' messages of Revelation 14. Young people so educated will know how to live an active life of service and to be invested in the life of the church.

With this model of education in view, the Seventh-day Adventist Church has developed a system that currently operates nearly 8,000 schools around the world, including elementary schools, secondary schools, colleges, and universities. These schools form the heart of one of the highest priorities in the Seventh-day Adventist Church—the salvation, character development, and missionary train-

> *Students are taught that the Bible is the Word of God.*

ing of our youth. Along with programs such as Pathfinders, Adventurers, summer camps, youth literature evangelism, annual youth conferences, and both local and conference youth departments, our schools are a means of investing in young people who will help to shape the church until Jesus comes.

Foreign Missions

During the 1850s and 1860s, Europeans who learned of the Adventist message while in America began to share the truth with their friends and family in Europe. In 1869, the church responded to a growing interest by forming the Foreign Mission Society to begin work in foreign lands. Then in 1871, Ellen White was shown in vision that "young men should be qualifying themselves for service by becoming familiar with other languages, that God may use them as mediums through which to communicate His saving truth to those of other nations" (*Life Sketches of Ellen G. White,* p. 204).

The vision given in 1871 led to significant changes in the scope of the work in the year 1874. Battle Creek College, our first college to train missionaries, was established. James White published *True Missionary,* the Adventist Church's first missionary publication, urging the need for foreign missionaries. Ellen White had an impressive dream in which she was told, "You are entertaining too limited ideas of the work for this time. You are trying to plan the work so that you can embrace it in your arms. You must take broader views. ... The message will go in power to all parts of the world, to Oregon, to Europe, to Australia, to the islands of the sea, to all nations, tongues, and peoples. ... It will grow to large proportions. Many countries are waiting for the advanced light the Lord has for them; and your faith is limited, it is very small. Your conception of the work needs to be greatly enlarged" (*Life Sketches of Ellen G. White,* pp. 208-209).

In September of 1874, John Nevins Andrews sailed for Switzerland as our first official overseas missionary, along with his two teenage children. Ellen White said that we had sent "the ablest man in our ranks" (*Manuscript Releases,* vol. 5, p. 436). Andrews established the Adventist press in Basel, Switzerland, but he died in Europe of tuberculosis in 1883, at the age of 54.

In the years that followed the work grew in Europe, Australia, New Zealand, and South Africa. Churches were raised up and publications in the languages of the people were distributed far and wide. The groundwork was laid for an explosion of missions. By the end of the 1890s, an Adventist presence was established on every continent and many islands of the sea. While it began in North America, the Seventh-day

Adventist Church is now a global movement with work established in more than 200 countries and areas of the world. Nearly 95% of its membership is currently outside of North America. Many parts of the world are still difficult to reach, and church leaders are working to spread the truth in these regions with the same spirit of foreign missions that inspired John Andrews so many years ago.

Media Development

The Seventh-day Adventist Church has for many years been at the forefront of Christian media ministries. Television, radio, and Internet ministries are operated by the church or by dedicated members with a burden for spreading the gospel.

Hope Channel is the official television channel of the Adventist Church and is translated in multiple languages to appeal to a wide, global audience. Three Angels Broadcasting Network, or 3ABN, is a supporting ministry of the church and the second largest Christian television network in North America. Adventist World Radio, Voice of Prophecy, It Is Written, Breath of Life, and Amazing Facts are media ministries that have utilized radio, television, or the Internet, to broadcast biblical truth for the last several decades. And while these organizations are among the largest, they are only a few of the many media ministries seeking to communicate the three angels' messages to today's world.

Practical Application

In the 1820s, long before the Seventh-day Adventist Church would be formed in 1863, a Baptist farmer named William Miller was convicted by the prophecies of Scripture that the coming of Jesus was near. He felt that it was his duty to share his discovery with others, but was afraid of how people would respond. For nine long years he wrestled with God, but the conviction only grew stronger. Through those years, one consistent message kept ringing in his ears: "Go and tell it to the world."

The burden that rested on the shoulders of William Miller still rests on every Seventh-day Adventist today. No one else will do this work for us. We alone can share our God-given message with the world. "Your duty cannot be shifted upon another. No one but yourself can do your work" (*Christian Service,* p. 100).

Pray this week that God will give *you* the strength to "Go, and tell it to the world."

Section 5

Christian Lifestyle

14

Something Better

The next several chapters of the *Discipleship Handbook* will focus on distinctive characteristics of Christian behavior. We will explore what the Bible teaches in the practical areas of Sabbath-keeping, reverence, financial stewardship, health, modesty, entertainment, and family relationships. Before entering into these practical and often sensitive topics, however, some common areas of confusion should be addressed.

Behavior Cannot Merit Salvation

First, it is important for every disciple of Christ to understand that our behavior can never earn salvation. Our salvation is based on the merits of Christ's life and sacrifice. Nothing we do or abstain from doing can gain for us favor with God. As the old hymn *Rock of Ages* says, "Not the labor of my hands, can fulfill Thy law's demands; could my zeal no respite know, could my tears forever flow, all for sin could not atone; Thou must save, and Thou alone."

Truly the blood of Jesus is our only basis for forgiveness and salvation. Yet when Jesus saves, it is *not* to offer freedom from having to submit to God's Word. On the contrary, when by faith we accept the sacrifice of Christ for our forgiveness, love for Jesus springs up in the heart and empowers us to obey Him! The acceptance of Christ as our personal Savior always gives birth to the pursuit of holiness, or Christlikeness. We cannot truly receive Jesus as our Savior without also receiving Him as our Lord and Master.

Still, because we cannot earn salvation by our works, many wonder if external matters are really important to God. When offering instruction in Christian behavior, questions are often raised: "Shouldn't we be focusing on a relationship with God instead of rules? Do such minor things really matter to God? Is this really a salvation issue?" These are important questions, which deserve careful answers.

Rules or Relationship?

We should be careful not to create an imaginary conflict between rules and relationship. Consider the example of marriage. If a husband seeks to improve his relationship with his wife, he will naturally seek to make positive changes in his behavior. He will stop doing things that cause conflict in the relationship and do more of what pleases her. By his change in behavior, she is able to see that he loves her. So it is in our relationship with Jesus. When the Holy Spirit reveals areas in which our behavior is separating us from Christ, we must repent and change our ways in order to strengthen the relationship. In so doing, we show that we love and trust God. As Jesus said, "If you love Me, keep My commandments." And "If you keep My commandments, you will abide in My love" (John 14:15, 15:10). We can maintain a positive *relationship* with Him ("abide in

SECTION 5 - CHRISTIAN LIFESTYLE   SOMETHING BETTER

My love"), only as we submit our *behavior* to His will ("keep My commandments").

There are those who say that a relationship with Christ is all that matters, and who speak critically of anyone who places importance on matters of external behavior. The truth, however, is that those who downplay Christian lifestyle and behavior only hinder their relationship with Christ. Behavioral instruction and our relationship with Jesus simply cannot be separated without causing untold harm. A focus on behavior without relationship can result in cold formalism, but a focus on relationship without behavior can result in a failure to acknowledge cherished sin.

Salvation Issues

So how do we answer the oft-asked question, "Is this really a salvation issue?" Once again, this question implies an artificial distinction that we should be careful to avoid. While it is true that the Word of God describes some sins as being weightier than others (see Matthew 23:23), we should never conclude that any biblical instruction is small in God's eyes. "God does not regard all sins as of equal magnitude; there are degrees of guilt in His estimation, as well as in that of man; but however trifling this or that wrong act may seem in the eyes of men, no sin is small in the sight of God. Man's

> *The acceptance of Christ as our personal Savior always gives birth to the pursuit of holiness, or Christlikeness.*

judgment is partial, imperfect; but God estimates all things as they really are" (*Steps to Christ*, p. 30). Because our judgment is imperfect, it would be presumptuous for us to claim the ability to discern which areas of God's Word are important to Him and which are not.

Many wrong actions that received punishment in the Bible would be considered no big deal by many today. Adam and Eve were punished for eating a piece of fruit. Cain was not accepted for one modification to what God asked him to use in worship. Uzzah was punished for reaching out and steadying the ark. Human perception may view these as small transgressions, but the reality was quite different. Not because what they did was intrinsically sinful, but because they manifested a lack of trust in God by disobeying His clear commands. We must be careful that we don't classify certain habits or behaviors as "little things" in an effort to rationalize disobedience. Often these are the very things that have the tightest grip on our lives. Therefore, if our relationship with Christ is to truly grow, we must come face to face with God's will in the practical areas of our daily lives.

> *It is for our good, and not our harm, that we are told to obey.*

The "salvation issue" question is often another way of asking, "Will this one thing keep me out of heaven?" Perhaps the question itself is looking at our Christian lives from a wrong perspective. Born again Christians do not ask how little they have to do to be accepted into heaven; they ask how they can please God and more fully conform to His will.

"God's Word is plain. Its teachings cannot be mistaken. Shall we obey it, just as He has given it to us, or shall we seek to find how far we can digress and yet be saved?" (*Evangelism*, p. 271). "Those who feel the constraining love of God, do not ask how little may be given to meet the requirements of God; they do not ask for the lowest standard, but aim at perfect conformity to the will of their Redeemer. ... A profession of Christ without this deep love is mere talk, dry formality, and heavy drudgery" (*Steps to Christ,* p. 44).

Something Vastly Better

Sometimes, when we learn that our lifestyle is contrary to God's Word, we are tempted to feel that God is taking away our joy. But the truth is exactly the opposite. Though our sinful natures make the surrender of habits and lifestyle difficult, it is for our good, and not our harm, that we are told to obey. "God does not require us to give up anything that it is for our best interest to retain. In all that He does, He has the well-being of His children in view" (*Steps to Christ,* p. 46).

God asks us to return tithes and offerings to build our faith and benevolence, and to save us from the destructive traits of selfishness and greed. He provides counsels on health to give us clarity of mind and quality of life, and to spare us the suffering of disease and addictions. He instructs His people in modesty of dress to develop meekness and humility, and to free us from the bondage of pride and insecurity. He encourages healthful recreation and forbids sinful entertainment to protect our minds from moral corruption. "Would that all ... might realize that He has something vastly better to offer them than they are seeking for themselves" (*Steps to Christ,* p. 46). Rather than questioning the practical counsels of the Bible, let us view them as they are—merciful blessings from our all-wise Creator.

Practical Application

If following Jesus in the practical areas of life has been a struggle for you, do not despair or become discouraged. Remember that you have a sympathetic and forgiving Savior. "Jesus loves to have us come to Him just as we are, sinful, helpless, dependent. We may come with all our weakness, our folly, our sinfulness, and fall at His feet in penitence. It is His glory to encircle us in the arms of His love and to bind up our wounds, to cleanse us from all impurity" (*Steps to Christ,* p. 52).

The purpose of biblical lifestyle instruction is not to condemn us, but to help us more fully reflect the life and character of Jesus and to strengthen our relationship with Him. As we follow this instruction, it provides us with essential protection from the dangers and entrapments of the world, from our own sinful natures, and from the enemy of souls.

Before reading the following chapters, ask God to give you a humble spirit and an honest desire to follow the truth. By trusting the biblical instruction found in these chapters, the Lord will bless you abundantly. "And all these blessings shall come upon you and overtake you, because you obey the voice of the Lord your God" (Deuteronomy 28:2).

15

Day of Delight

The Sabbath was made to be a blessing to mankind. It is not a day of drudgery, but a day of delight and rejoicing in the Lord. Jesus affirmed the blessing of the Sabbath when He said, "The Sabbath was made for man, and not man for the Sabbath" (Mark 2:27). The Sabbath does come with commands for its proper observance, but these are only given to protect and strengthen our relationship with Jesus. For the one who desires to be right with God, to seek first His kingdom, and to prepare for eternity, the Sabbath is a wonderful gift from heaven.

Keep It Holy

Perhaps the best summary of proper Sabbath observance is found in the biblical command to "keep it holy" (Exodus 20:8). In Genesis 2:3, the Bible says that God "blessed the seventh day and sanctified it." The seventh day is the only day of the week in all of Scripture that God sanctified or made holy. This is one reason that only the seventh day can be the true Sabbath. We can only *keep* a day holy if it has already been *made* holy.

When God appeared to Moses in a burning bush, the Lord commanded him, "Take your sandals off your feet, for the place where you stand is holy ground" (Exodus 3:5). The ground was not previously holy, but the presence of God had made it that way. Similarly, the Sabbath is holy because the presence of God is to be experienced in a special way on that day. And we can only keep the seventh day *holy* when the presence of the *Holy* Spirit is actively invited into our lives. We can be in the right place doing the right things on the right day and still fall short of keeping the Sabbath if our hearts are far from God. We must have Jesus dwelling in our hearts by faith (see Ephesians 3:17) if we would find joy in the spiritual emphasis of the Sabbath, and be brought into harmony with the command to "keep it holy."

Evening to Evening

In order to keep the seventh day holy, it is important to know when it begins and ends. According to Genesis 1, each day of creation consisted of "the evening and the morning." The evening was listed as the beginning of the 24-hour day. Other passages of Scripture confirm this understanding. Nehemiah commanded the gates of Jerusalem to be shut "as it began to be dark before the Sabbath" (Nehemiah 13:19). The implication is that once it was dark, the Sabbath would begin. In Leviticus 23:32, when describing the observance of an annual sabbath associated with the Day of Atonement, the Israelites were instructed, "From evening to evening, you shall celebrate your sabbath."

The Bible consistently teaches that the Sabbath begins when it becomes dark, or at sundown, on Friday evening, and ends at sundown on Saturday evening. The beauty of this plan is that we can welcome the Sabbath hours while we are still awake rather than having it begin while we are asleep. This provides a wonderful opportunity for families or groups of fellow believers to usher in and also close the Sabbath with prayer, singing, and reading God's Word. "Vespers," a term that means an evening religious service, is often used in the Seventh-day Adventist Church to describe these enjoyable family or church worship services that open or close the Sabbath.

A Day of Rest

Without a command to rest, many would allow the busyness of life to prevent them from spending ample time with God. But the fourth commandment unambiguously states, "Six days you shall labor and do all your work, but the seventh day is the Sabbath of the Lord your God. In it you shall do no work; you, nor your son, nor your daughter, nor your male servant, nor your female servant, nor your cattle, nor your stranger who is within your gates" (Exodus 20:9-10). This prohibition applies to any common labor performed on the seventh day, or between sundown Friday and sundown Saturday.

Some occupations, such as certain physicians and nurses, may require caring for those who are suffering on Sabbath. This kind of labor is in harmony with the statement of Jesus, "It is lawful to do good on the Sabbath" (Matthew 12:12). Inasmuch as this labor is to meet the urgent needs of humanity, rather than employment for income, it is recommended that wages earned for this Sabbath labor be donated as a freewill offering.

In addition to our own abstinence from work, the commandment also forbids labor by anyone within our sphere of influence. The reference to male and female servants could apply today to hired labor such as house cleaners, baby sitters, plumbers, landscapers, or builders. If we employ someone to work on home improvements, we should stipulate that no work is to be performed between Friday sundown and Saturday sundown. Or, if we run a business with workers whose hours we control, we are not innocent if we refrain from work on the Sabbath but still require it of our employees.

An associated application of the Sabbath command to refrain from labor pertains to common commerce or business transactions. According to Scripture, buying and selling on the Sabbath is also a violation of the sacredness of the day. When Nehemiah discovered the children of Judah selling goods on the Sabbath, he "warned them about the day on which they were selling provisions" (Nehemiah 13:15).

> *The primary reason that God is worthy of our worship is His claim upon us as our Creator.*

He also found them buying from merchants who brought their goods into Jerusalem on the Sabbath day. Nehemiah then "contended with the nobles of Judah," saying, "What evil thing is this that you do, by which you profane the Sabbath day?" (Nehemiah 13:17). He further stated that their practice of buying and selling on the Sabbath was bringing "added wrath on Israel" (Nehemiah 13:18). These verses indicate that common commerce, such as dining at a restaurant or shopping at a grocery store, is a violation of the Sabbath commandment.

Because God asks us to carefully limit the Sabbath to spiritual activities, we must plan ahead with regard to those things that are better suited for another day. This is why God said, "Remember the Sabbath day" (Exodus 20:8). We are to keep the Sabbath in view throughout the week, so that we are not unprepared when it arrives.

The Bible refers to the day before the Sabbath as the Preparation Day. This name implies that practical labor, commerce, and other preparations are especially suited for the day before the Sabbath. We should buy fuel for our car, prepare meals ahead of time to the extent that we can, clean and straighten our homes, or perform other practical preparations ahead of the Sabbath. By so doing, we will be free to focus on Jesus when the Sabbath arrives.

A Day to Worship the Creator

It is not uncommon to hear of someone endeavoring to keep the Sabbath by simply resting alone at home and refraining from work. While this is a good start, it falls short of the fullness of what Sabbath-keeping means. In Leviticus 23:3, the Sabbath is referred to as "a holy convocation," or a sacred assembly. This phrase reveals that part of the beauty of the Sabbath is in worshiping corporately with other believers.

Jesus Himself incorporated this important aspect of Sabbath-keeping into His own life. "And as His custom was, He went into the synagogue on the Sabbath day" (Luke 4:16). Jesus did not remain alone, but habitually attended corporate worship on the Sabbath. In the book of Hebrews, we find that this need for fellowship becomes increasingly important as we approach the second coming of Christ, "And let us consider one another in order to stir up love and good works, not forsaking the assembling of ourselves together, as is the manner of some, but exhorting one another, and so much the more as you see the Day approaching" (Hebrews 10:24-25). Even in the "new heavens and the new earth," we discover that "from one Sabbath to another, all flesh shall come to worship" (Isaiah 66:22-23) before God. Throughout eternity, the Sabbath will be a day for God's people to join together in the worship of their Creator.

"You are worthy, O Lord, to receive glory and honor and power; for You created all things, and by Your will they exist and were created" (Revelation 4:11). The primary reason that God is worthy of our worship is His claim upon us as our Creator. The Sabbath is a weekly reminder of this important relationship. The fourth commandment concludes with the following reason for our obedience: "For in six days the Lord made the heavens and the earth, the sea, and all that is in them, and rested the seventh day. Therefore the Lord blessed the Sabbath day and hallowed it" (Exodus 20:11). The Sabbath, as a memorial of creation, is therefore a wonderful day to spend time in nature. Walking in the woods, looking out on the ocean, listening to the birds, or smelling the flowers can point us to the One who in infinite love created it all for our happiness.

His Day

"If you turn away your foot from the Sabbath, from doing your pleasure on My holy day, and call the Sabbath a delight, the holy day of the Lord honorable, and shall honor Him, not doing your own ways, nor finding your own pleasure, nor speaking your own words, then you shall delight yourself in the Lord" (Isaiah 58:13-14).

Isaiah 58 gives an excellent description of how to truly keep the Sabbath, providing principles that can guide us in any situation. The prohibitions against doing our own ways, finding our own pleasure, or speaking our own words, are not given in order to take the joy out of the Sabbath. They invite us to find joy *in His presence* rather than by engaging in common thoughts, conversation, and activities that are not spiritual in nature. The Sabbath is not a day for our sports or hobbies, for keeping up on world news, or going to secular events. Rather, it is an opportunity to deepen our relationship with God, to spend valuable time with our children and families, and to fellowship with like-minded believers.

One important way to draw close to God is to minister to the physical and spiritual needs of humanity on the Sabbath. In this, the example of Christ is highly instructive. "Every working of Christ in miracles was essential, and was to reveal to the world that there was a great work to be done on the Sabbath day for the relief of suffering humanity, but the common work was not to be done" (*Selected Messages,* book 3, p. 258).

The beginning portions of Isaiah, chapter 58, while they reference fasting, may also apply to the observance of the Sabbath mentioned at the end of the chapter. Isaiah writes of the need to "loose the bonds of wickedness, to undo the heavy burdens, to let the oppressed go free, and that you break every yoke" (Isaiah 58:6). He appeals further, "If you extend your soul to the hungry and satisfy the afflicted soul, then your light shall dawn in the darkness, and your darkness shall be as the noonday" (Isaiah 58:10).

The Sabbath, as Jesus exemplified in His life, is a great time to minister to others. Practical ways to do this may include:

- Offering encouraging words and prayers for those going through difficulty at your church.
- Visiting those who are shut-in, sick, elderly, or hospitalized.

- Visiting those who desire Bible study
  or spiritual guidance.
- Going on organized church outreach activities.

Practical Application

A list of rules need not be made for the Sabbath, but God has given us principles to guide us in our efforts to keep the day holy. Now let us apply these principles to some challenging Sabbath day scenarios:

Helping a neighbor build a deck. While Jesus did say "it is lawful to do good on the Sabbath" (Matthew 12:12), the context was an *emergency* situation of a sheep falling into a pit. Good deeds that require manual or common labor, and which are not in response to an emergency situation, are not the lawful ones of which Jesus spoke.

Mandatory late Friday work only once a year. It may seem harmless to work on the Sabbath only once or twice a year, but every time we knowingly disobey God's law we weaken our character and make it easier to sin in the future. Even occasional disobedience will only prepare us for failure when greater tests come. It is much better to be open with your employer and take a stand. God will honor those who honor Him.

Watching or participating in secular activities. These could be work events (employer picnics, golf outings, etc.) or recreational hobbies and entertainment (little league games, hunting trips, college football, etc.). The Lord instructs, "turn away your foot from the Sabbath, from doing your pleasure on My holy day" (Isaiah 58:13). Others may not understand why we view these activities as being inappropriate on the Sabbath, yet we should still maintain our reverence for God's holy day. This will not lessen, but potentially increase our spiritual influence with those around us.

Staying in a hotel over a weekend. Travel that keeps us away from home on Sabbath is sometimes unavoidable. In such cases, meals can be prepared ahead of time, hotel payment arrangements can be handled before the Sabbath, and maid service can be declined during Sabbath hours. Leaving a Sabbath tract or a personal note sharing your Sabbath beliefs, along with a generous tip, is a good way to witness while traveling.

Attending a friend's wedding. While weddings are to be spiritual occasions, most weddings consist of many non-spiritual activities. Consider attending the spiritual portion of the service, greeting the bride and groom, giving a card and gift, and then leaving before the atmosphere becomes decidedly unspiritual.

Spouse who does not keep the Sabbath. One of the most common and yet challenging Sabbath scenarios is a spouse who insists on watching secular television, playing loud music, or otherwise being unmindful of the sacredness of the Sabbath. Sometimes different arrangements may be negotiated, but we should be careful not to demand an entire change in the lifestyle of those in our home simply to accommodate our beliefs. Time and opportunity must be given for our loved ones to see and respond to the truth for themselves. Sometimes, spending time with fellow Sabbath-keepers during the Sabbath hours can be a fruitful way to enjoy the Sabbath while not interfering with the plans of those in your home.

As you evaluate your own Sabbath observance, ask the following questions: Am I keeping up my spiritual interest with regular devotional time during the week so that I look eagerly to the spiritual blessings of the Sabbath? Am I opening and closing the sacred hours of the Sabbath with family or church worship? Have I been clear with my employer about my intention to never work during Sabbath hours? Is corporate worship a habitual part of my Sabbath observance? Am I preparing weekly for the Sabbath so that I do not need to do unnecessary work or to buy or sell on the Sabbath? Am I incorporating activities that minister to the physical or spiritual needs of others on the Sabbath? And most importantly, am I seeking to build my personal relationship with God on the Sabbath?

As you carefully guard the sacredness of God's holy day, remember that the reason for its proper observance is that we might more fully know God and delight ourselves in Him. "To know God is to love Him" (*The Desire of Ages*, p. 22). As you turn your eyes upon Jesus each Sabbath, the things of this earth will grow strangely dim. Your love for God will grow, and heaven will draw near.

16

Fear God

T he first of the three angels' messages of Revelation 14 begins with the words, "Fear God, and give glory to Him" (Revelation 14:7). This command to fear God, however, is not to be confused with the idea of being afraid of God. On the contrary, we learn from the Bible that "God is love" (1 John 4:8, 16), and that "there is no fear in love; but perfect love casts out fear" (1 John 4:18). The command to *not* be afraid occurs more than 50 times in the Bible.

What does it mean then, when the Bible tells us to fear God? What kind of fear can possibly co-exist with love and affection? Hebrews 12:28 gives us a clue when it instructs us to serve God "with reverence and godly fear." Here we find godly fear associated with "reverence," which is defined as showing great honor or profound awe, adoration, and respect. This reverence for God is the positive "fear" of which the Bible writers speak.

Solemn Joy

While rightly associated with a solemn attitude, true reverence should also reflect great joy. Reverence is being in awe not only of God's might and power, but also of His love and mercy. When Isaiah saw God, He said, "Woe is me, for I am undone! Because I am a man of unclean lips, and I dwell in the midst of a people of unclean lips; for my eyes have seen the King, the Lord of hosts" (Isaiah 6:5). Being in the presence of God inspired Isaiah with deep humility, and a greater appreciation of God's power than ever before. But it was also the revelation of God's *mercy,* in pardoning his sin, that inspired Isaiah to dedicate his life to sacrificial service for Him (see Isaiah 6:7-8). God's character is a perfect blend of justice and mercy, and true reverence includes a healthy appreciation for both.

Through the prophet Jeremiah, God revealed that when He would forgive and cleanse Judah and Israel of their sins, they would "fear and tremble for all the goodness and all the prosperity that I provide for it" (Jeremiah 33:9). Notice that the fear and trembling here described is for the abundant "goodness" and "prosperity" that comes from God. Similarly, the Psalmist writes, "Serve the Lord with fear, and rejoice with trembling" (Psalm 2:11). Biblical fear and trembling do not take away our joy. They do not reflect a believer who is petrified by fear of judgment, but one who is overwhelmingly thankful for love and forgiveness that is undeserved! When the Holy Spirit gives us a revelation of God's majestic character, and we sense that we are in the presence of One who is infinite in holiness and love, it is a solemn experience. At the same time, it should also inspire us with great hope and joy. As it is written, "In Your presence is fullness of joy" (Psalm 16:11).

> *Reverence is being in awe not only of God's might and power, but also of His love and mercy.*

Reverence For God's Name

The third commandment of the moral law reads, "You shall not take the name of the Lord your God in vain, for the Lord will not hold him guiltless who takes His name in vain" (Exodus 20:7). Because God is holy, we should treat His name with the utmost respect. We should not use the names of God or Jesus as empty expressions or slang, or even use euphemisms that sound similar to His name. As the Psalmist says, "Holy and awesome is His name" (Psalm 111:9).

While it is true that God is our Friend, He is not like our erring, mortal, human friends. He is the Almighty Creator and Sovereign over the entire universe. "You thought that I was altogether like you," the Lord declared in Psalm 50:21. But the Scripture is clear that in so very many ways, He is not like us. "'For My thoughts are not your thoughts, nor are your ways My ways,' says the Lord. 'For as the heavens are higher than the earth, so are My ways higher than your ways, and My thoughts than your thoughts'" (Isaiah 55:8-9). We make a terrible mistake if we view God or His name in a casual or common way. For this reason, Jesus taught us to pray, "Our Father in heaven, hallowed be Your name" (Matthew 6:9).

We must remember that the reason God's name is holy is that it represents His person and character. There is no special sanctity attached to the original Hebrew or Greek letters with which the Bible was written, or to finding the precise pronunciation of His name in those languages. God's name is holy because the God it represents is holy. We should be reverent, not flippant, when speaking any of the many names attributed to God. But the Scripture does not teach that we may only speak the names of God and Jesus in Hebrew, or that translating His name into other languages is wrong. This is an extreme view that confuses reverence for God with a reverence for human language.

Reverence in Prayer

When we pray, our posture and attitude should reflect our reverence for God. If we are physically able to kneel during our personal prayer time, this posture best impresses upon our own hearts and minds the idea of submission to God. For some, kneeling causes too much pain or difficulty in getting back up. God understands this and is most concerned that our hearts are humble before Him, regardless of our posture. Because the Bible admonishes us to "pray without ceasing" (1 Thessalonians 5:17), there will often be occasions when we will need to pray while standing, sitting, or walking. God hears every one of these prayers.

Nevertheless, the Scriptural examples of kneeling before God abound. This posture appears to be a positive sign of reverence, and an expression of humility in worship. "Oh come, let us worship and bow down; let us kneel before the Lord our Maker" (Psalm 95:6).

Reverence for God's Word

The apostle Paul counsels us to "work out your own salvation with fear and trembling" (Philippians 2:12). While we are not to be afraid of God, we are to take His Word seriously. We are to be afraid of the consequences of disregarding it. When the children of Israel quaked with fear at the glory of God's presence on Mount Sinai, Moses assured them, "Do not fear; for God has come to test you, and that His fear may be before you, so that you may not sin" (Exodus 20:20). At the same time that he told them, "Do not fear," Moses also desired that "His fear" —a healthy respect for God's commands—would protect the nation of Israel from the terrible results of sin.

Reverence is an attitude of trust in God and distrust in self, which manifests itself in obedience to God's Word. "On this one I will look; on him who is poor and of a contrite spirit, and who trembles at My word" (Isaiah 66:2). To tremble at the Word of God is to take time to read it regularly and to have a deep interest in the wisdom and instruction it provides. Even the physical handling of our Bibles should be given extra care in comparison to common books. We should not casually toss it around, or use it as a coaster for a drink. By treating it with respect outwardly, we impress our minds with the need to carefully heed the words on the inside.

Reverence for God's House

Another area in which reverence for God should be evident is in the way we relate to the house of worship. "God is greatly to be feared in the assembly of the saints, and to be held in reverence by all those around Him" (Psalm 89:7). We must remember that when we come into the sanctuary each Sabbath, we are coming to worship in the presence of God. "You shall keep My Sabbaths and reverence My sanctuary: I am the Lord" (Leviticus 19:30). Being aware of this will lead us to behave differently in the sanctuary.

"If when the people come into the house of worship, they have genuine reverence for the Lord and bear in mind that they are in His presence, there will be a sweet eloquence in silence. The whispering and laughing and talking which might be without sin in a common business place should find no sanction in the house where God is worshiped. The mind should be prepared to hear the word of God, that it may have due weight and suitably impress the heart" (*Testimonies for the Church,* vol. 5, p. 492).

We can maintain an atmosphere of reverence in the sanctuary by reserving casual conversation for outside its walls, muting cell phones during worship, instructing our children to never run or play in the sanctuary, and by always being attentive to those leading out in the worship service. This final aspect, that of paying close attention during worship and not distracting others from doing the same, is an underlying principle that should govern our behavior in the house of God. "When the word is spoken ... Listen attentively. Sleep not for one instant, because by this slumber you may lose the very words that you need most" (*Testimonies for the Church,* vol. 5, 493).

Reverence during worship includes more than being quiet or sitting still. It involves participating in the service with the whole heart, and being genuinely interested. It involves singing when it is time to sing, kneeling when it is time to kneel, following along in our Bibles, and even proclaiming a heartfelt "Amen!" or "Praise the Lord!" when the Word is preached. "The lifeless attitude of the worshipers in the house of God is one great reason why the ministry is not more productive of good" (*Testimonies for the Church,* vol. 5, p. 492). It is not merely noise or disruption in the sanctuary that is the heart of irreverence, but a lifeless indifference and disregard for the presence of God and the power of His Word!

> *Reverence during worship includes more than being quiet or sitting still.*

While attention and participation in worship are vital aspects of reverence, we should be careful to avoid artificial methods of bringing life into the worship service. When theatrics or levity are made the focus of sacred services in an effort to merely entertain the crowd or elicit applause, reverence is lost. An atmosphere of a secular performance steals from the quiet influence of the Spirit of God. Our sacred services should be full of enthusiasm and joy without compromising solemnity and order.

A final aspect of reverence in public worship is our appearance. It has become common in recent years to say that God doesn't care how we dress when we appear before Him in worship. It is certainly true that we should never exclude or look down on someone because of what he or she wears to church. But consider that in biblical times, the priests were given special instructions on exactly what to wear when ministering in the sanctuary (see Exodus 28). Notice, too, that God told the people to wash their clothes before meeting with Him to receive His law (see Exodus 19:10, 14).

These examples suggest that we should not be unmindful of our appearance before God, but should be clean, modest, and respectful in our attire. The most respectful attire may vary by culture, but we should appear before God in our best. It would be inconsistent to wear a suit to work, but jeans and a sweatshirt to appear before God. Furthermore, if angels cover themselves with their wings when in God's presence (see Isaiah 6:1-2), how much more should we properly cover ourselves by dressing modestly for public worship. Our choice of clothing for worship will impress both ourselves and others with the level of importance that we place upon God and His Word.

Practical Application

Reverence is an attitude of the heart that reflects profound love and respect for God. It leads us to treat that which God calls holy with special care. As you have read this chapter, perhaps God has revealed to you areas in which a casual attitude toward sacred things has crept into your own heart and life. Commit yourself to treating that which is sacred in an extra special way. Doing so will elevate God and His Word in your own mind and in the minds of those around you.

One area of caution, however, is that we should never cherish a critical spirit toward others because of a perceived lack of reverence in their lives. True reverence will lead us to say, as did Isaiah when in the presence of God, "Woe is me, for I am undone" (Isaiah 6:5). It is this humility that makes truly reverent people the most gracious and thoughtful when dealing with the weaknesses of others. Reverence is an area that can easily slip out of view for any of us if we are not watchful. So be kind and thoughtful if you see others who do not seem to reflect the Scriptural ideal for reverence. Rather than focusing on the weaknesses of others, endeavor to apply the message of Revelation 14:7 to your own life; "Fear God and give glory to Him, for the hour of His judgment has come." In so doing, you will experience the blessing that can only come with true reverence for God. "Happy is the man who is always reverent" (Proverbs 28:14).

17

Treasure in Heaven

God is the only being in the universe who has life inherent in Himself. Every other living thing receives its life from God and is continually sustained by Him. When the serpent came to Eve in the Garden of Eden, however, he lied to her about the source of life. By flattering her with the notion that she would not "surely die" (Genesis 3:4) despite God's warning, the serpent implied that humanity was not dependent upon God for life. Eve ate of the forbidden fruit because she was deceived into thinking that she could live her life *independent* of God.

Today, the deception that fooled our first parents continues to bear sway over humanity. Rather than see ourselves as managing that which belongs to God—our lives, our bodies, our children, our possessions—we are tempted to think that everything in this life is ours to do with as we please. The Bible tells a different story. "Or do you not know that your body is the temple of the Holy Spirit who is in you, whom you have from God, and you are not your own? For you were bought at a price; therefore glorify God in your body and in your spirit, which are God's" (1 Corinthians 6:19-20).

Accountable to God

In Luke Chapter 12, Jesus gives a parable in which a rich man becomes even richer when he is blessed with a bountiful harvest. The man had only God to thank for his riches. His ability to earn an income had come from God, and it was God who gave the sun and the rain and caused his crops to grow. But instead of considering how God might want him to use his riches—perhaps by ministering to those in need or by advancing the spread of the gospel—he decided to build a bigger barn and keep it all for himself so that he could live in ease. "But God said

> *The first step to understanding God's will in financial matters is to understand the unselfish nature of God.*

to him, 'Fool! This night your soul will be required of you; then whose will those things be which you have provided?' So is he who lays up treasure for himself, and is not rich toward God" (Luke 12:20-21). The man thought he was accountable to no one and that he could live "for himself." He was wrong. The moral of the story is that we will one day give an account to God of how we managed that which He has given us.

To manage or look after the property of someone else is the definition of a *steward*. This is a fit description of our role as beings created by God. While the Lord is happy to bless us with life and possessions, all of creation still technically belongs to Him (see Psalm 50:10). Therefore, as stewards of God's possessions, we need to consider His purposes before deciding how to use money and possessions. And the first step to understanding God's will in financial matters is to understand the unselfish nature of God.

The Benevolent Heart

The Bible refers to God as the One who gives us our lives and everything we need—our daily bread, repentance, forgiveness, victory, grace, love, wisdom, the Holy Spirit, the kingdom, and eternal life. He is also the One who "so loved the world that He gave His only begotten Son" (John 3:16). The heart of God is a heart of sacrifice and loving benevolence, because "God is love" (1 John 4:8, 16). Giving to others is a fundamental expression of His character. And if our goal is to be like Jesus, then we must learn to give, too.

Unfortunately, unselfish and sacrificial giving is not natural to the human heart. It is far more natural to spend money on unnecessary luxuries for ourselves and our loved ones. The devil preys upon this weakness and entices us with the "deceitfulness of riches" (Mark 4:19). We look for contentment in things, only to find that we are less content than ever. This leads to even more spending, which often spirals out of control and results in heavy burdens of debt (see Proverbs 22:7). For this reason Jesus warns us, "Take heed and beware of covetousness, for one's life does not consist in the abundance of the things he possesses" (Luke 12:15).

Hebrews 13:5 admonishes, "Let your conduct be without covetousness; be content with such things as you have. For He Himself has said, 'I will never leave you nor forsake you.'" This passage reminds us that a personal relationship with Jesus—the One who will never leave us nor forsake us—is the only thing that can bring true contentment. When Jesus is in the heart, our financial choices begin to reflect the benevolent heart of God. We become so thankful for our own salvation that rather than spend merely on temporal possessions for ourselves, we are compelled to invest in the eternal salvation of others. And how do we do this? To answer this question, we will now explore what the Bible says about tithes and offerings.

The Tithing System

The twelve tribes of Israel each received an inheritance in the land of Canaan—except for the Levites. The Levites were those chosen to lead out in the service of the sanctuary and the worship of God. There was a different plan for this tribe, which God explained in Numbers 18:21-24: "Behold, I have given the children of Levi all the tithes in Israel as an inheritance in return for the work which they perform, the work of the tabernacle of meeting. ... For the tithes of the children of Israel, which they offer up as a heave offering to the Lord, I have given to the Levites as an inheritance; therefore I have said to them, 'Among the children of Israel they shall have no inheritance.'"

Rather than inheriting land, the Levites were given "all the tithes in Israel as an inheritance in return for the work which they perform." The word tithe means "tenth." Each tribe was required to give a tenth of the increase of their produce, flocks, and herds to serve as the "inheritance" of the Levites for their work in the service of God. The tithe, then, was God's way of providing for those who were dedicated to religious activities and instruction and could not regularly engage in income-earning activities.

By faithfully returning tithe, we invest in the spreading of the gospel and partner with God in the mission of saving souls.

In 1 Corinthians 9:13-14, Paul asserts that the same system established to provide for the priests who ministered in the temple is today still needed for ministers of the gospel. "Do you not know that those who minister the holy things eat of the things of the temple, and those who serve at the altar partake of the offerings of the altar? Even so the Lord has commanded that those who preach the gospel should live from the gospel." Here Paul first speaks of those who "serve at the altar"—a reference to the priests—being sustained by the tithes and offerings brought to the temple. He then declares that "even so," or just as the priests were sustained by the tithe, "the Lord has commanded" that those who preach the gospel today should be provided for in the same way. By faithfully returning tithe, we invest in the spreading of the gospel and partner with God in the mission of saving souls.

Holy to the Lord

Leviticus 27:30 states that "all the tithe of the land … is the Lord's. It is holy to the Lord." The tithe belongs to God. Just as it was needed to provide for the priests in Old Testament times, it is today needed to support the pastors, evangelists, and others who are employed in the ministry of the gospel. Because it is "holy to the Lord"—designated by God for this sacred purpose—the tithe is not ours to do with as we please. The returning of God's tithe, therefore, is a matter of honesty and integrity.

Consider the vivid counsel given in the book of Malachi. It emphasizes not only the sacred nature of the tithe, but also the wonderful promises made to those who faithfully return it to God. "'Will a man rob God? Yet you have robbed Me! But you say, "In what way have we robbed You?" In tithes and offerings. You are cursed with a curse, for you have robbed Me, even this whole nation. Bring all the tithes into the storehouse, that there may be food in My house, and try Me now in this,' says the

Lord of hosts, 'If I will not open for you the windows of heaven and pour out for you such blessing that there will not be room enough to receive it'" (Malachi 3:8-10).

Common Questions Regarding Tithe

What is the amount on which I calculate my tithe? In the days of Israel, produce, flocks, and herds represented the "increase" upon which the tithe was calculated. Today, most people will simply pay 10% of their gross wages or other income. This would not represent the amount received on a paycheck after taxes are withheld, but the full wage paid before taxes. This is our true increase. Tax refunds and similar reimbursements or overpayments do not need to be tithed.

What if I don't have anything left for tithe after paying my bills? Proverbs 3:9 says, "Honor the Lord with your possessions, and with the firstfruits of all your increase." The tithe, or tenth of our increase, should be the first thing we pay—even before our bills. It belongs to God and should be promptly returned to Him. Keep in mind that God promises to "open for you the windows of heaven" (Malachi 3:10) if you faithfully return the tithe. We can have faith in that promise. In order to faithfully return 10% of our income along with freewill offerings, we may need to better manage our finances. But when we have done all we can, God promises that He will provide for us.

Is it okay to give less than 10%? To give less than 10% is not really tithing, since the word "tithe" means "tenth." The appeal of Malachi 3:10 is to bring "all the tithes" into the storehouse. If we do, we will receive "such blessing that there will not be room enough to receive it." This isn't a promise that we will get rich, but it does mean that God will provide for us, both spiritually and physically.

Where should I pay my tithe? In Old Testament times the tithes of the children of Israel went to the temple "storehouse" (Malachi 3:10) from which the priests and Levites were paid. God gave strict commands to His people not to take their tithes and offerings wherever they chose, "every man doing what is right in his own eyes" (Deuteronomy 12:8), but specifically to the place where the Lord was to "make His name abide" (Deuteronomy 12:11). This would be where the service of God was conducted by the Levites who were sustained from the tithe. Similarly, we should return our tithe to the Seventh-day Adventist Church, which employs the ministers, evangelists, and other workers sustained by the tithe. More specifically, each member should return his or her tithe to the local church where membership is held. From there, the tithe is forwarded to the local conference to be kept in the "storehouse" from which the workers are paid. A portion of this tithe is also distributed to higher levels of the church to support its worldwide work.

May I allocate a portion of my tithe to any worthwhile ministry? The tithe was sacredly set apart to provide for employed laborers in the work of God. Ellen White counseled, "God has given special direction as to the use of the tithe. … The portion that God has reserved for Himself is not to be diverted to any other purpose than that which He has specified. Let none feel at liberty to retain their tithe, to use according to their own judgment. They are not to use it for themselves in an emergency, nor to apply it as they see fit, even in what they may regard as the Lord's work" (*Testimonies for the Church*, vol. 9, p. 247). In light of this counsel, and the biblical use of the tithe, we should include a full 10% on the tithe line of our donation envelope.

Do pastors of big churches get rich while pastors of small churches struggle financially? In the Seventh-day Adventist Church, all pastors are paid the same base salary with only minor adjustments for years of service and cost of living. A pastor's salary will not be directly increased or decreased by the amount of tithe returned by the local church.

Should we still return tithe if the pastor or conference leadership becomes unfaithful? While we may sometimes disagree with the spiritual leaders who are paid from the tithe, we must remember that we do not return tithe to ministers, but to God. In the days of Malachi, when God instructed His people to return to Him by returning "all the tithes" (Malachi 3:10), the priests who were sustained by that tithe had become corrupt (see Malachi 2:7-9). Yet God still said that the people were robbing God if they withheld their tithe from Him. Ellen White provides wise counsel on how to relate to such a situation: "Some have been dissatisfied, and have said, 'I will not longer pay my tithe; for I have no confidence in the way things are managed at the heart of the work.' But will you rob God because you think the management of the work is not right? Make your complaint, plainly and openly, in the right spirit, to the proper ones. Send in your petitions for things to be adjusted and set in order; but do not withdraw from the work of God, and prove unfaithful, because others are not doing right" (*Counsels on Stewardship*, pp. 93-94).

Freewill Offerings

When carefully considering Malachi 3:8, we discover that robbing God happens not only when we withhold tithe, but also offerings. The children of Israel brought offerings with them every time they came to the temple—whether sin offerings, guilt offerings, burnt offerings, peace offerings, or grain offerings. They also gave special offerings for the building or repairing of the temple, the dedication of the altar and the sanctuary, and at the three annual pilgrimages to Jerusalem. The giving of offerings in addition to the 10% tithe was a regular part of the worship experience of God's people. "Every man shall give as he is able, according to the blessing of the Lord your God which He has given you" (Deuteronomy 16:17; see also 1 Corinthians 16:2).

The financial needs of the local church today are still sustained by the freewill offerings of its members—above and beyond the 10% designated as tithe. While no specific amount is commanded in the Bible for these offerings, it is best to give a fixed percentage of income to your local church. Those returning tithe for the first time may require an adjustment period before giving a substantial freewill offering percentage. They may begin with only 1-2%. Others may have the means to give 10-15%. Most Seventh-day Adventist Churches operate on an average of somewhere between 3-5% of their members' income being donated to the local church, above and beyond the tithe.

When contributing these offerings to the local church, it is recommended that you use the line on your tithe and offering envelope entitled, Combined Budget or Local Budget. Money designated to this fund will be used to pay for literature and other evangelistic materials, capital improvements and repairs to church property, utility costs, and many other operating expenses. In addition to local church needs, you may also consider giving to your local conference, world mission fields, media ministries, youth programs, and many other worthwhile endeavors.

The Bible encourages Christians to develop benevolent hearts by giving both liberally and cheerfully: "He who sows sparingly will also reap sparingly, and he who sows bountifully will also reap bountifully. So let each one give as he purposes in his heart, not grudgingly or of necessity; for God loves a cheerful giver" (2 Corinthians 9:6-7). There is a close connection between our financial support of the church and our love for the church. Those who are most invested financially *in* the cause of God will usually have the greatest sympathies *for* the cause of God.

Practical Application

One day, Jesus commended a woman for her exceptional benevolence. "And He looked up and saw the rich putting their gifts into the treasury, and He saw also a certain poor widow putting in two mites. So He said, 'Truly I say to you that this poor widow has put in more than all; for all these out of their abundance have put in offerings for God, but she out of her poverty put in all the livelihood that she had'" (Luke 21:1-4). Perhaps the key to a benevolent heart is not how much we give, but what we sacrifice to give it.

Take time to evaluate your financial stewardship. Are you being honest with God in your tithe—faithfully and consistently returning to Him 10% of your income? Are you being generous and sacrificial in your freewill offerings? In the light of eternity, prayerfully consider how much you are investing financially in the Lord's work. Remember, "where your treasure is, there your heart will be also" (Matthew 6:21).

18

Eight Laws of Health

"If you diligently heed the voice of the Lord your God and do what is right in His sight, give ear to His commandments and keep all His statutes, I will put none of the diseases on you which I have brought on the Egyptians. For I am the Lord who heals you" (Exodus 15:26).

From the beginning, God created us to live in harmony with His commandments. Not only does this include moral laws that govern our spiritual health, but also natural laws that govern our physical health. Only when we "give ear to His commandments" and seek to cooperate with these laws will we experience the healing of our entire person. By following God's directions for optimum physical health, we too can escape many of the diseases that afflicted the Egyptians, and which still cause much suffering in our world today.

Glorify God in Your Body

Purity of heart and mind are not the only important aspects of the Christian life. The Bible also teaches that we should care for our bodies. "Or do you not know that your body is the temple of the Holy Spirit who is in you, whom you have from God, and you are not your own? For you were bought at a price; therefore glorify God in your body and in your spirit, which are God's" (1 Corinthians 6:19-20).

While the kingdom of God is more than a matter of "eating and drinking" (Romans 14:17), choices affecting our physical health *are* important to God. "Whether you eat or drink, or whatever you do, do all to the glory of God" (1 Corinthians 10:31). The Lord desires our good, and He knows that our physical health affects how we think and act in spiritual matters. A healthy body results in a clear mind that is better able to comprehend truth, resist temptation, and face the spiritual battles of life. Furthermore, being physically healthy simply helps us to feel better, and God does not want us to experience any unnecessary suffering. "Beloved, I pray that you may prosper in all things and be in health, just as your soul prospers" (3 John 2).

Looking for a NEW START

When it comes to living healthfully, we all need encouragement. Ever since our first parents failed on the matter of appetite by eating that forbidden fruit, we have each inherited strong inclinations to make not-so-healthy choices. We eat too much of what we shouldn't and not enough of what we should. We don't exercise enough, don't drink enough water, and often become addicted to unhealthful habits and practices. All this has led to an increase in lifestyle-related sickness and disease, and for many it has resulted in strong feelings of guilt and the loss of much self-respect.

How comforting to know, however, that Jesus is a loving Savior who came into our world not to condemn but to save (see

John 3:17). He longs to help us find freedom from the habits that enslave us. We must remember that changing physical habits is a spiritual matter that requires help from God. Jesus' example taught us that it is only by maintaining a close connection with God that we can experience victory over temptation. He was victorious, even in the matter of appetite (see Luke 4:3-4), and He can and will help us to find victory, too!

> *Our physical health affects how we think and act in spiritual matters.*

To make positive changes in our physical health, it is important that we have a well-rounded view of a truly healthy lifestyle. Therefore, we will now explore eight important laws of health, each represented by a different letter in the acronym NEW START.

"N" for Nutrition

One of the most important factors in our physical health is to make good choices in the things we eat. But with so many diets being promoted today, how are we to know what is best? While discussing marriage, Jesus taught that divorce was not in God's plan with the words, "But from the beginning it was not so" (Matthew 19:8). Just like God's ideal for marriage, we can find the ideal diet by looking back to God's instruction in "the beginning."

"And God said, 'See, I have given you every herb that yields seed which is on the face of all the earth, and every tree whose fruit yields seed; to you it shall be for food. Also, to every beast of the earth, to every bird of the air, and to everything that creeps on the earth, in which there is life, I have given every green herb for food'; and it was so" (Genesis 1:29-30).

From the dietary instruction given by God to our first parents, we discover that mankind was never intended to eat the animals. Even after Adam and Eve sinned, God still instructed humanity to live on a vegetarian diet (see Genesis 3:18). Concessions allowing the eating of clean meats were made at the time of the flood, but this was primarily due to the absence of vegetation. Today, it is still God's ideal to avoid the eating of meat whenever possible. After all, we're preparing to live in the New Earth, where there will be no more death and everyone will be vegetarian (Revelation 21:4)!

The eating of meat, with its high concentrations of protein, cholesterol, and fat, has been closely tied to high-blood pressure, heart disease, cancer, and many other diseases. Much benefit could be gained if we would adopt a diet free from meat but rich in fruits, nuts, vegetables, grains, and legumes. If meat is eaten, it should never include the unclean animals that the Bible refers to as abominable (see Leviticus 20:25), most of which are scavengers. These include swine (pork bacon, ham, pepperoni, sausage, lard, etc.), shellfish, lobster, crab, shrimp, and many other animals (see Leviticus 11).

While some argue that Jesus removed any restrictions regarding the eating of unclean animals, there is no evidence that this is the case. He did refute the idea that food was unclean for merely ceremonial reasons, such as unwashed hands (Mark 7:2), but never did He remove the instruction regarding clean and unclean animals. This distinction is first mentioned in the Bible when clean animals entered the ark in sevens while the unclean entered in twos (see Genesis 7:2), an event that occurred long before the temporary ceremonial laws were given to the Jewish nation. Even in the New Testament church, when Peter was given a vision of unclean creatures to teach him not to call "any man common or unclean" (Acts 10:28), the biblical distinction between clean and unclean meats was by no means abolished.

In addition to entirely abstaining from unclean meats and promoting a vegetarian diet, Seventh-day Adventists also encourage many other beneficial dietary habits. These include taking care not to eat too much sugar or refined foods, avoiding the habit of eating between meals, eating heavier at breakfast and lunch than the evening meal (some benefit from only two meals a day), and eating several hours before going to bed for optimum sleep and improved digestion.

"E" for Exercise

One of the most beneficial habits to develop is regular exercise. The conveniences of today's society have had the unfortunate side effect of reducing the physical labor required in our day-to-day lives. Consequently, we are becoming more and more sedentary. We sit at work, we sit at home, and then we go to bed. Obesity has become a problem of epidemic proportions.

God designed humanity to be active. Adam and Eve were given the blessing of work when they were told to "tend and keep" (Genesis 2:15) the Garden of Eden. Even after sin entered, God said that the ground was cursed "for your sake" (Genesis 3:17). It was for the good of mankind to work hard and be physically active.

Regular physical exercise reaps incredible benefits. It provides increased energy, endurance, and muscle strength. It reduces stress, cholesterol, blood pressure, and the corresponding risk of disease. It improves sleep and mood. And it helps us to maintain a healthy weight. So what are you waiting for? You may need to start slow, but plan now to begin getting regular, daily exercise. It will change your life!

"W" for Water

More than half of our body is made up of water. Drinking at least seven or eight glasses of water each day improves metabolism and helps our body to perform many important functions, including the filtering of toxins and poisons through our kidneys. Most people wouldn't go too long without showering their bodies with water. A few days without showering and the oil and dirt would build up until we couldn't hide our uncleanliness anymore. And yet how often we fail to shower the inside of our bodies, making sure that all of our internal organs are clean and efficient, by drinking ample quantities of water every day!

Waiting until you are thirsty is not the best way to decide when to drink water. Thirst is generally an indicator that we have waited too long and are becoming dehydrated. To avoid drinking too much juice or soda, neither of which is a substitute for pure water, the best plan is to keep a water bottle with you so you are reminded to drink from it throughout the day.

"S" for Sunlight

We have all heard many warnings about getting too much sunlight. But sometimes, in an effort to avoid this, we have neglected to see the incredible benefits that only the sun can provide! Sunlight stimulates the production of essential Vitamin D, gives us healthier skin, improves our immune systems, and helps to relax our nerves. Most people have experienced the improved mood that results from a clear, sunny day, while areas that receive very little sunlight have been tied to higher rates of depression.

Too much sun, without proper protection, can be harmful to the skin. Still, we should not allow this risk to keep us out of the sun altogether. We have been blessed by God to be given such a bright, warm sun to cheer our days. Getting at least a few minutes of sunlight every day is essential to our overall physical health.

"T" for Temperance

Temperance means self-control, and generally refers to avoiding harmful substances and using only in moderation those things that are good. As Seventh-day Adventists, we are known for our longevity due in large part to abstaining from alcohol, tobacco, caffeine, and illegal drugs. Anything mind-altering or addictive, which is not prescribed by a doctor, should be entirely avoided by Christians.

Some people believe that wine or alcohol in moderation, or a cup of coffee every morning, is harmless. However, even the smallest amounts of alcohol impair judgment and weaken the area of the brain responsible for our moral decisions. Caffeinated beverages, while not as potent as other drugs, create an artificial stimulation that eventually leaves the body with *less* energy. Even moderate coffee drinkers will begin to require caffeine to elevate their energy to the level they enjoyed before they ever started drinking coffee in the first place.

Ample rest, good nutrition, plenty of water, and regular exercise provide benefits that are both immediate and long-lasting. The perceived benefits of addictive drugs, on the other hand, are temporary and come with harmful side effects. Therefore, we should be careful to abstain from any addictive substance, determining as did Paul, "I will not be mastered by anything" (1 Corinthians 6:12 NIV).

Ellen White affirms that while some articles of diet are not ideal and should be taken only moderately, the rule for others should be total abstinence. "Tea, coffee, tobacco, and alcohol we must present as sinful indulgences. We cannot place on the same ground, meat, eggs, butter, cheese, and such articles placed upon the table. These are not to be borne in front, as the burden of our work. The former—tea, coffee, tobacco, beer, wine, and all spiritous liquors—are not to be taken moderately, but discarded. The poisonous narcotics are not to be treated in the same way as the subject of eggs, butter, and cheese" (*Selected Messages,* book 3, p. 287).

> *Temperance, or self-control, is avoiding harmful substances and using only in moderation those things that are good.*

"A" for Air

Everyone knows that we need air to breathe and live. But the quality of the air we breathe is also important. Avoid spending all your time in tight, closed-in quarters or in areas with second-hand smoke. Regularly open windows for good ventilation and spend time outdoors each day, breathing deeply of clean, fresh air. The 100 trillion oxygen-needing cells in your body will thank you.

"R" for Rest

Proper rest and relaxation is becoming more and more difficult in today's fast-paced society. Still, there is no substitute for a good night's sleep. The average adult needs at least seven or eight hours of quality sleep every day. Without it, our bodies and minds quickly lose their energy and efficiency. Going to sleep well before midnight, and rising early in the morning, has proven to be more effective than staying up late and sleeping in late.

If you struggle to get good sleep, consider eliminating one of these common culprits from your life:

Drinking caffeinated beverages. Caffeine that you drink in the morning will remain in your system even into the night and disrupt the depth and quality of your sleep.

Eating late. Even if you fall asleep, your body will still be working to complete the digestive process, robbing you of valuable rest.

Lack of exercise. Exercise prepares your body to crave rest when you lie down to sleep.

Too much stress. Eliminating unnecessary stressors from your life is important to obtain good quality sleep.

"T" for Trust in God

Of all the keys to our spiritual and physical health, none are as important as maintaining an active life of faith and trust in God. "You will keep him in perfect peace, whose mind is stayed on You, because he trusts in You" (Isaiah 26:3). When our lives are surrendered to Christ, it eases the mind and brings peace to the soul. It is a lack of that peace, or ease, that creates *dis*-ease in both mind and body.

Jesus gives our lives purpose and inspires us to serve our fellow men. When we become co-laborers with Him, the tension caused by this world's pressures and demands rolls away. Only in Jesus can we find health and salvation for the whole person. He promises, "Come to Me, all you who labor and are heavy laden, and I will give you rest. Take My yoke upon you and learn from Me, for I am gentle and lowly in heart, and you will find rest for your souls" (Matthew 11:28-29).

Practical Application

Throughout His ministry, Jesus cared for the physical needs of humanity. His was a ministry of healing. But while miracles of healing still happen today, God would have us to understand that our potential for better health lies to a great degree within our own lifestyle choices.

"Do not be deceived, God is not mocked; for whatever a man sows, that he will also reap" (Galatians 6:7). One application of this text is that bad lifestyle habits will produce bad results. But it also means that if we sow seeds of good health through proper nutrition, exercise, water, sunlight, temperance, fresh air, rest, and trust in God, we will prevent many of the diseases that plague our society. Our minds will be clearer and better able to resist temptation and serve God.

Evaluate your own habits and lifestyle in the light of the eight laws of health discussed in this chapter. Begin making changes this week to improve in at least one area of NEW START. As you do, remember that you have a never-failing Savior who is by your side to help you. Take comfort in the words of the apostle Paul, "I can do all things through Christ who strengthens me" (Philippians 4:13).

19

The Beauty of Modesty

Jesus taught His disciples a fundamental principle when He said, "You will know them by their fruits" (Matthew 7:16). What is in the heart will often be manifested in observable areas of our lives, including our appearance. "Dress is an index of the mind and heart. That which is hung upon the outside is the sign of what is within" (*Mind, Character, and Personality,* vol. 1, p. 289).

The reason we hear so little of what the Bible says about dress and appearance is not because it is a minor, unimportant matter, but because it is highly personal and very important to the majority of people in this world. This makes it a subject that is not always welcome. For many, allowing Jesus into the area of their outward appearance is to allow Him deeper into their hearts than ever before.

We must remember that our value is not found in how we look, or what we wear, but in who we are as children of God. The Christian finds worth and security in the One who says, "I have loved you with an everlasting love" (Jeremiah 31:3). Rather than dressing to draw attention or to gain acceptance with the world, the Christian is to "put on" Christ and "make no provision for the flesh" (Romans 13:14).

Dressing for God's Glory

Because of our sinful hearts, we can be tempted to draw attention to ourselves through what we wear. In contrast, the Bible teaches that Christians should "adorn themselves in modest apparel" (1 Timothy 2:9). Modesty is dressing and acting in such a way that our outward appearance does not distract others from seeing the character of Christ manifested in our lives. As Christians, we should be ever seeking to glorify God and to draw attention to Him rather than to ourselves. Paul wrote, "For you were bought at a price; therefore glorify God in your body and in your spirit, which are God's" (1 Corinthians 6:20).

Modesty is a virtue that demonstrates self-respect, while also showing love and respect for those who are tempted by immodesty. Jesus taught that "whoever looks at a woman to lust for her has already committed adultery with her in his heart" (Matthew 5:28). Yet the fashion industry often designs clothing with the *express purpose* of eliciting sexual thoughts. In spite of societal pressures, the Christian will strive to live out the unselfish spirit of Romans 14:13—"Therefore let us

> *In the matter of dress, we should prayerfully look to God's Word as our guide.*

not judge one another anymore, but rather resolve this, not to put a stumbling block or a cause to fall in our brother's way." When we take care not to *expose* or *emphasize* sensual parts of our bodies, we protect both ourselves and the spiritual commitments of others.

While principles of modesty should prevent us from dressing like the world in many respects, this does not mean that we should go out of our way to be different. Ellen White wisely counsels, "Christians should not take pains to make themselves gazingstocks by dressing differently from the world. … If the world introduces a modest, convenient, and healthful mode of dress, which is in accordance with the Bible, it will not change our relation to God or to the world to adopt such a style of dress" (*The Review and Herald,* January 30, 1900). There is nothing wrong with adopting current styles of dress as long as they reflect biblical principles of modesty.

When selecting your clothing, consider how it will affect your witness to others. Ask yourself, "Am I dressing merely to fit in with current fashion? Am I seeking to draw undue attention to myself?" Or, "Will this clothing contradict my witness by making people notice and desire me sexually?" In the matter of dress, as in all other practical areas, we should prayerfully look to God's Word as our guide.

External versus Internal Adornment

While one aspect of modesty is being adequately clothed, the apostle Paul's appeal for modesty also includes a prohibition against the wearing of jewelry. He counsels in 1 Timothy 2:9-10, "In like manner also, that the women adorn themselves in modest apparel, with propriety and moderation, not with braided hair or gold or pearls or costly clothing, but, which is proper for women professing godliness, with good works."

Before directly discussing the reference to jewelry in this passage, we note the following:

- The principle of modesty and the instruction here given to women applies equally to men.
- Based on the context, the "braided hair" here prohibited is not a simple braid, but an elaborate hairstyle intended to draw attention.
- This passage is addressing articles worn for display or ornamentation. It does not forbid items with a function, such as watches or tie clips, as long as they are simple and modest.

Now let us consider Paul's counsel against the wearing of jewelry in 1 Timothy 2:9-10. He writes that we are to dress modestly, "not with braided hair or gold or pearls or costly clothing." Notice that unlike hair or clothing, which are preceded by adjectives to describe how they can *become* immodest, ornamenting our bodies with "gold or pearls" is *by nature* immodest. The Bible does not prohibit only *excessive* gold, or *costly* pearls, but instead teaches that anything worn merely for ornamentation violates the principle of modesty by drawing unnecessary attention to self. Yet while the wearing of jewelry is not "proper for women professing godliness," it certainly *is* proper to be adorned with "good works." The Bible here makes an important contrast between the artificial and the genuine; between outward appearance and true character.

> *Modesty and humility are "precious in the sight of God."*

The apostle Peter also counsels against elaborate hair styles, artificial display of jewelry, and costly clothing. Instead, he encourages our adornment to be "the hidden person of the heart, with the incorruptible beauty of a gentle and quiet spirit, which is very precious in the sight of God" (1 Peter 3:4). While jewels are regarded as precious in the eyes of the world, modesty and humility are "precious in the sight of God." Again, we see a contrast between the outward adornment that brings glory to self, and the inward adorning that gives glory to God.

In the book of Revelation, the consistent instruction of Paul and Peter is illustrated in the visions given to the apostle John. Two women, each representing churches, are there depicted. The first, found in Revelation 12, represents God's church. The appearance of this woman is striking, as she is clothed with the natural light of the "sun," "moon," and "stars" (Revelation 12:1). In the Bible, these cosmic symbols are referred to as the heavens; "The heavens declare the glory of God" (Psalm 19:1). Appearing as clothing on a symbolic woman, these symbols represent the glory, or character, of Christ, as reflected in His true church. Conspicuously absent in her attire, however, is *any* artificial adornment.

The other woman of Revelation is the harlot of chapter 17, who represents an unfaithful church. Her appearance is an exact reversal of that of the true church. She is "adorned with gold and precious stones and pearls" (Revelation 17:4), but with none of the natural light of the heavens. Because she does not have a Christ-like character, she courts the favor of the world using artificial attraction. While the pure woman is clothed with the glory or character of God, and no jewels, the harlot woman is clothed with jewelry, and none of God's glory. Which one should we emulate?

The consistent teaching of the New Testament is not that of limiting jewelry, but of avoiding it altogether. It is presented as being opposed to the principles of modesty and Christ-like humility. One distracts from God and glorifies self, while the other denies self to give glory to God. "Self-denial in dress is a part of our Christian duty. To dress plainly, and abstain from display of jewelry and ornaments of every kind is in keeping with our faith" (*Evangelism,* p. 269).

The Wedding Ring

In light of the New Testament teaching on jewelry, a commonly asked question is whether or not the wearing of a wedding ring is appropriate. Commenting on this, the *Seventh-day Adventist Church Manual* states, "In some countries and cultures the custom of wearing the wedding ring is considered imperative, having become, in the minds of the people, a criterion of virtue, and hence it is not regarded as an ornament. Under such circumstances we do not condemn the practice." The difference between the wedding ring and most jewelry is that the wedding ring may in certain places be considered imperative, thus making it functional rather than ornamental. Whether this is true in a particular culture is a matter that the church has left for the individual conscience, guided by the Bible and Spirit of Prophecy counsel (see *Testimonies to Ministers and Gospel Workers,* p. 180).

While many Adventists do not wear wedding rings, those who do base their practice on the understanding that it is merely functional and "not regarded as an ornament." Therefore, if a wedding ring is worn, it follows that such a ring would be a modest, simple band rather than one ornamented with jewels.

Jewelry in the Old Testament

It is true that God's people did, at times, wear jewelry in the Old Testament era. We must be careful, however, not to read the *descriptions* of biblical characters as being *prescriptive* for us today. Even sins such as polygamy and unjustified divorce were not uncommon among God's people in Old Testament times.

Still, God did not leave us without Old Testament examples that express His will regarding outward adornment. For instance, when Jacob was searching his heart on his way to meet his brother Esau, he cleansed his family of both idols and jewelry; "And they gave unto Jacob all the strange gods which were in their hand, and all their earrings which were in their ears; and Jacob hid them under the oak which was by Shechem" (Genesis 35:4). Many years later, when the children of Israel were told that God's presence could not go among them due to their disobedience, they repented and "stripped themselves of their ornaments, from Mount Horeb onward" (Exodus 33:6 ESV). Though Israel would eventually return to the practices of surrounding nations, God had revealed His will regarding the wearing of jewelry and would later reaffirm it in the clear teachings of the New Testament.

When Those of Experience Lose Their Way

"The idolatry of dress is a moral disease. It must not be taken over into the new life. In most cases, submission to the gospel requirements will demand a decided change in the dress" (*Evangelism,* p. 312). Many new Seventh-day Adventists have made changes in the way they dress in order to bring their lives into harmony with God's Word. After becoming part of the church, however, they are surprised to find long-time church members who do not take seriously the biblical teachings on modesty and adornment. We should not become discouraged, nor should we feel justified in returning to worldly fashion ourselves, merely because we see a lack of commitment among those of greater experience.

Ellen White relates the true story of a woman who had lived a worldly lifestyle before accepting Christ and becoming a member of the church. While visiting an Adventist institution, this woman was disappointed by the prevalence of jewelry worn by those of experience who worked there. Ellen White writes:

"Mrs. D, a lady occupying a position in the institution, was visiting at Sr. __'s room one day, when the latter took out of her trunk a gold necklace and chain, and said she wished to dispose of this jewelry and put the proceeds into the Lord's treasury. Said the other [Mrs. D], 'Why do you sell it? I would wear it if it was mine.' 'Why,' replied Sr. __, 'when I received the truth, I was taught that all these things must be laid aside. Surely they are contrary to the teachings of God's Word.' And she cited her hearer to the words of the apostles, Paul and Peter. ...

"In answer, the lady [Mrs. D] displayed a gold ring on her finger, given her by an unbeliever, and said she thought it no harm to wear such ornaments. 'We are not so particular,' said she, 'as formerly. Our people have been overscrupulous in their opinions upon the subject of dress. The ladies of this institution wear gold watches and gold chains, and dress like other people. It is not good policy to be singular in our dress; for we cannot exert so much influence.'"

Ellen White's response to Mrs. D's far-too-common attitude toward God's Word is highly instructive:

"Is this in accordance with the teachings of Christ? Are we to follow the Word of God, or the customs of the world? Our sister decided that it was the safest to adhere to the Bible standard. Will Mrs. D and others who pursue a similar course be pleased to meet the result of their influence, in that day when every man shall receive according to his works?

"God's Word is plain. Its teachings cannot be mistaken. Shall we obey it, just as He has given it to us, or shall we seek to find how far we can digress and yet be saved? ...

"Conformity to the world is a sin which is sapping the spirituality of our people, and seriously interfering with their usefulness. It is idle to proclaim the warning message to the world, while we deny it in the transactions of daily life" (*Evangelism,* pp. 270-272).

Grace Toward Others

We should be careful not to condemn others for their outward appearance. Many honest-hearted people have not fully known God's will in the matter of dress, or are still studying to understand. Others may be struggling with deeper issues of which we are not fully aware. While we should be careful and conscientious in our personal decisions, we should be patient and full of grace toward others.

Ellen White wisely taught, "There are many who try to correct the life of others by attacking what they consider are wrong habits. They go to those whom they think are in error, and point out their defects. They say, 'You don't dress as you should.' They try to pick off the ornaments, or whatever seems offensive, but they do not seek to fasten the mind to the truth. Those who seek to correct others should present the attractions of Jesus. ... There is no need to make the dress question the main point of your religion. There is something richer to speak of. Talk of Christ, and when the heart is converted, everything that is out of harmony with the Word of God will drop off" (*Evangelism,* p. 272).

Practical Application

Seventh-day Adventists have certainly not been the only ones to uphold the clear teachings of Scripture in regard to modesty. Many Protestant churches believed and taught the truth of God's Word regarding dress and jewelry before eventually becoming influenced by the pressures of culture. Notable preachers among them were John Wesley, one of the founders of Methodism, Charles Spurgeon, the Baptist "Prince of Preachers," and Presbyterian minister Charles Finney, one of the leaders of the Second Great Awakening in the United States.

For the disciple, however, Jesus is the ultimate Example. When casting lots for His clothing, the soldiers at the foot of the cross found no gold chain or other jewelry. He had only garments and a seamless tunic. Jesus no doubt avoided wearing jewelry because He wanted nothing to distract from the beauty and simplicity of His character. As the Bible says, "He had no beauty or majesty to attract us to Him, nothing in His appearance that we should desire Him" (Isaiah 53:2 NIV).

The primary reason that Seventh-day Adventists do not wear jewelry is that our goal is to be like Jesus, the One who is *meek* and *lowly* in heart. He invites us, "Come to Me, all you who labor and are heavy laden, and I will give you rest" (Matthew 11:28). We are called to lay aside striving for the world's approval and to find our rest, security, and acceptance in Him.

This week, ask God to help you know if your clothing and appearance is giving honor and glory to Him. As you seek to be faithful in every aspect of your life, God promises to give strength for victory and a peace that passes all understanding.

20

The Pure in Heart

As Seventh-day Adventists, we look forward to the day when we will see our Lord face to face. Jesus Himself promised, "Blessed are the pure in heart, for they shall see God" (Matthew 5:8). These words provide wonderful assurance to all who are preparing their hearts for the coming of Jesus. Hebrews 12:14 also urges us, "Pursue peace with all people, and holiness, without which no one will see the Lord." Finally, knowing that every evidence of sin will one day be destroyed, the apostle Peter asks, "What manner of persons ought you to be in holy conduct and godliness, looking for and hastening the coming of the day of God?" (2 Peter 3:11-12).

> *We are called to purity of heart and life.*

We are called to purity of heart and life as we prepare for our soon coming Savior. Still, we live in a broken and sinful world, surrounded by immorality and corruption. Even that which appears pure is often tainted by hypocrisy, selfish motives, pride, and a desire for human praise. The Bible exposes the underlying cause of this sinfulness and corruption when it says, "The heart is deceitful above all things, and desperately wicked" (Jeremiah 17:9).

The Heart Problem

The powerfully honest declaration of Jeremiah, that our own hearts are "desperately wicked," is a reminder that selfishness and pride have been the inheritance of the human race ever since the fall of Adam and Eve. This bent toward sin and evil is referred to in the Bible as "the flesh," the "sinful nature," the "carnal mind," and the "old man" (Galatians 5:16; Romans 8:13 NIV; Romans 8:6-7; Colossians 3:9).

So pervasive is the impurity of our natural hearts that the apostle Paul declares, "For I know that in me (that is, in my flesh) nothing good dwells" (Romans 7:18). Apart from God, the height of mankind's righteousness is still entirely impure. "We are all like an unclean thing, and all our righteousnesses are like filthy rags" (Isaiah 64:6). The natural heart, or mind, is so hopelessly hostile toward God that it cannot be cured. Paul writes, "The carnal mind is enmity against God; for it is not subject to the law of God, nor indeed can be. So then, those who are in the flesh cannot please God" (Romans 8:7-8).

A New Heart

If the carnal mind with which we are born cannot possibly be brought into harmony with God, where is our hope of being among the pure in heart who will one day see the Lord face to face? King David, a man with the same sinful nature that is common to all humanity, recognized this need when he cried out, "Create in me a clean heart, O God, and renew a steadfast spirit within me" (Psalm 51:10).

This desperate prayer, "Create in me a clean heart," is our only hope of finding the purity we seek. Having been born with a corrupt and sinful nature, we are helpless apart from God (see Ephesians 2:1-3). We must have an entire transformation, but we are unable to change ourselves. We need a Savior, and thanks be to God, we have One who is abundant in mercy. Jesus offers to dwell in our hearts by His Spirit, making us "partakers of the divine nature, having escaped the corruption that is in the world through lust" (2 Peter 1:4). Only in this way can we be among the pure in heart. Jesus plainly states, "Unless one is born again, he cannot see the kingdom of God" (John 3:3).

Asking God for a clean heart is only the first step toward obtaining one. We must also read the Bible and exercise faith in its promises. "Having been born again, not of corruptible seed but incorruptible, through the word of God which lives and abides forever" (1 Peter 1:23). When the Spirit of God impresses the Word upon the mind, a newfound hunger

> *We must have an entire transformation, but we are unable to change ourselves.*

for God is born in the heart. The Bible and spiritual themes are no longer considered boring or uninteresting. The love of Jesus manifested on Calvary's cross, the plan of salvation offered so freely but at so high a cost, becomes the central theme that occupies the mind.

Two Natures

This new birth is more than a mere modification of what we once were. The apostle Paul declares, "If anyone is in Christ, he is a new creation; old things have passed away; behold, all things have become new" (2 Corinthians 5:17). The book *Steps to Christ* beautifully describes this dramatic change: "Those who become new creatures in Christ Jesus ... will no longer fashion themselves according to the former lusts, but by the faith of the Son of God they will follow in His steps, reflect His character, and purify themselves even as He is pure. The things they once hated they now love, and the things they once loved they hate" (*Steps to Christ*, p. 58).

Although being born again involves becoming a new creature in Christ, it is important to recognize that there are now two natures striving for mastery in the heart. "For the flesh lusts against the Spirit, and the Spirit against the flesh; and these are contrary to one another, so that you do not do the things that you wish" (Galatians 5:17). Though a love for Jesus and a desire for purity will be born in the heart through the divine nature, the old sinful nature ("the flesh") will continue to war against us until Jesus comes.

Set Your Mind

How do we gain the victory over the flesh, so that we maintain a love for God and His Word? The Bible offers a consistent answer to this question. "Walk in the Spirit, and you shall not fulfill the lust of the flesh" (Galatians 5:16). "Those who live according to the flesh set their minds on the things of the flesh, but those who live according to the Spirit, the things of the Spirit. For to be carnally minded is death, but to be spiritually minded is life and peace" (Romans 8:5-6). "Set your mind on things above, not on things on the earth" (Colossians 3:2).

The Bible teaches that the secret to developing and maintaining purity of heart is to "set your mind" on heavenly things rather than earthly. By reading, watching, listening to, and meditating upon spiritual things, the "fleshly lusts which war against the soul" (1 Peter 2:11) lose their strength and we find victory over temptation. This is why it is so important that we surround ourselves with spiritual influences.

Proverbs 4:23 wisely admonishes, "Keep your heart with all diligence, for out of it spring the issues of life." It is not enough that we receive a new heart through a saving relationship with Jesus. We must carefully "keep" our hearts by guarding our senses—the avenues to the soul by which the devil attempts to arouse the sinful passions of our carnal natures. For this reason, the apostle counsels, "Finally, brethren, whatever things are true, whatever things are noble, whatever things are just, whatever things are pure, whatever things are lovely, whatever things are of good report, if there is any virtue and if there is anything praiseworthy— meditate on these things" (Philippians 4:8).

> *"Set your mind on things above, not on things on the earth."*

By Beholding

Ellen White wrote, "The mind of a man or woman does not come down in a moment from purity and holiness to depravity, corruption, and crime. It takes time to transform the human to the divine, or to degrade those formed in the image of God to the brutal or the satanic. By beholding we become changed" (*The Adventist Home*, p. 330). These words reveal that beholding sinful behavior causes us to become desensitized to the same behavior in our own lives (see Matthew 6:22-23; 2 Corinthians 3:18).

Rather than feeding the soul with spiritual food that purifies the heart, many people in today's generation are only strengthening their sinful natures by what they watch in movies and on television. While these media are not inherently evil, Christians should abstain from beholding any entertainment that glorifies violence or vice, promotes godless behavior, provokes envy or lust, uses inappropriate language, or in any other way dishonors God.

"There is no influence in our land more powerful to poison the imagination, to destroy religious impressions, and to blunt the relish for the tranquil pleasures and sober realities of life than theatrical amusements. The love for these scenes increases with every indulgence, as the desire for intoxicating drinks strengthens with its use" (*The Adventist Home,* p. 516). Not only the content, but the emotional excitement created by many television programs and movies has the effect of lessening our interest in the Bible. Dramatic productions can become so "intoxicating" that we begin to lose interest in more "tranquil pleasures."

Unlike the intellectual strength gained from reading Scripture or even from spending time in conversation with others, watching television can lead to an almost hypnotic state of "vegging out." The activity in the frontal lobe—the portion of the brain responsible for spiritual values and moral judgment—decreases markedly when watching television and movies. In fact, the word "amusement" is a combination of the prefix "a," meaning "not," and the word "muse," meaning "think." Amusement, then, has the effect of causing us to not think.

Now, as never before, we should guard against drifting off to spiritual sleep by allowing ungodly entertainment to shape our thinking for us. "Therefore let us not sleep, as others do, but let us watch and be sober" (1 Thessalonians 5:6).

Trapped by the Net

In generations past, the temptations of the carnal heart were to some degree hindered by a lack of easy access to many evils. But with the dawn of the Internet, all that has changed. Today, most people spend an average of five hours or more online each day. Social media, streaming entertainment, blogs, and countless other websites absorb our time and affections. Through this avenue, the dark curiosity and secret vices of the sinful nature now have unlimited access to all manner of evil. Thousands have become addicted to social media sites, engaged in emotional affairs online, or have been trapped by the lure of pornography.

Christians who want to be ready for the coming of Jesus must get serious about the potentially damaging influence of the Internet on themselves and their families. As with all media, the Internet can be a rich blessing. Within proper guidelines, social media can be a helpful form of communication, and can be used to shed a positive influence upon others. The Internet also contains a wealth of positive educational and spiritually uplifting articles, videos, and websites. However, to gain this benefit without being negatively influenced requires vigilant effort. Here are several ideas to consider:

- Set Internet time limits for you and your family, including certain times in which all electronic devices are off limits.
- Keep your computers in areas visible to others.

- Use software that filters website content and refuses access to certain types of sites.
- Make a covenant to set nothing wicked before your eyes (see Psalm 101:3; Job 31:1).
- Go to bed early so that you will be able to get up in the morning for your devotional time with God.

The Allure of Fantasy

The Bible says, "Trust in Him at all times, you people; pour out your heart before Him; God is a refuge for us" (Psalm 62:8). Instead of turning to Jesus as our place of refuge, a growing number of Christians are turning to fiction and fantasy. Through video games, social media, and fictional novels, many are seeking an alternate reality rather than striving to be content and productive in their own lives. The devil uses these escapes, which can be highly addictive, to keep God's people from the practical duties of life and from sharing the gospel with the world. Precious moments, even days, weeks, months, and years, are wasted away focusing on a world that is entirely imaginary.

Christians should be watchful and sober (1 Peter 1:13), avoiding anything that might fuel discontent with the real circumstances of their lives. Let us pray with the Psalmist, "Turn away my eyes from looking at worthless things, and revive me in Your way" (Psalm 119:37).

Making Melody to the Lord

The Bible encourages Christians to "be filled with the Spirit, speaking to one another in psalms and hymns and spiritual songs, singing and making melody in your heart to the Lord" (Ephesians 5:18-19). Our God is musical (see Zephaniah 3:17), and He has given us the blessing of music to brighten our lives. Nevertheless, the devil knows how to take that which is good and distort it for our harm. "When turned to good account, music is a blessing; but it is often made one of Satan's most attractive agencies to ensnare souls" (*Testimonies for the Church,* vol. 1, p. 505).

Much of today's music excites the listener with adrenaline, overstimulates the emotions, and generates a strong bodily response. While many downplay its negative effects, even society has admitted the link between such music and an immoral lifestyle. "Sex, drugs and Rock & Roll" was a phrase that characterized an entire generation.

While many do not see a problem with any form of music as long as the lyrics are appropriate, the book *The Adventist Home* reveals that some musical styles *do* have a negative effect. Ellen White writes, "I feel alarmed as I witness everywhere the frivolity of young men and young women who profess to believe the truth. God does not seem to be in their thoughts. Their minds are filled with nonsense. Their conversation is only empty, vain talk. They have a keen ear for music, and Satan knows what organs to excite to animate, engross, and charm the mind so that Christ is not desired. The spiritual longings of the soul for divine knowledge, for a growth in grace, are wanting" (*The Adventist Home,* p. 407).

Not only does Satan influence through inappropriate or immoral lyrics, but he also chooses musical instrumentation that will "excite" the "organs" so that "Christ is not desired." This unhealthy excitement often leads to an increased desire for the stimulation provided by the music, and less time and thought given to devotional activities such as prayer and Bible study.

Christians should choose music that does not overstimulate the senses, engross the mind, or diminish the spiritual longings of the soul. We should also never listen to music with lyrics that are immoral, distasteful, or in any other way dishonor God. Good music will be elevating and harmonious and lead us to more closely follow our Savior.

Love Not the World

The apostle John warns, "Do not love the world or the things in the world. If anyone loves the world, the love of the Father is not in him. For all that is in the world—the lust of the flesh, the lust of the eyes, and the pride of life—is not of the Father but is of the world. And the world is passing away, and the lust of it; but he who does the will of God abides forever" (1 John 2:15-17).

The devil is constantly working to draw our affections to the things of the world. He wants us to be among those who profess to be Christians at the end of time, but who in heart are "lovers of pleasure rather than lovers of God" (2 Timothy 3:4).

For many Christians, materialism is an idol that steals the heart from God. They become addicted to riches, fashion, or the adrenaline rush of buying something new. For others, sports have become their god. They follow every headline and care more about the statistics of their favorite team or player than they care about Scripture or saving the lost.

> *"If we are Christ's, our thoughts are with Him."*

Whatever the idol may be, we must surrender it to Jesus Christ and give Him our whole heart.

In a spirit of self-examination, every Christian should regularly consider, "Who has the heart? With whom are our thoughts? Of whom do we love to converse? Who has our warmest affections and our best energies? If we are Christ's, our thoughts are with Him, and our sweetest thoughts are of Him. All we have and are is consecrated to Him. We long to bear His image, breathe His spirit, do His will, and please Him in all things" (*Steps to Christ*, p. 58).

Practical Application

In Acts chapter 19, the account is given of certain believers in Ephesus who had either continued, or fallen back into, occult practices since their conversion to Christianity. Upon being convicted of their lack of wholehearted devotion, they brought their magic books and "burned them in the sight of all" (Acts 19:19). The result of their newfound purity of heart was immediate, "So the word of the Lord grew mightily and prevailed" (Acts 19:20).

Christians today are no different than those believers in Ephesus. In order for the word of the Lord to grow mightily and prevail in our lives, we too must burn our "magic books." This week, consider what might need to be removed from *your* life. Think not only of sinful habits and practices that pollute the heart, but also of those things that may not be inherently evil but which steal your best energies and affections from God. It could be movies or music that dishonor the Lord, Internet or sports that occupy your time and receive your deepest interest, video games or novels that weaken your desire for spiritual things, or anything that strengthens your carnal nature rather than helping you to maintain purity and singleness of heart.

After addressing any idols that may exist in your heart and life, consider what positive influences could be put in their place. Be a regular attendee at prayer meeting and other church functions. Open your home for a small group Bible study. Get regular exercise, and try to remain active. Spend more time with your family. If you need ideas for replacing worldly entertainment with healthful recreation, or understanding what options are available for Christian programming and music, talk to your mentor or pastor.

The following counsel is an invaluable guide for every Christian, "The true Christian will not desire to enter any place of amusement or engage in any diversion upon which he cannot ask the blessing of God" (*The Adventist Home*, p. 515). Remember, it is the pure in heart who will one day see God. So pray with David, "Create in me a clean heart," and then ask God for the strength to keep it pure for Him.

21

Love at Home

One of the most important truths of Scripture is that "God is love" (1 John 4:8, 16). Unselfish love is not only the foundation of His character, but of the universe. God created everything, whether animate or inanimate, to unselfishly give of itself for the benefit of someone or something else.

When Adam and Eve fell, everything changed. Every one of us has inherited a selfish nature that wars against God's original plan for His creation. Only through the hope of salvation can we now be "partakers of the divine nature" (2 Peter 1:4). The born again Christian, though living on earth, can still experience the love of heaven when Christ dwells in the heart. And when every member of the family is humble and striving to be like Jesus, the home can be a foretaste of heaven. It can model the glorious truth that "God is love."

Choosing a Marriage Partner

The beginning of the home life, that which above all else establishes its atmosphere, is the quality of the relationship between husband and wife. It is important, then, that young men and women are very careful when choosing a life partner.

The home can be the happiest place on earth when both husband and wife are committed to God and to one another. However, the apostle Paul wisely counsels, "Do not be unequally yoked together with unbelievers" (2 Corinthians 6:14). In obedience to Scripture, Seventh-day Adventists should only consider marrying someone within the Seventh-day Adventist Church—someone who shares their beliefs and convictions.

We must remember, however, that it is not merely denominational affiliation that makes a happy home, but the Spirit of God reigning in the hearts of both husband and wife. Those seeking marriage should ask questions such as: Does my prospective partner regularly pray and read the Bible? Does he regularly attend church services and functions? Does she regularly speak familiarly about the Lord, indicating a personal relationship with Him? Is he conscientious in following biblical instructions regarding the Sabbath, Christian lifestyle and service? They should also ask highly practical questions such as: Is she compatible in personality, habits and future goals? Is he responsible and financially stable?

> *Marriage is an institution created and defined by God.*

Those who fail to ask important questions about a future spouse, especially in regard to spiritual compatibility, will often experience untold difficulties after marriage. Rather than improving the spiritual condition of a less committed spouse, an unequal union will more often result in spiritual decline for the one who had been more faithful. Differing values and goals can also lead to the couple living somewhat separate lives, confiding in like-minded friends more than in husband or wife, and fighting over decisions in the home. All of these difficulties are only multiplied when children are brought into the situation.

Because romantic relationships can blind even the most faithful Christians, it is wise to seek counsel early and often from parents, pastors, and strong spiritual mentors, and to take their counsel seriously. The choice of a spouse is undoubtedly one of the most important decisions we ever make.

The Sanctity of Marriage

Marriage, while it does involve the recognition of the state and the declaration of a minister, is not primarily defined by these characteristics. When a man and woman become husband and wife, it is "what God has joined together" (Matthew 19:6). Marriage is an institution created and defined by God as a loving and exclusive union of one man and one woman that is to last for the rest of their lives. Efforts to define marriage as anything other than this are contrary to the clear testimony of the Bible.

Still, our world is broken. Many struggle with temptations to same-sex relationships, pornography, fornication, and many other impure thoughts and actions. We should never condemn those who have been overcome by these temptations, but should instead offer sympathy and help. We can be caring friends to those who feel alone, confused, or guilty due to impure desires or past moral failures. More importantly, we can commend to every tempted soul a compassionate and all-powerful Savior.

In sensitive and often-addictive areas such as sexuality, we should not give the impression that one can simply offer up a prayer and the impure desires will immediately go away.

Boundaries, accountability, and even professional counseling will often be needed in order to break free from deeply entrenched patterns of thought and action. Yet with persevering prayer and effort, we can find victory over any and every temptation through Jesus Christ. We can even find victory over the sexual sins that defile the mind and, far too often, destroy the home.

For Better or For Worse

While marriage is a blessing, it can also be very difficult to maintain love and affection when faced with the pressures of family and work, with unexpected tragedies, or with the nagging temptations of our own hearts. For this reason, it is vitally important that husbands and wives see the importance of maintaining spiritual closeness, open communication, regular affirmation, and ongoing romance in the marriage relationship. When these practices are followed, a strong marriage will be the result, and together, the husband and wife will be able to successfully navigate the storms of life.

Even marriages that are founded on biblical principles, where husband and wife are committed to each other, will encounter difficulties. For many couples, periodically attending marriage enrichment retreats or reading books on how to have a healthy marriage can be helpful in addressing minor problems before they become major ones. Problems or differences that are faced and handled with a loving, unselfish spirit will often make the marriage stronger.

Even so, thousands of marriages end in divorce every year. So is there ever a time when divorce is permissible? Jesus gives us the answer. "Moses, because of the hardness of your hearts, permitted you to divorce your wives, but from the beginning it was not so. And I say to you, whoever divorces his wife, except for sexual immorality, and marries another, commits adultery; and whoever marries her who is divorced commits adultery" (Matthew 19:8-9).

While it is not *required* for a victim of adultery to divorce his or her spouse, adultery is the one instance in which Jesus says an innocent spouse may divorce and remarry. Other reasons often given for divorce, such as emotional abuse, neglect, lying, or financial failures, are not biblically justified. For Christians who are bound by God's Word, marriage is a lifelong covenant for better or for worse, for richer or for poorer, in sickness and in health. What God has joined together, we are not to separate.

In marriages that have become physically or emotionally unhealthy for spouse or children, separation is often advisable while sorting through difficulties with a reputable Christian marriage counselor. Even when circumstances are not so desperate, finding such a counselor during the early stages of difficulty in marriage is important. Do not procrastinate in seeking help if you feel your marriage is in trouble.

"Though difficulties, perplexities, and discouragements may arise, let neither husband nor wife harbor the thought that their union is a mistake or a disappointment. ... Let there be mutual love, mutual forbearance. Then marriage, instead of being the end of love, will be as it were the very beginning of love. The warmth of true friendship, the love that binds heart to heart, is a foretaste of the joys of heaven" (*The Ministry of Healing*, p. 360).

The Law of Kindness

One of the clearest manifestations of love in the home is what the Bible refers to as the "law of kindness" (Proverbs 31:26). Kind words, courtesy, and patience are virtues often reserved for public settings where it would reflect poorly on us to act differently. But the genuine Christian will be thoughtful and kind with his or her spouse, children, parents, and siblings. True character is not revealed by who we are at work, church, or school. The true "you" is who you are at home with your family, and in your private life.

Husbands, wives, and children should communicate their love freely, and never lift their voices in anger. They should protect the feelings of one another and manifest sympathy and patience for one another's weaknesses. They should guard each other's reputation and speak positively of one another in the presence of others. Finally, they should maintain a sacred family circle and avoid sharing private matters that would make any member of the family feel uncomfortable.

> *One of the clearest manifestations of love in the home is the "law of kindness."*

"The wife should have no secrets to keep from her husband and let others know, and the husband should have no secrets to keep from his wife to relate to others. The heart of his wife should be the grave for the faults of the husband, and the heart of the husband the grave for his wife's faults. Never should either party indulge in a joke at the expense of the other's feelings. Never should either the husband or wife in sport or in any other manner complain of each other to others. ... I have been shown that there should be a sacred shield around every family" (*The Adventist Home*, p. 177).

Equal but Different

Mutual love and respect between husband and wife is the clear teaching of Scripture, with neither spouse being superior to the other. This full equality can be seen as far back as the creation account. "Eve was created from a rib taken from the side of Adam, signifying that she was not to control him as the head, nor to be trampled under his feet as an inferior, but to stand by his side as an equal, to be loved and protected by him" (*The Adventist Home,* p. 25).

Of course, not everything about men and women is the same. In addition to differences in size, strength, and physical anatomy, men and women are also different in how they think and feel. Both husband and wife have distinct roles that utilize their natural strengths and abilities. We should remember that God created both male and female for a reason, notwithstanding the efforts of the current generation to blur the lines between the sexes.

The Husband and Father

The Bible sets a high standard for husbands when it says, "Husbands, love your wives, just as Christ loved the church and gave Himself for her" (Ephesians 5:25). The husband and father is to follow Jesus as his pattern in manifesting self-sacrificing love for his wife and children.

"All members of the family center in the father. He is the lawmaker, illustrating in his own manly bearing the sterner virtues: energy, integrity, honesty, patience, courage, diligence, and practical usefulness" (*The Adventist Home,* p. 212). The father is the primary lawmaker of his family due to the "manly bearing" and "sterner virtues" with which he was created.

"It was God's plan for the members of the family to be associated in work and study, in worship and recreation, the father as priest of his household, and both father and mother as teachers and companions of their children" (*Child Guidance,* p. 535). Notice that while both father and mother are to be teachers and companions, only the father has the special designation of "priest of his household." Therefore, every husband and father should feel a special responsibility to pray for his wife and children, give spiritual guidance, set the example in having daily personal devotions, and lead the family in regular family worship, church attendance, and witnessing activities.

It cannot be overstated, however, how important it is for the husband and father to manifest humility and gentleness toward his wife and children. The Bible admonishes, "Fathers, do not provoke your children, lest they become discouraged" (Colossians 3:21). And Ellen White counsels further, "It is no evidence of manliness in the husband for him to dwell constantly upon his position as head of the family. It does not increase respect for him to hear him quoting Scripture to sustain his claims to authority. It will not make him more manly to require his wife, the mother of his children, to act upon his plans as if they were infallible. The Lord has constituted the husband the head of the wife to be her protector; he is the house-band of the family, binding the members together, even as Christ is the head of the church. ... Christ's authority is exercised in wisdom, in all kindness and gentleness; so let the husband exercise his power and imitate the great Head of the church" (*The Adventist Home,* p. 215).

The Wife and Mother

While the husband and father is more naturally endowed with the sterner virtues, the wife and mother is blessed with a blend of internal strength and the sweeter graces of tenderness and empathy. The mother's caring, nurturing way gives her an influence with her children that cannot be equaled. "The tenderest earthly tie is that between the mother and her child. The child is more readily impressed by the life and example of the mother than by that of the father, for a stronger and more tender bond of union unites them" (*The Adventist Home,* p. 240).

Ellen White consistently spoke of the lofty importance of women in both the family and the church. "The king upon his throne has no higher work than has the mother" (*The Adventist Home,* p. 231). "We may safely say that the distinctive duties of woman are more sacred, more holy, than those of man. … She should feel that she is her husband's equal—to stand by his side, she faithful at her post of duty and he at his" (*ibid.*). "The Saviour will reflect upon these self-sacrificing women the light of His countenance, and this will give them a power that will exceed that of men. They can do in families a work that men cannot do, a work that reaches the inner life. They can come close to the hearts of those whom men cannot reach. Their work is needed" (*Testimonies for the Church,* vol. 9, p. 128).

In addition to fulfilling her own unique responsibilities, the Bible also instructs the wife to be supportive of her husband's leadership in the home. "Wives, submit to your own husbands, as to the Lord" (Ephesians 5:22; see also v. 33). This submission is not unconditional, but "as to the Lord." A wife should never feel obligated to submit to the judgment of her husband if by so doing she would be disobeying God, putting herself or her children in danger, or surrendering her individual dignity.

Only the Spirit of God can enable husbands and wives to relate to one another as heaven designed. "We must have the Spirit of God, or we can never have harmony in the home. The wife, if she has the spirit of Christ, will be careful of her words; she will control her spirit, she will be submissive, and yet will not feel that she is bondslave, but a companion to her husband. If the husband is a servant of God, he will not lord it over his wife; he will not be arbitrary and exacting. We cannot cherish home affection with too much care; for the home, if the Spirit of the Lord dwells there, is a type of heaven" (*The Adventist Home,* p. 118).

> "The home, if the Spirit of the Lord dwells there, is a type of heaven."

A Heritage From the Lord

Children, whom the Bible calls a "heritage from the Lord" (Psalm 127:3), are wonderful gifts from God. They bring life and joy into the home. The Bible instructs parents to bring up children in the "training and admonition of the Lord" (Ephesians 6:4). Higher than any other missionary responsibility is that of leading our own children to love and obey Jesus. For this reason, parents should allow nothing to prevent them from giving the time, affection, and loving discipline to their children that is so needed. It requires patience, prayer, and a faithful example to mold the characters of our children for heaven. Yet the Lord promises, "Train up a child in the way he should go, and when he is old he will not depart from it" (Proverbs 22:6). What a wonderful assurance!

For their part, children (whether old or young) are to show gratitude and appreciation for their parents by obeying the commandment, "Honor your father and your mother" (Exodus 20:12; see also Ephesians 6:1-3). Sadly, the Bible says that many professed Christians in the last days will be "disobedient to parents" (2 Timothy 3:2). Disrespect toward parental authority is a shameful characteristic of our age that will inevitably lead to disrespect for God and His Word. Our children should be taught early to not only obey their parents, but to show respect for teachers and church leaders, and to give deferential treatment to the elderly. Both parents and children must guard against the proud spirit of the age and remain humble and respectful toward God and toward one another.

Practical Application

While this chapter has sought to describe the ideal of a Christ-centered home, most of our families have already been marred by failures, tragedies, or pain. A vast number of people, for instance, have experienced the pain of divorce. In many homes, children have been neglected or abused. Some young people have not been supported in their biblical convictions. Some parents have come to Christ at a late age and now feel guilty for not raising their children to follow God. Still others wonder if failures in their own example have caused their children to leave the church. If you can relate to any of these circumstances, know that you are not alone. Turn to the Lord Jesus and He will provide sympathy, forgiveness, repentance, strength, and whatever else may be needed for the journey ahead. When we surrender to the will of God, the future becomes full of hope.

The truth is that all Christians face weaknesses, and at times struggle with bad habits. We lament failed promises or other imperfections in both ourselves and our family members. But we must not become discouraged or give up to despair. Instead, follow these important steps:

1. Put Jesus first, humbly obeying God even if your family objects (see Matthew 10:34-37).
2. Pray daily for your own character development and for the salvation of each member of your family.
3. Acknowledge your own weaknesses and do not delay in making positive changes.
4. Forgive others and be patient with their weaknesses.
5. Finally, trust God—it is never too late to see healing in your family no matter what your stage in life. If Jesus dwells in *your* heart, you can always have love at home.

Section 6

Cycle of Evangelism

$$\boxed{22}$$

Send Forth Laborers

"A sower went out to sow" (Luke 8:5). "The fields are … already white for harvest" (John 4:35). "The harvest truly is plentiful, but the laborers are few" (Matthew 9:37).

These are just a few of the many places where Jesus used practical examples from the cycle of planting and harvesting to illustrate the process of making disciples. Just as the agricultural cycle includes soil preparation, seed planting, cultivation, harvesting, and preservation, the "Cycle of Evangelism" requires equivalent phases that are essential for true success.

It is not uncommon for Christians to express disappointment at meager results from their efforts to win souls. The problem often lies in failing to realize that evangelism is a process involving multiple steps, each of which demands careful planning and hard work. If even one step is overlooked, results will suffer.

Preparing the Soil

The first step in the growing season is getting the ground ready for seed. The hard clods of earth must be broken up in order for the seed to take root. In the parable of the sower (see Matthew 13:1-23), Jesus taught that the seed represented the Word of God that was to be planted in the human heart. Just as the hard ground must be broken up so the seed can take root, the human heart must be softened to receive the truths of God's Word.

Ellen White observes, "As the garden must be prepared for the natural seed, so the heart must be prepared for the seed of truth. ... No one settles upon a raw piece of land with the expectation that it will at once yield a harvest. Diligent, persevering labor must be put forth in the preparation of the soil, the sowing of the seed, and the culture of the crop. So it must be in the spiritual sowing" (*The Adventist Home,* pp. 145-146).

The Scripture record tells us that in order to accomplish this, Jesus "went about doing good" (Acts 10:38). By loving ministry to the needs of others, He opened their hearts to the spiritual truths He longed to implant. In following His example, we too will find success in reaching hearts. When we demonstrate genuine love and care by ministering to the needs of those in our communities, we can make lasting friendships, build trust, and bring down defenses. Then, when the seed of God's Word is sown, it will find hearts that are fertile and open to receiving the truth.

Planting the Seed

No farmer intends to till the soil indefinitely. The preparation of the soil is only for the purpose of sowing the seed. Without planting seed, there will be no harvest. The apostle Paul reminds us, "He who sows sparingly will also reap sparingly, and he who sows bountifully will also reap bountifully" (2 Corinthians 9:6).

Many Christians do well at building friendships with others, but they never get around to sharing the Word. When the time comes to discuss matters of faith or to share a piece of truth-filled literature, we often fear jeopardizing our friendships by being too spiritual. Yet just as the farmer must plant the seed if he expects a harvest, a true Christian friend will not fail to plant seeds of truth in the hearts of those for whom he labors.

Cultivating

Once the seed has taken root, the new plant must be cultivated. This includes watering, fertilizing, weeding, and otherwise nurturing to promote healthy growth. This is by far the most time-consuming and labor-intensive phase of the growing cycle. Where soil preparation and seed-sowing may take a day or two, cultivation requires continued effort over weeks or months.

In the spiritual realm, the primary way to nurture the growth of the Word in someone's heart is by giving regular Bible studies. The apostle Peter admonished new believers to "desire the pure milk of the word, that you may grow thereby" (1 Peter 2:2). It is the regular study and application of the Word that fosters spiritual growth, causing the weeds of error and sinful habits to be uprooted from the heart. It is through patient labor that the new spiritual plant is brought to harvest.

Harvesting

The harvest is what the farmer has been laboring for all season long! Only after the work of preparing the soil, planting the seed, and cultivating the crop has been faithfully done can he look forward to the harvest. And only when the soul-winner has carefully followed each phase of the evangelism cycle may he look forward to a harvest of souls taking their stand for Christ in baptism.

Just as the ripe grain must be picked at the time of harvest, so a person contemplating a decision to follow Christ must be *invited* to act. This is why Jesus urged us to "pray the Lord of the harvest to send out laborers into His harvest" (Matthew 9:38). Jesus saw that it would take more than tillers, sowers, or cultivators to get the job done. He would need workers who knew how to harvest!

Ellen White describes this need to "harvest" decisions for Christ: "Many are convicted of sin, and feel their need of a sin-pardoning Saviour; but they are merely dissatisfied with their pursuits and aims, and if there is not a decided application of the truth to their hearts, if words are not spoken at the right moment, calling for decision from the weight of evidence already presented, the convicted ones pass on without identifying themselves with Christ. ... The people should be urged to decide just now to be on the Lord's side" (*Evangelism,* p. 283).

Preserving

Once the crop has been harvested, the grain must be preserved that it may "give seed to the sower and bread to the eater" (Isaiah 55:10). Every soul won to Christ is to be a blessing and encouragement to the church (bread to the eater) and to work for the salvation of other souls (seed to the sower). When the evangelism cycle comes full circle, it accomplishes its purpose of making disciples who in turn make other disciples.

The Great Commission calls for new believers to be taught "to observe all things" (Matthew 28:20) that Christ commanded.

This calls for an intentional and systematic approach to mentoring those who have been newly baptized, integrating them into the church, and teaching them how to work for the salvation of souls. When this is accomplished, the cycle continues uninterrupted, with even more laborers joining in the work of God. "One soul, won to the truth, will be instrumental in winning others, and there will be an ever-increasing result of blessing and salvation" (*Christian Service*, p. 121).

Practical Application

The soul-winning efforts of many Christians could be compared to the baseball player who always swings for a home run. They're looking for that special event or program that will result in exponential growth. But Jesus' symbolic use of the agricultural cycle teaches us that evangelism is a process, not a one-time event. Like the farmer, the soul-winner must labor with patience and consistency through every phase of the evangelism cycle, trusting God to reward his labors with a bountiful harvest.

> *As a disciple of Christ, God wants to use you to win souls.*

"In proportion to the enthusiasm and perseverance with which the work is carried forward, will be the success given" (*Christian Service*, p. 262).

There are no shortcuts when it comes to winning souls for Christ. We must prepare the soil of the heart, plant the seed of God's Word, cultivate spiritual interest with ongoing Bible studies, harvest decisions to follow Christ, and preserve those decisions through systematic discipleship.

Most importantly, we must remember that it is only God who "gives the increase" (see 1 Corinthians 3:6). Nothing should drive us to our knees and convince us of our dependence upon God like working for the salvation of others. "Through much prayer you must labor for souls, for this is the only method by which you can reach hearts. It is not your work, but the work of Christ who is by your side, that impresses hearts" (*Evangelism*, p. 341).

As a disciple of Christ, no matter how unqualified you may feel, God wants to use you to win souls. "God often uses the simplest means to accomplish the greatest results. ... The humblest worker, moved by the Holy Spirit, will touch invisible chords, whose vibrations will ring to the ends of the earth, and make melody through eternal ages" (*The Desire of Ages*, pp. 822-823). Jesus sorrowfully declares, "The harvest truly is plentiful, but the laborers are few" (Matthew 9:37). Will you be a co-laborer with Him?

23

Preparing the Soil

Every farmer knows that the most important factor in a successful growing season is the soil. If the soil is not ready for the seed, the harvest will be meager at best. This was the point Jesus emphasized in the parable of the sower: "Behold, a sower went out to sow. And it happened, as he sowed, that some seed fell by the wayside … some fell on stony ground … some seed fell among thorns. … But other seed fell on good ground and yielded a crop that sprang up, increased and produced: some thirtyfold, some sixty, and some a hundred" (Mark 4:3-8). The only harvest came from seeds that were planted in "good ground."

As we learned in the last chapter, the seed represents the Word of God, while the ground represents the soil of the human heart (see Mark 4:14-20). Before the heart will be ready to receive the seed of truth, it must be softened. In an age when people tend to be skeptical about religion, they must be approached in a way that inspires confidence in the one sharing the truth before they will be open to receiving it. This is best accomplished by drawing close to people in personal ministry.

Christ's Method

"The sowers of the seed have a work to do in preparing hearts to receive the gospel. ... There is need of personal labor for the souls of the lost. In Christlike sympathy we should come close to men individually, and seek to awaken their interest in the great things of eternal life. Their hearts may be as hard as the beaten highway, and apparently it may be a useless effort to present the Saviour to them; but while logic may fail to move, and argument be powerless to convince, the love of Christ, revealed in personal ministry, may soften the stony heart, so that the seed of truth can take root" (*Christ's Object Lessons,* p. 57).

Personal ministry was the proven method of Christ. "Christ's method alone will give true success in reaching the people. The Saviour mingled with men as one who desired their good. He showed His sympathy for them, ministered to their needs, and won their confidence. Then He bade them, 'Follow Me'" (*The Ministry of Healing,* p. 143). Dr. Philip Samaan, in his book *Christ's Method Alone,* summarizes this method of ministry as socializing, sympathizing, serving, and saving.

Socializing

Jesus didn't wait for people to come to Him; He sought them out. He mingled with them. He spent His time among them. He showed an interest in what interested them. "He sought them in the public streets, in private houses, on the boats, in the synagogue, by the shores of the lake, and at the marriage feast. He met them at their daily vocations, and manifested an interest in their secular affairs" (*The Desire of Ages,* p. 151). Christ was both spiritual and social, mingling with people in the hope of ultimately reaching their hearts with the gospel.

This pattern is given for us to follow. We too must be intentional about being spiritually social with people to show we care and to discover how we can best minister to them. Job said it this way, "I was a father to the poor, and I searched out the case that I did not know" (Job 29:16). We must seek to develop an interest in what interests others. And while those we are trying to reach may not be immediately open

> *Personal ministry was the proven method of Christ.*

to spiritual things, there are plenty of common activities that can serve as beginning points for building relationships. Helping your neighbor to rake leaves, inviting a co-worker to dinner, or going for a bike ride with an unbelieving relative are just a few examples of how we can come close to those for whom we labor. "By being social and coming close to the people, you may turn the current of their thoughts more readily than by the most able discourse" (*Gospel Workers,* p. 193).

Sympathizing

To sympathize is to enter into another's feelings. It is impossible to sympathize with those with whom we are unwilling to socialize. "It is acquaintance that awakens sympathy, and sympathy is the spring of effective ministry" (*Education,* p. 269).

A prominent feature of older homes, regardless of size, is the accommodating front porch. People used to spend more time socializing. People knew who their neighbors were, and had real relationships with them. Times have changed. We live in an increasingly impersonal society. Much of our contact with others comes in the form of text messages and emails. As a result, sympathy for our fellow man can die out of the heart and cause us to become more and more self-absorbed.

There's an old saying that until people know how much you care, they won't really care how much you know. Multitudes feel too overwhelmed by financial woes, marital struggles, health problems, and a general dissatisfaction with life to be interested in what they consider just another religious theory. They feel that no one else cares or understands, and that it is their lot to carry these burdens alone.

For this reason, Ellen White instructs, "If we would humble ourselves before God, and be kind and courteous and tenderhearted and pitiful, there would be one hundred conversions to the truth where now there is only one" (*Testimonies for the Church,* vol. 9, p. 189). "The world needs today what it needed nineteen hundred years ago—a revelation of Christ" (*The Ministry of Healing,* p. 143). Just as the Savior was seen by the sickbed, among the poorer classes, and seeking to uplift the disheartened, so His followers should reveal His sympathy in their interaction with their fellow man.

Serving

As Jesus came close to the people and sympathized with their burdens, He was able to minister to their needs "as one who desired their good." It is an undeniable responsibility of the Christian Church to minister to the needs of humanity. Concerning this responsibility, the Bible teaches, "Is it not to share your bread with the hungry, and that you bring to your house the poor who are cast out; when you see the naked, that you cover him. ... If you extend your soul to the hungry and satisfy the afflicted soul, then your light shall dawn in the darkness, and your darkness shall be as the noonday" (Isaiah 58:7-10).

This instruction was later repeated by Jesus when He said, "I was hungry and you gave Me food; I was thirsty and you gave Me drink; I was a stranger and you took Me in; I was naked and you clothed Me; I was sick and you visited Me; I was in prison and you came to Me. … Assuredly, I say to you, inasmuch as you did it to one of the least of these My brethren, you did it to Me" (Matthew 25:35-36, 40).

It is in ministering to the needs of people that we gain their confidence and prepare the soil of the heart to receive the truth of the gospel.

Saving

Upon gaining the confidence of people through socializing, sympathizing, and serving, Jesus then invited them, "Follow Me." This is what He had been working toward all along! While the farmer takes great care to prepare the soil, he does it with the clear intent of sowing the seed.

There is a danger of allowing a needs-based ministry to eclipse the sharing of the gospel message. Some people never go beyond ministering to physical and emotional needs, because it doesn't carry the same risk of offending as does sharing unpopular truth. However, unless those for whom we labor are invited to follow Jesus and His Word, all will be lost. The gospel is still the world's greatest

> *While the farmer takes great care to prepare the soil, he does it with the clear intent of sowing the seed.*

need. "It is not hardship, toil, or poverty that degrades humanity. It is guilt, wrongdoing. This brings unrest and dissatisfaction. Christ would have His servants minister to sin-sick souls" (*The Desire of Ages*, p. 822).

Even when suffering from illness or disease, the greatest and most urgent need is often the healing of the soul. Christ's pronouncement to the paralytic that his sins were forgiven, which he made *prior* to healing his body, provides a striking example of this (see Mark 2:1-12). "The paralytic found in Christ healing for both the soul and the body. He needed health of soul before he could appreciate health of body. Before the physical malady could be healed, Christ must bring relief to the mind, and cleanse the soul from sin. This lesson should not be overlooked" (*The Ministry of Healing*, p. 77).

If we socialize, sympathize, and serve, but never save, we are making friends for this life only. But God would have us make friends for eternity.

Practical Application

The method of Christ cannot be improved upon. Only genuine sympathy and ministry to those around us will open hearts to receive and accept the truth. "There is need of coming close to the people by personal effort. If less time were given to sermonizing, and more time were spent in personal ministry, greater results would be seen. The poor are to be relieved, the sick cared for, the sorrowing and the bereaved comforted, the ignorant instructed, the inexperienced counseled. We are to weep with those that weep, and rejoice with those that rejoice. Accompanied by the power of persuasion, the power of prayer, the power of the love of God, this work will not, cannot, be without fruit" (*The Ministry of Healing*, pp. 143-144).

Consider the people in your own life, as well as those in your community, who are battling grief, poverty, illness, or temptation. Ask yourself what you can do to minister to their needs, lift their burdens, encourage them in their journey, and show the sympathy of Christ. Remember, "Your success will not depend so much upon your knowledge and accomplishments, as upon your ability to find your way to the heart" (*Christian Service,* p. 122). This week, draw close to someone in loving, personal ministry. In so doing, you will win hearts and prepare them to respond favorably to the seeds of truth.

Practical Ways to Prepare the Soil of the Heart

- Take time to build a friendship by striking up a conversation and being a good listener.

- Minister to a need (mow lawns, prepare a meal during sick times, babysit, provide transportation, etc.).

- Give a gift that would be meaningful.

- Do an activity together of particular interest to your friend.

- Go out to a restaurant together or invite your friend home for a meal.

- Take time to help with a project (home repair, gardening/landscaping, craft project, car repair, etc.)

- Be sensitive to periods of stress and crisis in your friend's life and go out of your way to offer support.

- Pray for the Holy Spirit to open your friend's heart to spiritual things.

24

Sowing the Seed

The importance of soil preparation, often referred to as
"friendship evangelism," cannot be overstated. Yet no
farmer endlessly tills the soil. He tills for the purpose of planting
seeds. Jesus said, "The seed is the word of God" (Luke 8:11).
There must come a time when we begin to share the truths of
the Bible with our friends. Without the seed being planted, the
results of the harvest will suffer. Therefore, we are encouraged
to "sow beside all waters" (Isaiah 32:20), or to sow God's Word
wherever we go.

Where to Begin

Before we can plant the seed, we must have an idea of
where to plant it. For this, we need only to look around us. The
Lord places His followers in their particular families, neighborhoods, and jobs in order to reach others through their influence
(see Acts 17:24-28).

Jesus told the disciples that they would be His witnesses
"in Jerusalem, and in all Judea and Samaria, and to the end of
the earth" (Acts 1:8). Commenting on this, Ellen White writes,

"Here is a lesson to all who have a message of truth to give to the world: Their own hearts must first be imbued with the Spirit of God, and their labors should commence at home; their families should have the benefit of their influence. … Then the circle should widen; the whole neighborhood should perceive the interest felt for their salvation, and the light of truth should be faithfully presented to them; for their salvation is of as much importance as that of persons at a distance. From the immediate neighborhood, and adjoining cities and towns, the circle of the labors of God's servants should widen, till the message of truth is given to the uttermost parts of the earth" (*The Spirit of Prophecy,* vol. 3, p. 240).

The Home Mission Field

While our first mission field is our family, sharing the gospel with relatives can sometimes prove to be very challenging. Those who are most familiar with our background and past experience, or with our faults and weaknesses, may use these as an excuse to reject the truth we share with them. This is what Jesus was referring to when He said, "A prophet is not without honor except in his own country, among his own relatives, and in his own house" (Mark 6:4).

On the other hand, because those nearest to us know our weaknesses, they are likely more aware of the positive changes the Lord has made in our lives. These changes cannot help but have an effect. Studies have shown that approximately three out of four Christians come to Christ because of the influence of a friend or relative, and over half of those who join the Seventh-day Adventist Church do so after being invited to a church event by someone they know.

Seeking and Saving the Lost

While ministering to those close to us is important, the Lord would have us to extend our sphere of labor beyond our friends and family. The Great Commission commands us to "Go" (Matthew 28:19). Jesus' method was to "seek" (Luke 19:10) the lost. These texts describe an intentional effort to reach those who we do not currently know. Scripture promises, "Those who sow in tears shall reap in joy. He who continually goes forth weeping, bearing seed for sowing, shall doubtless come again with rejoicing, bringing his sheaves with him" (Psalm 126:5-6). We must be willing to "go forth" if we want to find hearts receptive to the truth. We should cultivate the mindset of Christ: "Every soul was precious in His eyes. … In all men He saw fallen souls whom it was His mission to save" (*Steps to Christ,* p. 12).

> *"In all men He saw fallen souls whom it was His mission to save."*

For most people, being warm and kind in an effort to make new friends for Jesus is not the problem. The difficulty comes in knowing just how and when to transition to spiritual conversation. Many Christians, paralyzed by uncertainty and fear, simply never get around to sharing biblical truth.

Because everyone is different, it can be difficult to know the best time to turn the topic to spiritual things, or whether the individual will respond positively when we do. In spite of this, we must at some point step out in *faith* and plant the seed! We call this "testing the soil."

Testing the Soil

Some people wrongly assume that they must spend years building a relationship with someone before he or she will be open to spiritual truth. They point to the method of Jesus in mingling with and ministering to the people (see previous chapter), and they assume that any method that does not include a long time for building relationships before bringing up spiritual matters (evangelistic meetings, door-to-door ministry, etc.) must be ineffective. However, the length of time needed for soil preparation depends on the individual. It could take years, but it could also take months, weeks, days, or as in the case of Jesus with the woman of Samaria, only a matter of minutes (see John 4:1-26).

Jesus' entire ministry only lasted a period of three and a half years. So while He regularly befriended others through kindness and personal ministry, He did not waste opportunities to speak about eternal realities—even early in the relationship. He knew that while some people would require much time and personal ministry before opening their hearts to the truth, many others would require much less effort due to the work that the Holy Spirit was already doing in their lives. In the same way, there are those around us today whom the Holy Spirit has already been preparing. They just need someone to share the truth with them.

The best way to know if a person is ready for the truth is to "test the soil." One personal and non-threatening way to begin doing this is to simply mention spiritual topics or activities, and see how the person responds. Give a report of your weekend and include the church functions you attended. Mention something you heard in a sermon or prayer meeting. Offer to pray with someone who is discouraged. Share a short portion of your testimony. If the response is positive, such as questions or comments that indicate an interest, gradually begin to bring more spiritual insights and biblical truth into your conversations with the individual. If the response is one of indifference or avoidance, keep in mind that things can change quickly in a person's life—so don't be afraid to test the soil periodically.

Silent Messengers

Sharing a spiritual tract, book, magazine, or DVD is an excellent way to test the soil by planting the seed of God's Word. Rather than sharing spiritual literature only on rare occasions, Ellen White counsels, "Publications must be multiplied, and scattered like the leaves of autumn. These silent messengers are enlightening and molding the minds of thousands" (*Colporteur Ministry*, p. 5).

The phrase, "silent messengers," is a fitting description of the quiet influence of books and tracts, which do not fight or argue with the reader. This "silence" allows a person to wrestle alone with God, unencumbered by feelings of pride and reputation that often rise up when hearing the truth from another person. Many people will read literature, set it aside, and then come back to it again and again as they privately grapple with the truth. The value of sharing literature with others will only be fully known in eternity. Ellen White writes, "More than one thousand will soon be converted in one day, most of whom will trace their first convictions to the reading of our publications" (*Colporteur Ministry*, p. 151).

> *"Publications must be multiplied, and scattered like the leaves of autumn."*

Through the distribution of tracts, books, magazines, and DVDs, many people who might not have otherwise looked into the Bible are led to do so. "If there is one work more important than another, it is that of getting our publications before the public, thus leading them to search the Scriptures" (*Colporteur Ministry*, p. 7).

If we are unsure about sharing literature with someone, the safest route is to give it a try. We may be surprised to find a receptive heart where we least expected. "Our literature is to be distributed everywhere. The truth is to be sown beside all waters; for we know not which will prosper, this, or that. In our erring judgment we may think it unwise to give literature to the very ones who would accept the truth the most readily. We know not what may be the results of giving away a leaflet containing present truth" (*Colporteur Ministry*, p. 4).

Awakening an Interest

We are not only to plant seeds of truth for the purpose of discovering those already interested in eternal things. Sharing our personal testimony or giving someone a piece of biblical literature can also *awaken* interest where there was none previously. "We must in our work not only strike the iron when it is hot but make the iron hot by striking" (*Evangelism*, p. 647).

While we should seek to build trust and confidence through our caring ministry for others, we cannot wait for them to come asking for truth-filled literature. "I want to say, brethren and sisters, that we must labor for the wandering where they are. You need not expect those who have the chilling influence of the world upon them to manifest anxiety for their own souls. We must manifest it for them" (*Manuscript Releases*, vol. 18, p. 284).

A Life and Death Message

Most Christians worry far too much about what people might think of them. Yet those who live for the world have no problem telling Christians all kinds of things we would rather not know! They tell us of their weekend exploits, their favorite movies, and many other things that matter to them. While we should never seek to offend, we should be as enthusiastic about telling others what is important to us as they are about telling us what is important to them. Most of all, we must never forget that the things that interest us are the very things that those in the world need if they would avoid being eternally lost.

If we do not understand the eternal value of our own message, we will be far less likely to risk our reputations to share it. Ellen White wrote, "You must respect your own faith in order successfully to introduce it to others" (*Fundamentals of Christian Education,* p. 194).

Because Jesus understood the value of the gospel, He shared it with many who did not yet know they needed it. He told the Samaritan woman, "If you knew the gift of God, and who it is who says to you, 'Give Me a drink,' you would have asked Him, and He would have given you living water" (John 4:10). Jesus explained that if she only knew what He knew, she would be asking Him for it!

This same Jesus has entrusted us with a message that is vital for this time. If the world only knew the importance of what God has revealed to us in His Word, they would be asking us for it. "Our message is a life and death message, and we must let it appear as it is, the great power of God. We are to present it in all its telling force. Then the Lord will make it effectual" (*Manuscript Releases,* vol. 1, p. 57).

Practical Application

In the parable of the sower, Jesus described a man who went out to plant seeds. Some of the seeds fell by the wayside, some fell on stony ground, some fell among thorns, but only the seed that fell on good ground bore fruit. From this parable, we discover that it was not the farmer, the type of seed, or the method of planting that determined success. The success of the harvest depended instead upon the type of soil in which the seed was planted. This lesson should give encouragement and instruction to every disciple of Christ. It is not primarily our eloquence, timing, ability, or exact methodology that determines the success of our soul-winning efforts. What is more important is the condition of the heart in the one for whom we labor. The more seed we sow, the more likely we are to find "good ground"—a heart prepared for the seeds of truth to grow and bear fruit to salvation.

The Bible tells us that "He who observes the wind will not sow, and he who regards the clouds will not reap" (Ecclesiastes 11:4). In other words, if we put off the spiritual sowing and reaping because we are waiting for the *perfect* time or conditions for sharing, we will never see fruit from our labors. The next verses go on to say, "As you do not know what is the way of the wind … so you do not know the works of God who makes everything. In the morning sow your seed, and in the evening do not withhold your hand; for you do not know which will prosper, either this or that, or whether both alike will be good" (Ecclesiastes 11:5-6).

We cannot read the heart. We cannot know the perfect time to open a spiritual conversation, or to share a tract or other piece of literature. Therefore, the inspired counsel is to sow seed "in the morning" and "in the evening." It is an eternal principle that "He who sows sparingly will also reap sparingly, and he who sows bountifully will also reap bountifully" (2 Corinthians 9:6).

This week, stock up on tracts, books, magazines, and DVDs for sharing. Keep them in your car or some other location where they are readily available. Start a habit of keeping several tracts in your pocket at all times so that you can scatter them like the "leaves of autumn." Then, determine to "test the soil" with someone you know. Pray for wisdom and boldness, and for God to orchestrate "divine appointments" with those open to the truth. As you go forth to sow precious seeds of truth, may God help you to return with rejoicing, bringing your "sheaves" (Psalm 126:6) with you.

Practical Ways to Sow Seeds of Truth

- Share something God has done in your life either in the past or the present.

- Tell the story of how you came to know Christ and became a Seventh-day Adventist.

- Offer to pray with someone.

- Share Bible promises when someone you know is facing a difficult situation.

- Distribute small sharing tracts (GLOW, Balanced Living, etc.) by leaving them places, handing them to strangers, and giving them to those with whom you are already acquainted.

- Share truth-filled CDs and DVDs and follow up to determine the level of interest.

- Post spiritual thoughts on social media or share links to websites and online media that promote the truth.

- Bring up in conversation a Bible verse or topic you have recently read or studied.

- Distribute evangelistic sharing books or Bible study enrollment cards.

- Invite to church services or events (Sabbath worship, prayer meeting, concerts, seminars, evangelistic meetings, etc.).

- Invite to local conference events (women's or men's retreats, marriage retreats, summer camps, etc.).

25

Cultivation

O nce the soil has been prepared and the seeds have been planted, the cultivation phase begins. Cultivation is the process of helping plants to grow. It includes giving them adequate sunlight and water, proper nutrients, removing weeds that would choke out their growth, and protecting them from the elements. The cultivation phase is in some respects the most vital part of the entire growth process because it requires more time and labor than any other phase. While it only takes a few days to prepare the soil, plant the seeds, or harvest the crop, the cultivation of new plants takes several months.

Once the heart has been softened through soil preparation, and interest has been generated by planting seeds of truth, the next step is to cultivate the interest by engaging in regular Bible studies. Here is where the one for whom you are laboring grows in his or her understanding and application of the Word. The truth of God's Word provides the "nutrients" needed to grow, and gives light and power to remove the "weeds" of false doctrines and sinful habits.

> *God's Word provides the "nutrients" needed to grow.*

The Importance of Giving Bible Studies

One of the greatest needs in the church today is the need for church members who will cultivate spiritual interests by giving Bible studies. Few understand the incredible potential that exists in the church if only more of its members would commit to giving one Bible study per week.

It is possible for someone who has never attended a health ministry event to still become a baptized member. It is also entirely feasible that someone might never attend a church social, a Vacation Bible School, or an evangelistic meeting before baptism. However, there is one thing that every Seventh-day Adventist must do, to one degree or another, before being baptized.

> *In the evangelism process, the bottleneck is often Bible studies.*

Every one must go through Bible studies. Here is where the truth grips the heart and decisions are made to believe and practice in harmony with the Seventh-day Adventist Church.

In the manufacturing industry, a bottleneck is the part of the production process with the slowest rate of output. A company can waste a lot of time and money increasing efficiencies in other areas, because the total output will still never be greater than the amount produced by the area identified as the bottleneck. The only way to increase the total output is to increase the rate of output in that particular area.

In the evangelism process, the bottleneck is often Bible studies. While many church members volunteer in other worthwhile areas, only a small percentage are involved in this vital ministry. We can increase our labors in every other area, but most of our churches will never see a significant increase in the harvest until more of their members are giving Bible studies. When this happens, it will open the bottleneck and our growth will be exponential.

A Bible Study Reformation

God Himself inspired the question-and-answer Bible study format, which is so common today, so that church members could have a simple way to share Bible truth. The discovery of this simple method goes back to the early years of the Seventh-day Adventist Church.

It was the summer of 1883, and at that time the truth was spread primarily by tracts and literature or by preaching to crowds. Elder S. N. Haskell was preaching in a tent meeting in Southern California when a severe storm arose. The thunder was so loud that the people could not hear the speaker, and there was thought of canceling the meeting, when Elder Haskell was struck with a divinely-inspired idea. He called the people to crowd around him in the center of the tent and began to call out a question followed by a text, which they were encouraged to look up. Then he would call on one or another to read the text aloud. In this way he was able to conclude his message, and the effect was powerful! The people had seen many of their questions answered straight from their own Bibles and were deeply impressed with the truth.

After the guests had dispersed, one of them—Elder W. C. White—shared with his mother what had taken place that night. On the next day, Ellen White met with Elder Haskell and the other ministers and told them that the meeting described to her was in harmony with the light she had received from the Lord. God had shown her a vision in which she saw hundreds and thousands of Seventh-day Adventists going into homes and sharing the truth in this same way.

A description of the vision is given in *Christian Service,* page 42. "In visions of the night representations passed before me of a great reformatory movement among God's people. ... Hundreds and thousands were seen visiting families, and opening before them the word of God. Hearts were convicted by the power of the Holy Spirit, and a spirit of genuine conversion was manifest." This powerful vision revealed God's plan for a mighty reformation among His people—a Bible study reformation!

A Heaven-Born Idea

Elder Haskell was inspired by Ellen White's vision to provide simple instruction for sharing the Bible using the same question-and-answer format that he had used. In October of that same year, he established a ten-day Bible Reading Institute for the training of lay people ("Bible studies" were then called "Bible readings").

A general announcement to all Adventists was given in one of our leading papers, encouraging them to attend the training. It read, "Not only young men and women are wanted, but men of mature years; even if their heads are sprinkled with gray hairs, they are none too old to visit families and tell what God has done for them, and read the Scriptures" (S. N. Haskell, in *The Signs of the Times,* October 18, 1883, p. 465). Ellen White would later write, "The plan of holding Bible readings was a heaven-born idea. There are many, both men and women, who can engage in this branch of missionary labor" (*Christian Service,* p. 141).

It is worth noting who was being recruited to give Bible studies. Old and young, men and women—anyone who could tell what God had done for them, and read the Scriptures. Here was the genius, the "heaven-born" wisdom, of the Bible study method. Here was the secret to the excitement it generated in the church. No longer was the church dependent upon the ministers alone to spread the truth. Here was a method that would empower thousands of lay people and be an important means of finishing the work.

Discovering the Power

There are some who view the giving of personal Bible studies as being simplistic or mechanical. Nothing could be further from the truth. Those who hold this view have not understood the tremendous power of giving Bible studies, which are perfectly suited to meet the needs of a sin-sick world.

First, Bible studies employ the power of the Word. The Lord has promised, "My word ... shall not return to Me void, but it shall accomplish what I please, and it shall prosper in the thing for which I sent it" (Isaiah 55:11). We must never forget that it is the Word of God that creates spiritual life in the soul. Peter reminds us that we are born again, "not of corruptible seed but incorruptible, through the word of God which lives and abides forever" (1 Peter 1:23). Ellen White concurs, "The creative energy that called the worlds into existence is in the word of God. This word imparts power; it begets life. ... It transforms the nature and re-creates the soul in the image of God" (*Education,* p. 126). This power is in the personal Bible study!

Second, giving Bible studies binds us to the hearts of those for whom we labor. Occasional deeds of kindness are often lauded for their expressions of love, but they do not compare to the love conveyed by giving someone a regular weekly Bible study. While it may not feel like a sacrifice to study with someone week after week, the one with whom we are studying takes note of the tremendous amount of personal time being invested in his or her salvation and spiritual growth. The time spent communicates love in a way that few other actions could. Furthermore, giving Bible studies is not merely for disseminating information, but to offer help in discovering and applying the salvation offered in God's Word. It is an intimate experience to struggle alongside someone as the Bible speaks to the deepest needs of the soul.

Finally, giving personal Bible studies is essential for the growth of the one *giving* the study. This is why Ellen White wrote, "Among the members of our churches there should be more house-to-house labor in giving Bible readings and distributing literature. A Christian character can be symmetrically and completely formed only when the human agent regards it as a privilege to work disinterestedly in the proclamation of the truth" (*Testimonies for the Church,* vol. 9, p. 127). And again, "Let ministers teach church members that in order to grow in spirituality, they must carry the burden that the Lord has laid upon them—the burden of leading souls into the truth" (*Christian Service,* p. 69).

> *The best way to remember what we know, and to grow in our knowledge of the truth, is to share the knowledge we already have.*

The best way to remember what we know, and to grow in our knowledge of the truth, is to share the knowledge we already have. "He who begins with a little knowledge, in a humble way, and tells what he knows, while seeking diligently for further knowledge, will find the whole heavenly treasure awaiting his demand. The more he seeks to impart light, the more light he will receive. The more one tries to explain the word of God to others, with a love for souls, the plainer it becomes to himself. The more we use our knowledge and exercise our powers, the more knowledge and power we shall have" (*Christ's Object Lessons,* p. 354).

Do Not Forget to Ask

We can typically find Bible study interests among those with whom we have been preparing the soil and sowing the seed. These might be family, friends, co-workers, neighbors, church visitors, or those who have attended an evangelistic meeting or other church event. Bible study interests are also often found through literature evangelism and other door-to-door outreach, or by mailing Bible study invitation cards to those in your community. While the sentiment of many today is that people "just aren't interested in the Bible anymore," we must let the words of Jesus be our guide. He told us "the fields … are already white for harvest" (John 4:35). He also said, "The harvest truly is plentiful" (Matthew 9:37). Do we believe Him? Though it will sometimes require searching, there is no shortage of people who are open to studying the Bible.

"All over the world men and women are looking wistfully to heaven. Prayers and tears and inquiries go up from souls longing for light, for grace, for the Holy Spirit. Many are on the verge of the kingdom, waiting only to be gathered in" (*The Acts of the Apostles,* p. 109).

Here are a few ways that you might ask someone to join you for a series of Bible studies:

- "I recently came across a set of Bible study guides that answers the most commonly asked questions about the Bible. I'd like to go through them and I'm wondering if you would have an interest in doing them with me."
- "I am looking for someone who would be interested in studying the Bible together with me and I thought of you. Would you be interested in meeting once a week for an hour or so to study God's Word?"
- "I have been going through a discipleship program at my church and one of the things they are asking us to do is go through a series of Bible lessons with someone. Would you be willing to go through a set of topical Bible study guides with me?"

The reason most people never find someone with whom to study the Bible is that they never ask. Regardless of the method you use, the secret to getting Bible studies is the same. Ask!

How to Give a Bible Study

Giving a Bible study is much simpler than most people realize. It is not necessary to be a seasoned Bible scholar. All it takes is a willing heart and a love for souls. Ongoing Bible studies can be given in either a personal or small group setting, generally with the aid of a printed lesson. There are many lesson guides from which to choose that are in a simple, question-and-answer format. Other resources that may be used include a marked Bible, personal notes, or video presentations. Here are some simple steps to giving a Bible study:

1. **Prepare your heart** (Psalm 37:5). Pray for the converting power of the Holy Spirit in your own life. "Without a living faith in Christ as a personal Saviour, it is impossible to make your faith felt in a skeptical world. If you would draw sinners out of the swift-running current, your own feet must not stand on slippery places" (*Gospel Workers,* p. 274).

2. **Prepare the lesson.** Choose a set of Bible study guides and go through the first lesson on your own. Fill in the blanks, if applicable. Thoroughly familiarize yourself with it. Highlight the two or three most important points and circle the questions that address these. Make personal notes of a few thoughts and personal experiences you can share during the study.

3. **Work with a partner.** Invite another church member to accompany you to the study. This way you can encourage one another, connect the Bible study interest to more than one person, and have someone to fill in if you cannot make it to the study. For these and many other reasons, Jesus sent His own disciples out two-by-two (see Luke 10:1; *The Desire of Ages,* p. 350).

4. **Arrive at the study on time.** This shows that you value your Bible study interest's time, and helps build trust.

5. **Socialize before the study.** Socializing is an important part of giving personal Bible studies. It helps you to relate better to your Bible study interest on a personal level. Socializing before the study, rather than after, allows you to leave on a spiritual note.

6. **Pray before you begin the study**. Ask the Holy Spirit to guide you into all truth (see John 16:13).

7. **Keep the study interesting by encouraging involvement.** Ask each question in the lesson study and invite your study interest to read the text that provides the answer. Then ask the question again, inviting the interest to answer from what was just read. If necessary, help guide to the answer in the text, but try to avoid actually giving the answer. You want your study interest to get the answer from the Bible rather than from you.

8. **Keep the study moving.** You will not be able to spend significant time on every question in the study. You should move along at a steady pace through most of the questions, only taking more time on the key questions you circled when preparing for the study. You should aim to keep your study time to one hour.

9. **Be personal.** Weave a few personal experiences into your study. These will help make the truth practical, make you more relatable and genuine, and endear you to the heart of your Bible study interest.

10. **Do not pretend you are an expert.** You will be asked questions you cannot immediately answer, but do not be discouraged. Even a small child can ask a question an adult cannot answer. If you do not know the answer, just say, "You know, I haven't thought of that before. Let me study into that and I'll share what I find at our next study." If a question will be answered in an upcoming study, simply say, "That's a great question, and we actually have an entire lesson coming up on that topic."

11. **Ask if the study was clear**. As you summarize your study at the end, ask if it was clear. You might say, "Is it clear from our study that the dead are asleep, awaiting the resurrection

at Jesus' coming?" Or, "Is it clear that the biblical form of baptism is full immersion?"

12. **Ask for a decision.** Most Bible study lessons conclude with a question that asks for a commitment to be made based on the topic of the study. Do not pass over this question without giving an opportunity for your study interest to respond.

13. **Confirm the time of the next study**. Never leave without knowing the date and time of your next study.

14. **Close with prayer.** As you pray, incorporate your study interest's decision into the prayer.

Practical Application

A study was done in which violin students were divided into three categories: famous violinists, good performers, and violin teachers. The single determining factor for which level a violinist would achieve, was found to be the number of hours of practice. The teachers had practiced four thousand hours in their lifetime, the good performers had practiced eight thousand hours, and those who became famous had practiced at least ten thousand hours. The fascinating part was that there was not a single violinist who had practiced ten thousand hours who had not also become famous. Ten thousand hours of practice was nearly a guarantee that you would become a renowned musician.

As the old adage says, "practice makes perfect." There is no task in which a person cannot gain proficiency by practice. If you are nervous about giving a Bible study, go along on a study that someone else is leading out so that you can observe. Then, try practicing on a fellow church member. Choose a Sabbath afternoon or some evening during the week, and try out the steps given in this chapter. Do this as many times as it takes to start feeling comfortable. With earnest prayer and plenty of practice, you will so excel at giving Bible studies that it will become one of your greatest joys.

Make no mistake, "It is in the water, not on the land, that men learn to swim" (*Education*, p. 268). You will never know how to give a Bible study until you step out in faith and actually start doing it. Angels are waiting to bless our humble efforts. Make a decision right now that you will begin looking for a spiritual interest with whom you can study the Bible. The Lord will open the way and give you the strength and wisdom you need if you will only go forward in faith.

Practical Ways to Cultivate Interests

- Meet once a week to go through a series of Bible lessons together.

- Give Bible lessons to an interest to study on his or her own.

- Invite to a weekly small group Bible study.

- Watch a series of evangelistic DVDs and discuss.

- Bring to Sabbath school, church, or prayer meeting.

- Invite to an evangelistic series.

- Invite to your local conference camp meeting.

- Encourage your study interest to regularly watch or listen to Adventist television or radio programming.

- Pray regularly that your Bible study interest would experience the life-changing power of Christ and His Word.

26

Harvest and Preserve

The most rewarding part of the cycle of evangelism is when the months and even years of soil preparation (friendship evangelism), seed-sowing (sharing truth), and cultivation (Bible studies) result in a *harvest* of life-transforming decisions and a public stand for Christ through baptism. It is in the harvest phase that belief is put into action and the individual takes up the cross to follow Jesus fully (see Matthew 16:24; Luke 9:23). There is "joy in the presence of the angels of God" (Luke 15:10), and in our own hearts too, when we see a person make such a commitment.

Unfortunately, we often do not experience this joy because we fail to see when the one for whom we labor is ready to become part of God's end-time church. Jesus addresses this common mistake when He says, "Do you not say, 'There are still four months and then comes the harvest'? Behold, I say to you, lift up your eyes and look at the fields, for they are already white for harvest!" (John 4:35). There are many who never make a decision, not because they were not ready, but because no one ever took the opportunity to *ask* for a decision! We must see the importance of making loving appeals to the heart and inviting the soul to surrender to Christ. Many will respond if we do.

While we are to courageously share the truth and ask people to follow it, we must never forget that a harvest of decisions for Christ does not come "by might, nor by power, but by My Spirit says the Lord of hosts" (Zechariah 4:6). Only the Holy Spirit can convict the heart and provide the power to change. This power comes through the Word of God (see Hebrews 4:12). "It is the Spirit who gives life; the flesh profits nothing. The words that I speak to you are spirit, and they are life" (John 6:63). We must depend upon the Bible to answer questions, meet objections, and lead to positive decisions for Christ. God's Word can convict where our words are powerless!

> *God's Word can convict where our words are powerless!*

Public Appeals

Some of the best opportunities to gain decisions for Jesus are during a public meeting such as the Sabbath worship service or an evangelistic meeting. Here the preaching of the Word brings deep conviction to hearts and the speaker invites the hearers to respond to the invitation of the Spirit. Never should a sermon be preached that does not include an appeal for the listeners to follow Christ and His Word.

Regarding the importance of these appeals, Ellen White writes, "If there is not a decided application of the truth to their hearts, if words are not spoken at the right moment, calling for decision from the weight of evidence already presented, the convicted ones pass on without identifying themselves with Christ, the golden opportunity passes, and they have not yielded, and they go farther and farther away from the truth, farther away from Jesus and never take their stand on the Lord's side" (*Evangelism,* p. 283).

The human tendency to procrastinate in responding to the conviction of the Holy Spirit is a highly risky one. "When persons who are under conviction are not brought to make a decision at the earliest period possible, there is danger that the conviction will gradually wear away" (*Evangelism,* p. 229). This is why the Scriptures appeal to us, "Today, if you will hear His voice, do not harden your heart" (Hebrews 4:7).

One-on-One Decisions

While public meetings can be very effective in gaining decisions, appeals made during home visits and Bible studies are perfect for gaining first-time decisions, sealing decisions made during a public meeting, or calling for a higher level of commitment than what was made in the public setting. The personal visit or study provides the opportunity to apply the truth to an individual's exact situation, to offer personalized words of encouragement, to discuss specific obstacles, and to capitalize on the trust gained through a personal relationship.

As soul-winners we are not called to coerce or manipulate anyone's will, but we must understand how a person's will works so that we can enlist it in making a decision. We can observe how the Spirit is working on the heart in order to help the individual to recognize this and respond to His promptings. Here are some simple steps you can take in asking for decisions:

1. **Look for signs of conviction.** These might be tears of sorrow or of joy, sincere inquiries, or a peaceful countenance. Negative responses such as hesitation, avoidance, or even

resistance are also signs of conviction. Whether they appear positive or negative, responses that indicate more than indifference are usually evidences of conviction.

2. **Ask commitment questions.** "Is there anything that would prevent you from keeping the Sabbath (or, returning God's tithe, being baptized, becoming a member of God's remnant church, etc.)?" This can bring to light any obstacles to following Jesus that might exist. Help the individual to outline a plan of action and pray together for strength to proceed.

3. **Share the benefits of obeying God and the dangers of delay.** God's Word is full of promises to the obedient and warnings to those who put off conviction. Encourage the individual to experience God's blessings through obedience.

4. **Make an appeal that focuses on Jesus.** Jesus is the greatest motivation for making any decision. Remind the individual that it is Jesus appealing to the heart—no one else. For example, you might say, "Jesus is inviting you to follow His example in being baptized. How would you like to respond to His invitation?"

If you take these steps while manifesting genuine interest and love, you will be a rich blessing to the soul for whom you labor. You are there as a friend, encouraging a positive response to the call of Jesus. Remember that decisions to follow God's Word are necessary in order to experience spiritual growth.

Preparation for Membership

The goal of the harvest stage of the evangelism cycle is joining God's remnant church through baptism or profession of faith. Once a person makes this decision, you should arrange to meet and review the 28 fundamental beliefs of the Seventh-day Adventist Church as listed in the baptismal certificate. The simplest way to do this is to use a baptismal preparation card that summarizes each one of our fundamental beliefs. Read and discuss each point on the card, looking up the accompanying Scriptures, and asking questions to assess the understanding.

As you go through the final baptismal preparation process, consider three key areas to evaluate the person's readiness for baptism and membership:

1. **The Heart**—Does the candidate manifest a genuine interest in Jesus and His Word?

2. **The Mind**—Does the candidate have an accurate understanding of the fundamental teachings of the Bible?

3. **The Life**—Is the candidate's life in harmony with the teachings of God's Word?

Before baptism, Bible truth should not only be understood and believed, but also practiced. Jesus taught, "But these are the ones sown on good ground, those who hear the word, accept it, and bear fruit" (Mark 4:20). Those who hear and accept the Word give evidence of doing so by bearing the fruit of obedience. The apostle Paul describes baptism as "the body of sin" being "done away with, that we should no longer be slaves of sin" (Romans 6:6). This

> *Jesus is the greatest motivation for making any decision.*

means that practicing the truth and putting away sin are both signs of genuine conversion. While candidates for baptism will never be perfect, they should be committed to obeying Bible truth.

Therefore, in addition to asking if your candidate understands a biblical truth, you will also want to ask if they have begun to obey it. For example, after reviewing what the Bible says about keeping the Sabbath, you might say, "Have you begun keeping the Sabbath in this way? Have you had to make any changes or adaptations in your life in order to do so?" Sympathize with obstacles and difficulties, relating your own experience in a kind and caring way, while at the same time giving vital instruction in how to find victory. Sometimes practical decisions to follow Bible teachings are not truly made until one is preparing for baptism.

A thorough baptismal preparation process might seem unnecessary, but nothing could be further from the truth. "Too much hasty work is done in adding names to the church roll. Serious defects are seen in the characters of some who join the church. Those who admit them say, 'We will first get them into the church, and then reform them.' But this is a mistake. The very first work to be done is the work of reform. Pray with them, talk with them, but do not allow them to unite with God's people in church relationship until they give decided evidence that the Spirit of God is working on their hearts" (*The Review and Herald,* May 21, 1901).

It is not greater numbers that we need in our churches, but truly converted disciples of Christ. "God would be better pleased to have six thoroughly converted to the truth than to have sixty make a profession and yet not be truly converted" (*Christian Service,* p. 104).

Church Membership Not the Final Goal

The ultimate goal of evangelism is to make disciples, who in turn make other disciples. Baptism and its corresponding entrance into church membership are only the early steps in this process. But how often do we rejoice when new members are baptized and then neglect to invest time mentoring and training them afterwards? How often are they left to figure out what it means to be genuine disciples of Christ on their own?

Ellen White counsels, "New converts will need to be instructed by faithful teachers of God's Word, that they may increase in a knowledge and love of the truth, and may grow to the full stature of men and women in Christ Jesus. They must now be surrounded by the influences most favorable to spiritual growth" (*Evangelism,* p. 337).

Evangelism does not end when a person has been saved from sinful practices, worldly philosophies, and doctrinal errors. There must also be an intentional process of discipleship in which the new member is given further instruction from God's Word, taught to apply its teachings, encouraged to develop strong spiritual habits, integrated into the life of the church, and given training in personal witnessing and church ministries. In this way, the new member will continue to grow and mature into a vibrant, active disciple of Christ.

Preserving the Harvest

The final phase of the cycle of evangelism is called *preservation.* In this critical phase, new members are mentored, equipped, and then sent out to make other disciples. This helps ensure that the harvest of souls is not lost and that the cycle will be replicated again and again.

New members often face many challenges after baptism. Non-Adventist friends or relatives may oppose the changes the new member has recently made. It can be hard to make friends and integrate into a new church. Living in harmony with the high standards of the Bible can also be a challenge. And then there are the winds of false doctrine that threaten to unsettle those new to the faith. Any or all of these can lead to discouragement, disillusionment, and distractions, resulting in the proverbial "back door" through which new members all too frequently slip out of the church.

Only through intentional, systematic, and diligent efforts at discipleship can the harvest be preserved. Ellen White counsels, "After individuals have been converted to the truth, they need to be looked after. ... These newly converted ones need nursing, watchful attention, help, and encouragement. These should not be left alone, a prey to Satan's most powerful temptations; they need to be educated in regard to their duties, to be kindly dealt with, to be led along, and to be visited and prayed with" (*Evangelism*, p. 351).

New members need spiritual mentors who will help them through challenges, assist them in developing spiritual habits, and integrate them into the local church. This *Discipleship Handbook* and its accompanying *Mentor's Guide* have been specifically designed to help in these areas.

> *Only through intentional, systematic, and diligent efforts at discipleship can the harvest be preserved.*

Discipleship, though, is not complete until the new member is sharing his or her faith with others. Jesus summarized it this way, "Go therefore and make disciples of all the nations, baptizing them in the name of the Father and of the Son and of the Holy Spirit, teaching them to observe all things that I have commanded you" (Matthew 28:19-20). Notice that disciples were commissioned to make other disciples. The spiritual health of every member is dependent upon sharing the truth with others. For this reason, Ellen White writes, "When souls are converted, set them to work at once. And as they labor according to their ability, they will grow stronger. It is by meeting opposing influences that we become confirmed in the faith" (*Evangelism*, p. 355). And in another place, "Let all be taught how to work. Especially should those who are newly come to the faith be educated to become laborers together with God" (*Christian Service*, p. 69).

Practical Application

No matter how long you have been a Seventh-day Adventist, you can have a part in winning souls for Christ. All around us there are people looking for truth and light. "Many are on the verge of the kingdom, waiting only to be gathered in" (*The Acts of Apostles*, p. 109).

Rather than pray merely for an abundant harvest, Jesus identifies an even greater need. "The harvest truly is great, but the laborers are few; therefore pray the Lord of the harvest to send out laborers into His harvest" (Luke 10:2). Far too often, we emphasize prayer for the harvest when Jesus said our greatest need is laborers. The world is dying for the want of genuine disciples, redeemed by the grace of Christ, who will feel a burden for the lost.

By remaining active in God's work and mentoring others newer to the faith than yourself, you can keep the cycle of evangelism going until Jesus comes. "One soul is of infinite value; for Calvary speaks its worth. One soul, won to the truth, will be instrumental in winning others, and there will be an ever-increasing result of blessing and salvation" (*Christian Service*, p. 121).

Practical Ways to Harvest and Preserve

- Make personal appeals during in-home Bible studies, giving an invitation to surrender fully to Christ and His Word.

- Provide examples from your own experience of the blessing of following Bible truth.

- Accompany an interest to a series of evangelistic meetings and encourage positive decisions for Christ.

- Help your friend prepare for baptism.

- Volunteer to help at the next evangelistic series at your church.

- Participate in a community outreach and invite a new church member to accompany you in service.

- Make friends with someone new to the church.

- Invite a new member to your home for Sabbath lunch or to join you in a social activity.

- Encourage a new member by sharing your testimony.

- Invite a new member to help you in a church ministry in which you are involved.

- Mentor a new member using this *Discipleship Handbook*.

Appendix A

Bible & Spirit of Prophecy Reading Plan

Reading Plan Introduction

D aily communion with God through prayer and Bible study is the most important spiritual habit we can develop. The writings of Ellen G. White, often referred to as the "Spirit of Prophecy" (see Revelation 12:17; 19:10), provide an inspired commentary on the Bible that can help you to discover the power and beauty of God's Word. In the pages that follow, you will find a daily Bible reading plan that incorporates corresponding passages in *Patriarchs and Prophets, Prophets and Kings, Steps to Christ, The Desire of Ages, Christ's Object Lessons, Thoughts from the Mount of Blessing, The Acts of the Apostles,* and *The Great Controversy.*

Special tribute is here gratefully given to Elder Arl V. Voorheis for spending over two decades refining these correlations between the Bible and the writings of Ellen White. Elder Voorheis developed three plans, each differing in the amount of time scheduled for daily reading, and published them in the book *Correlated Bible Readings.* You may obtain a copy of this helpful resource from Adventist Heritage Ministry (www.adventistheritage.org or 269-965-5600). The reading plan in this appendix is an adaptation of one of the three plans found in *Correlated Bible Readings,* and is used by permission from Adventist Heritage Ministry.

Using the Reading Plan

Read the information below for important instructions on how to use the Bible and Spirit of Prophecy reading plan:

- The reading plan consists of four sections of equal length, listed in chronological order. Each section will guide you through a different portion of the Bible and one or more Spirit of Prophecy books. The subheading of each section gives the biblical time period covered and the books needed for that section. You may begin at any section in the plan.

- Each day's reading assignment is based on approximately 15-20 minutes of reading. Assuming the plan is used five days a week, each of the four sections would take one year for a total of four years to finish the plan. The additional two days each week could be used for other reading, such as a Sabbath school lesson. Of course, using the plan seven days a week or doubling up on daily readings would shorten the total time considerably. You may also choose to order *Correlated Bible Readings,* which contains two faster plans, from Adventist Heritage Ministry (www.adventistheritage.org or 269-965-5600).

- SOP is an abbreviation for "Spirit of Prophecy," and refers to different books by Ellen G. White. Some days include only Scripture reading, some include only Spirit of Prophecy reading, but most include both.

- To use the plan, simply read the Scripture and corresponding Spirit of Prophecy passage shown in the same row as the day of your reading assignment.

- Highlighting key passages in your daily reading can help to deepen the impression of the statements that impact you the most. It can also help you to stay focused while reading and to more readily find important passages later. Please refer to the end of chapter two for other helpful suggestions for your devotional life.

- The chapter titles of each day's Spirit of Prophecy reading are displayed next to the book title and page numbers.

- The page numbers listed represent the original page numbers for the Spirit of Prophecy books. Some versions of these books do not follow the original page numbering. In these cases, chapter titles are helpful in approximating your daily reading.

- When page numbers are followed by a letter (e.g., "39a"), this means that the chapter is being broken up into more than one day of reading. You may stop or begin with the corresponding paragraph on that page ("39a" is the first paragraph on page 39, "39b" is the second paragraph, etc.).

- The abbreviations used for Spirit of Prophecy books, in the order in which they appear in the plan, are as follows:

  > PP = *Patriarchs and Prophets*
  > PK = *Prophets and Kings*
  > SC = *Steps to Christ*
  > DA = *The Desire of Ages*
  > COL = *Christ's Object Lessons*
  > MB = *Thoughts from the Mount of Blessing*
  > AA = *The Acts of the Apostles*
  > GC = *The Great Controversy*

May God bless you abundantly as you commit to spending at least 30 minutes each day (15 minutes of prayer and 15 minutes of inspired reading) in communion with Him!

Section One

Bible: Creation to King David
Spirit of Prophecy: *Patriarchs and Prophets*

✓ Day	Bible Reading	SOP Reading	SOP Chapter Title
☐ 1		PP Introduction xiii-xvii,b	
☐ 2		PP Introduction xvii, c-xxii	
☐ 3		PP 33-39a	Why Was Sin Permitted?
☐ 4		PP 39b-43	Why Was Sin Permitted?
☐ 5	Gen 1	PP 44-45	The Creation
☐ 6	Gen 2	PP 46-51	The Creation
☐ 7	Gen 3:1-6	PP 52-57a	The Temptation and Fall
☐ 8	Gen 3:7-24	PP 57b-62	The Temptation and Fall
☐ 9		PP 63-67a	The Plan of Redemption
☐ 10		PP 67b-70	The Plan of Redemption
☐ 11	Gen 4:1-16	PP 71-79	Cain and Abel Tested
☐ 12	Gen 4:16-5:17	PP 80-84b	Seth and Enoch
☐ 13	Gen 5:18-6:2	PP 84c-89	Seth and Enoch
☐ 14	Gen 6:3-13	PP 90-92b	The Flood
☐ 15	Gen 6:14-7:3	PP 92c-97c	The Flood
☐ 16	Gen 7:4-19	PP 97d-101a	The Flood
☐ 17	Gen 7:20-24	PP 101b-104	The Flood

✓ Day	Bible Reading	SOP Reading	SOP Chapter Title
☐ 18	Gen 8	PP 105-106a	After the Flood
☐ 19	Gen 9:1-17	PP 106b-110	After the Flood
☐ 20	Gen 10	PP 111-116	The Literal Week
☐ 21	Gen 9:18-29; 11:1-4	PP 117-119a	The Tower of Babel
☐ 22	Gen 11:5-9	PP 119b-124	The Tower of Babel
☐ 23	Gen 11:10-12:5	PP 125-127b	The Call of Abraham
☐ 24	Gen 12:6-20	PP 127c-131	The Call of Abraham
☐ 25	Gen 13-14	PP 132-136b	Abraham in Canaan
☐ 26	Gen 15; 17: 1-15	PP 136c-138b	Abraham in Canaan
☐ 27	Gen 18:1-8, 16-33	PP 138c-140c	Abraham in Canaan
☐ 28	Gen 20	PP 140d-144	Abraham in Canaan
☐ 29	Gen 16; 17:16-27; 18:9-15; 21:1-21	PP 145-147b	The Test of Faith
☐ 30	Gen 21:22-22:14	PP 147c-153a	The Test of Faith
☐ 31	Gen 22:15-24	PP 153b-155	The Test of Faith
☐ 32	Gen 19:1-3	PP 156-159a	Destruction of Sodom
☐ 33	Gen 19:4-22	PP 159b-161b	Destruction of Sodom
☐ 34	Gen 19:23-29	PP 161c-167b	Destruction of Sodom
☐ 35	Gen 19:30-38; 23	PP 167c-170	Destruction of Sodom
☐ 36	Gen 24:1-58	PP 171-173d	The Marriage of Isaac
☐ 37	Gen 24:59-67	PP 173e-176	The Marriage of Isaac
☐ 38	Gen 25:1-26:33	PP 177-179c	Jacob and Esau

✓ Day	Bible Reading	SOP Reading	SOP Chapter Title
☐ 39	Gen 26:34-27:40	PP 179d-182	Jacob and Esau
☐ 40	Gen 27:41-28:22	PP 183-188b	Jacob's Flight and Exile
☐ 41	Gen 29:1-30	PP 188c-190a	Jacob's Flight and Exile
☐ 42	Gen 29:31-30:24	PP 190b-192c	Jacob's Flight and Exile
☐ 43	Gen 30:25-31:55	PP 192d-194	Jacob's Flight and Exile
☐ 44	Gen 32	PP 195-198b	The Night of Wrestling
☐ 45	Gen 33	PP 198c-203	The Night of Wrestling
☐ 46	Gen 34:1-35:15	PP 204-206c	The Return to Canaan
☐ 47	Gen 35:16-36:8	PP 206d-209a	The Return to Canaan
☐ 48	Gen 37	PP 209b-212	The Return to Canaan
☐ 49	Gen 36:9-43; 38		
☐ 50	Gen 39	PP 213-218	Joseph in Egypt
☐ 51	Gen 40:1-41:16	PP 219-220b	Joseph in Egypt
☐ 52	Gen 41:17-52	PP 220c-223	Joseph in Egypt
☐ 53	Gen 41:53-42:38	PP 224-227a	Joseph and His Brothers
☐ 54	Gen 43:1-44:2	PP 227b-229a	Joseph and His Brothers
☐ 55	Gen 44:3-45:15	PP 229b-231b	Joseph and His Brothers
☐ 56	Gen 45:16-46:27	PP 231c-232	Joseph and His Brothers
☐ 57	Gen 46:28-48:22	PP 233-235b	Joseph and His Brothers
☐ 58	Gen 49	PP 235c-237c	Joseph and His Brothers
☐ 59	Gen 50	PP 237d-240	Joseph and His Brothers
☐ 60	Job 1-3		

✓ Day	Bible Reading	SOP Reading	SOP Chapter Title
☐ 61	Job 4-10		
☐ 62	Job 11-14		
☐ 63	Job 15-17		
☐ 64	Job 18-21		
☐ 65	Job 22-24		
☐ 66	Job 25-28		
☐ 67	Job 29-31		
☐ 68	Job 32-34		
☐ 69	Job 35-37		
☐ 70	Job 38-39		
☐ 71	Job 40-42		
☐ 72	Ex 1:1-2:9	PP 241-244a	Moses
☐ 73	Ex 2:10-22	PP 244b-251a	Moses
☐ 74	Ex 2:23-3:22	PP 251b-253f	Moses
☐ 75	Ex 4:1-26	PP 253g-256	Moses
☐ 76	Ex 4:27-6:1	PP 257-260c	The Plagues of Egypt
☐ 77	Ex 6:2-7:25	PP 260d-265b	The Plagues of Egypt
☐ 78	Ex 8:1-9:16	PP 265c-269b	The Plagues of Egypt
☐ 79	Ex 9:17-11:3	PP 269c-272	The Plagues of Egypt
☐ 80	Ex 11:4-12:17	PP 273-278b	The Passover
☐ 81	Ex 12:18-33	PP 278c-280	The Passover
☐ 82	Ex 12:34-14:14	PP 281-284b	The Exodus

✓ Day	Bible Reading	SOP Reading	SOP Chapter Title
☐ 83	Ex 14:15-15:21	PP 248c-290	The Exodus
☐ 84	Ex 15:22-16:3	PP 291-294c	From the Red Sea to Sinai
☐ 85	Ex 16:4-36	PP 294d-297c	From the Red Sea to Sinai
☐ 86	Ex 17	PP 297d-300b	From the Red Sea to Sinai
☐ 87	Ex 18	PP 300c-302	From the Red Sea to Sinai
☐ 88	Ex 19	PP 303-305a	The Law Given to Israel
☐ 89	Ex 20:1-21	PP 305b-310a	The Law Given to Israel
☐ 90	Ex 20:22-23:19	PP 310b-311d	The Law Given to Israel
☐ 91	Ex 23:20-24:18	PP 311e-313b	The Law Given to Israel
☐ 92	Ex 25-26		
☐ 93	Ex 27:1-28:30		
☐ 94	Ex 30:11-31:18	PP 313c-314	The Law Given to Israel
☐ 95	Ex 32:1-14	PP 315-319c	Idolatry at Sinai
☐ 96	Ex 32:15-29	PP 319d-326a	Idolatry at Sinai
☐ 97	Ex 32:30-33:18	PP 326b-328c	Idolatry at Sinai
☐ 98	Ex 33:19-34:35	PP 328d-330	Idolatry at Sinai
☐ 99		PP 331-336	Satan's Enmity Against the Law
☐ 100		PP 337-342	Satan's Enmity Against the Law
☐ 101	Ex 35:1-36:7	PP 343-347a	The Tabernacle and Its Services
☐ 102	Ex 36:8-37:29	PP 347b	The Tabernacle and Its Services

✓ Day	Bible Reading	SOP Reading	SOP Chapter Title
☐ 103	Ex 38-39	PP 347c-348b	The Tabernacle and Its Services
☐ 104	Ex 40	PP 348c-350a	The Tabernacle and Its Services
☐ 105	Ex 28:31-30:10	PP 350b-352b	The Tabernacle and Its Services
☐ 106	Lev 4	PP 352c-355a	The Tabernacle and Its Services
☐ 107	Lev 16	PP 355b-358	The Tabernacle and Its Services
☐ 108	Lev 1-3; 5-6		
☐ 109	Lev 7-9; 12		
☐ 110	Lev 10	PP 359-362	The Sin of Nadab and Abihu
☐ 111	Lev 13		
☐ 112	Lev 14		
☐ 113	Lev 11; 15		
☐ 114	Lev 17-19		
☐ 115	Lev 20-22		
☐ 116	Lev 24:1-9; 25		
☐ 117	Lev 26	PP 363-366b	The Law and the Covenants
☐ 118		PP 366c-373	The Law and the Covenants
☐ 119	Num 1-2		
☐ 120	Num 3-4		
☐ 121	Num 5-6		

✓	Day	Bible Reading	SOP Reading	SOP Chapter Title
☐	122	Num 7:1-9:14		
☐	123	Num 9:15-10:36	PP 374-376c	From Sinai to Kadesh
☐	124	Num 11:1-23	PP 376d-381c	From Sinai to Kadesh
☐	125	Num 11:24-12:16	PP 381d-386	From Sinai to Kadesh
☐	126	Num 13:1-14:10	PP 387-390c	The Twelve Spies
☐	127	Num 14:11-45	PP 390d-394	The Twelve Spies
☐	128	Num 15:1-31; 16:1-3	PP 395-398c	The Rebellion of Korah
☐	129	Num 16:4-35	PP 398d-401c	The Rebellion of Korah
☐	130	Num 16:36-17:13	PP 401d-405	The Rebellion of Korah
☐	131	Lev 24:10-23; Num 15:32-41; 20:1	PP 406-410	In the Wilderness
☐	132	Num 18-19		
☐	133	Num 20:2-5	PP 411-417a	The Smitten Rock
☐	134	Num 20:6-13	PP 417b-421	The Smitten Rock
☐	135	Num 20:14-29	PP 422-427d	The Journey Around Edom
☐	136	Num 21:1-20	PP 427e-432	The Journey Around Edom
☐	137	Num 21:21-23; Deut 1:1-2:31	PP 433-435a	The Conquest of Bashan
☐	138	Num 21:24-35; Deut 2:32-3:11	PP 435b-437	The Conquest of Bashan
☐	139	Num 22:1-20	PP 438-441b	Balaam
☐	140	Num 22:21-23:10	PP 441c-447	Balaam

✓ Day	Bible Reading	SOP Reading	SOP Chapter Title
☐ 141	Num 23:11-24:25	PP 448-452	Balaam
☐ 142	Num 25-26	PP 453-456b	Apostasy at the Jordan
☐ 143	Num 31:1-24	PP 456c-461	Apostasy at the Jordan
☐ 144	Num 27:1-11; 30; 36; Lev 27:1-29		
☐ 145	Num 31:25-54; 32; Deut 3:12-20; 4:41-49		
☐ 146	Num 33-35		
☐ 147	Num 27:12-23; Deut 3:21-4:40	PP 462-463	The Law Repeated
☐ 148	Deut 5:1-7:11	PP 464-466a	The Law Repeated
☐ 149	Deut 28	PP 466b-468	The Law Repeated
☐ 150	Deut 7:12-10:22		
☐ 151	Deut 11-13		
☐ 152	Deut 14-17		
☐ 153	Deut 18-21		
☐ 154	Deut 22-26		
☐ 155	Deut 27; 29-30		
☐ 156	Deut 31:1-32:47	PP 469-470c	The Death of Moses
☐ 157	Deut 32:48-33:29	PP 470d-471c	The Death of Moses
☐ 158	Deut 34	PP 471d-478b	The Death of Moses
☐ 159	Ps 90	PP 478c-480	The Death of Moses

✓ Day	Bible Reading	SOP Reading	SOP Chapter Title
☐ 160	Josh 1:1-3:5	PP 481-484a	Crossing the Jordan
☐ 161	Josh 3:6-5:12	PP 484b-486	Crossing the Jordan
☐ 162	Josh 5:13-6:20	PP 487-491c	The Fall of Jericho
☐ 163	Josh 6:21-7:6	PP 491d-494a	The Fall of Jericho
☐ 164	Josh 7:7-26	PP 494b-498	The Fall of Jericho
☐ 165	Josh 8	PP 499-504	The Blessings and the Curses
☐ 166	Josh 9	PP 505-507c	League With the Gibeonites
☐ 167	Josh 10:1-39	PP 507d-509	League With the Gibeonites
☐ 168	Josh 10:40-12:24	PP 510-511b	The Division of Canaan
☐ 169	Josh 13-14	PP 511c-513c	The Division of Canaan
☐ 170	Josh 15-17	PP 513d-514c	The Division of Canaan
☐ 171	Josh 18-19	PP 514d-515b	The Division of Canaan
☐ 172	Josh 20-21	PP 515c-517d	The Division of Canaan
☐ 173	Josh 22	PP 517e-520	The Division of Canaan
☐ 174	Josh 23-24	PP 521-524	The Last Words of Joshua
☐ 175	Lev 27:30-34	PP 525-529	Tithes and Offerings
☐ 176		PP 530-536	God's Care for the Poor
☐ 177	Lev 23:1-22; Num 28	PP 537-540a	The Annual Feasts
☐ 178	Lev 23:23-44; Num 29	PP 540b-542	The Annual Feasts
☐ 179	Jud 1-2	PP 543-545b	The Earlier Judges

✓ Day	Bible Reading	SOP Reading	SOP Chapter Title
☐ 180	Jud 3:1-6:1	PP 545c	The Earlier Judges
☐ 181	Jud 6:2-40	PP 545d-548c	The Earlier Judges
☐ 182	Jud 7	PP 548d-554b	The Earlier Judges
☐ 183	Jud 8:1-9:6	PP 554c-557a	The Earlier Judges
☐ 184	Jud 9:7-10:18	PP 557b-558c	The Earlier Judges
☐ 185	Jud 11:1-13:1	PP 558d-559	The Earlier Judges
☐ 186	Jud 13:2-23	PP 560-562b	Samson
☐ 187	Jud 13:24-15:20	PP 562c-564c	Samson
☐ 188	Jud 16	PP 564d-568	Samson
☐ 189	Jud 17-18		
☐ 190	Jud 19-21		
☐ 191	Ruth 1-4		
☐ 192	1 Sam 1:1-23	PP 569-571a	The Child Samuel
☐ 193	1 Sam 1:24-2:11	PP 571b-574	The Child Samuel
☐ 194	1 Sam 2:12-26	PP 575-577b	Eli and His Sons
☐ 195	1 Sam 2:27-36	PP 577c-580	Eli and His Sons
☐ 196	1 Sam 3-4	PP 581-585d	The Ark Taken by the Philistines
☐ 197	1 Sam 5:1-6:18	PP 585e-589a	The Ark Taken by the Philistines
☐ 198	1 Sam 6:19-7:17	PP 589b-591	The Ark Taken by the Philistines
☐ 199		PP 592-596b	The Schools of the Prophets

✓ Day	Bible Reading	SOP Reading	SOP Chapter Title
☐ 200		PP 596c-602	The Schools of the Prophets
☐ 201	1 Sam 8	PP 603-608a	The First King of Israel
☐ 202	1 Sam 9:1-10:16	PP 608b-611a	The First King of Israel
☐ 203	1 Sam 10:17-11:15	PP 611b-613b	The First King of Israel
☐ 204	1 Sam 12	PP 613c-615	The First King of Israel
☐ 205	1 Sam 13	PP 616-622	The Presumption of Saul
☐ 206	1 Sam 14	PP 623-626	The Presumption of Saul
☐ 207	1 Sam 15:1-23	PP 627-631c	Saul Rejected
☐ 208	1 Sam 15:24-35	PP 631d-636	Saul Rejected
☐ 209	1 Sam 16:1-13	PP 637-642	The Anointing of David
☐ 210	1 Sam 16:14-17:27	PP 643-645c	David and Goliath
☐ 211	1 Sam 17:28-58; Ps 8; 19; 23	PP 645d-648	David and Goliath
☐ 212	1 Sam 18:1-19:1	PP 649-652b	David a Fugitive
☐ 213	1 Sam 19:2-24	PP 652c-654b	David a Fugitive
☐ 214	1 Sam 20	PP 654c-655c	David a Fugitive
☐ 215	1 Sam 21:1-22:19; Ps 133	PP 655d-659	David a Fugitive
☐ 216	Ps 42; 52; 54; 57; 59; 107; 142; 1 Sam 22:20-23:15	PP 660a, b	The Magnanimity of David
☐ 217	1 Sam 23:16-25:1; Ps 11; 121	PP 660c-664b	The Magnanimity of David
☐ 218	1 Sam 25:2-17	PP 664c-666a	The Magnanimity of David

✓ Day	Bible Reading	SOP Reading	SOP Chapter Title
☐ 219	1 Sam 25:18-35; Ps 120; 141	PP 666b-667d	The Magnanimity of David
☐ 220	1 Sam 25:36-27:4	PP 667e-673b	The Magnanimity of David
☐ 221	1 Sam 27:5-28:2; Ps 7; 13; 27; 31; 56; 63	PP 673c-674	The Magnanimity of David
☐ 222	1 Chr 12:1-22; 1 Sam 28:3-14	PP 675-679	The Death of Saul
☐ 223	1 Sam 28:15-25; 31; 1 Chr 10	PP 680-682	The Death of Saul
☐ 224		PP 683-689	Ancient and Modern Sorcery
☐ 225	1 Sam 29:1-30:8	PP 690-693c	David at Ziklag
☐ 226	1 Sam 30:9-31; 2 Sam 1	PP 693d-696	David at Ziklag
☐ 227	1 Chr 1-2		
☐ 228	1 Chr 3-5		
☐ 229	1 Chr 6:1-7:19		
☐ 230	1 Chr 7:20-8:40; 9		
☐ 231	2 Sam 2:1-3:27	PP 697-699c	David Called to the Throne
☐ 232	2 Sam 3:28-5:3; 1 Chr 11:1-3; 12:23-40	PP 699d-702	David Called to the Throne
☐ 233	2 Sam 5:4-6:11; 1 Chr 11:4-9; 13-14; Ps 30	PP 703-706b	The Reign of David

✓ Day	Bible Reading	SOP Reading	SOP Chapter Title
☐ 234	2 Sam 6:12-19; 1 Chr 15:1-28; 16; Ps 24	PP 706c-708d	The Reign of David
☐ 235	2 Sam 6:20-7:29; 1 Chr 15:29; 17	PP 708e-713a	The Reign of David
☐ 236	2 Sam 8-9; 1 Chr 18; Ps 60	PP 713b, c	The Reign of David
☐ 237	2 Sam 10; 1 Chr 19	PP 713d-715c	The Reign of David
☐ 238	Ps 18; 20; 21; 33; 44	PP 715d-716	The Reign of David
☐ 239	Ps 9-10; 101; 2 Sam 11:1-25	PP 717-720b	David's Sin and Repentance
☐ 240	2 Sam 11:26-12:25	PP 720c-723d	David's Sin and Repentance
☐ 241	Ps 32; 51	PP 723e-726	David's Sin and Repentance
☐ 242	2 Sam 13:1-15:1	PP 727-729d	The Rebellion of Absalom
☐ 243	2 Sam 15:2-37	PP 729e-735	The Rebellion of Absalom
☐ 244	2 Sam 16	PP 736-739b	The Rebellion of Absalom
☐ 245	2 Sam 17; Ps 3	PP 739c-742d	The Rebellion of Absalom
☐ 246	2 Sam 18:1-19:8	PP 742e-745	The Rebellion of Absalom
☐ 247	Ps 4-5; 35; 61; 84		
☐ 248	2 Sam 23:8-39; 1 Chr 11:10-47		
☐ 249	2 Sam 19:9-20:26; 1 Chr 20	PP 746a	The Last Years of David
☐ 250	2 Sam 12:26-31; 21-22		

✓ Day	Bible Reading	SOP Reading	SOP Chapter Title
☐ 251	2 Sam 24; 1 Chr 21	PP 746b-749a	The Last Years of David
☐ 252	1 Ki 1	PP 749b-750a	The Last Years of David
☐ 253	1 Chr 23-25		
☐ 254	1 Chr 26-27		
☐ 255	1 Chr 22; 28:1-29:9	PP 750b-752a	The Last Years of David
☐ 256	1 Ki 2; 1 Chr 29:10-30	PP 752b-753	The Last Years of David
☐ 257	2 Sam 23:1-7; Ps 72; 89; 103	PP 754-755	The Last Years of David
☐ 258	Ps 6; 12; 14-17; 22; 25-26; 28		
☐ 259	Ps 29; 34; 36-40		
☐ 260	Ps 41; 43; 50; 53; 55; 58; 62; 64		

Section Two

Bible: King Solomon to the close of the Old Testament
Spirit of Prophecy: *Prophets and Kings*

✓ Day	Bible Reading	SOP Reading	SOP Chapter Title
☐ 1	Ps 65-66; 68-71; 77; 86		
☐ 2	Ps 108-110; 122; 124		
☐ 3	Ps 119		
☐ 4	Ps 131; 138-140; 143-150		
☐ 5	Ps 1-2; 45-49; 67; 73-74		
☐ 6	Ps 78-79; 81-82; 85; 87		
☐ 7	Ps 88; 91-98; 100		
☐ 8	Ps 102; 106; 111-115		
☐ 9	Ps 116-118; 123; 125; 128-130; 132; 134-136		
☐ 10		PK 15-22	Intro - The Vinyard of the Lord
☐ 11	Ps 72	PK 25-27a	Solomon
☐ 12	1 Ki 3:1-15; 2 Chr 1:1-12	PK 27b-31d	Solomon

✓	Day	Bible Reading	SOP Reading	SOP Chapter Title
☐	13	1 Ki 3:16-4:34; 2 Chr 1:13-17	PK 31e-34	Solomon
☐	14	1 Ki 5; 2 Chr 2; Ps 127	PK 35a, b	The Temple and Its Dedication
☐	15	1 Ki 6; 2 Chr 3-4	PK 35c-36	The Temple and Its Dedication
☐	16	1 Ki 7; 2 Chr 5:1	PK 37-38a	The Temple and Its Dedication
☐	17	1 Ki 8:1-11; 2 Chr 5:2-14	PK 38b-39a	The Temple and Its Dedication
☐	18	1 Ki 8:12-34; 2 Chr 6:1-25; Ps 99	PK 39b-40	The Temple and Its Dedication
☐	19	1 Ki 8:35-61; 2 Chr 6:26-7:3	PK 41-45a	The Temple and Its Dedication
☐	20	1 Ki 8:62-9:9; 2 Chr 7:4-22	PK 45b-50	The Temple and Its Dedication
☐	21	1 Ki 9:10-28; 11:1-4; 2 Chr 8	PK 51-56b	Pride of Prosperity
☐	22	1 Ki 11:5-8	PK 56c-60	Pride of Prosperity
☐	23		PK 61-65b	Results of Transgression
☐	24	1 Ki 10:1-13; 2 Chr 9:1-12	PK 65c-68a	Results of Transgression
☐	25	1 Ki 10:14-24; 2 Chr 9:13-23	PK 68b-71b	Results of Transgression
☐	26	1 Ki 10:25-29; 2 Chr 9:23-28	PK 71c-74	Results of Transgression

✓ Day	Bible Reading	SOP Reading	SOP Chapter Title
☐ 27	1 Ki 11:9-10; Eccl 1-2	PK 75-76	Solomon's Repentance
☐ 28	1 Ki 11:11-28	PK 77-78a	Solomon's Repentance
☐ 29	Eccl 3-5		
☐ 30	Eccl 6-7		
☐ 31	Eccl 8-10	PK 78b-79a	Solomon's Repentance
☐ 32	Eccl 11-12	PK 79b-86	Solomon's Repentance
☐ 33	Prov 1-4		
☐ 34	Prov 5-8		
☐ 35	Prov 9-12		
☐ 36	Prov 13-16		
☐ 37	Prov 17-20		
☐ 38	Prov 21-24		
☐ 39	Prov 25-28		
☐ 40	Prov 29-31		
☐ 41	Solomon 1-4		
☐ 42	Solomon 5-8		
☐ 43	1 Ki 11:29-12:15; 2 Chr 9:29-10:15	PK 87-90b	The Rending of the Kingdom
☐ 44	1 Ki 12:16-24; 2 Chr 10:16-11:17	PK 90c-93a	The Rending of the Kingdom
☐ 45	1 Ki 14:21-31; 2 Chr 11:18-13:1	PK 93b-98	The Rending of the Kingdom
☐ 46	1 Ki 12:25-13:6	PK 99-105b	Jeroboam

✓ Day	Bible Reading	SOP Reading	SOP Chapter Title
☐ 47	1 Ki 13:7-34	PK 105c-107b	Jeroboam
☐ 48	1 Ki 14:1-20; 2 Chr 13:2-22	PK 107c-108	Jeroboam
☐ 49	1 Ki 15:1-11, 25-31; 16:1-28; 2 Chr 14	PK 109-112a	National Apostasy
☐ 50	1 Ki 15:12-24, 32-34; 2 Chr 15-16	PK 112b-113	National Apostasy
☐ 51	1 Ki 16:29-34	PK 114-116	National Apostasy
☐ 52	1 Ki 17:1-4	PK 119-123a	Elijah the Tishbite
☐ 53	1 Ki 17:5-7	PK 123b-128	Elijah the Tishbite
☐ 54	1 Ki 17:8-24	PK 129-132	The Voice of Stern Rebuke
☐ 55	Ps 104	PK 133-137b	The Voice of Stern Rebuke
☐ 56	1 Ki 18:1-18	PK 137c-142	The Voice of Stern Rebuke
☐ 57	1 Ki 18:19-29	PK 143-150d	Carmel
☐ 58	1 Ki 18:30-40	PK 150e-154	Carmel
☐ 59	1 Ki 18:41-19:2	PK 155-159c	From Jezreel to Horeb
☐ 60	1 Ki 19:3-8	PK 159d-166	From Jezreel to Horeb
☐ 61	1 Ki 19:9-18	PK 167-170b	What Doest Thou Here?
☐ 62		PK 170c-176	What Doest Thou Here?
☐ 63		PK 177-183c	In the Spirit and Power of Elias
☐ 64		PK 183d-189	In the Spirit and Power of Elias
☐ 65	2 Chr 17	PK 190-192b	Jehoshaphat

✓ Day	Bible Reading	SOP Reading	SOP Chapter Title
☐ 66	1 Ki 22:1-17; 2 Chr 18:1-16	PK 192c-196a	Jehoshaphat
☐ 67	1 Ki 22:18-36; 2 Chr 18:17-19:11	PK 196b-198c	Jehoshaphat
☐ 68	2 Chr 20:1-19; Ps 83	PK 198d-201c	Jehoshaphat
☐ 69	1 Ki 22:41-50; 2 Chr 20:20-37	PK 201d-203	Jehoshaphat
☐ 70	1 Ki 20:1-21:4	PK 204-205c	The Fall of the House of Ahab
☐ 71	1 Ki 21:5-29; 22:37-40	PK 205d-207d	The Fall of the House of Ahab
☐ 72	1 Ki 22:51-53; 2 Ki 1	PK 207e-212b	The Fall of the House of Ahab
☐ 73	2 Ki 3; 8:16-24; 2 Chr 21	PK 212c-214a	The Fall of the House of Ahab
☐ 74	2 Ki 8:25-10:29; 2 Chr 22:1-9	PK 214b-215b	The Fall of the House of Ahab
☐ 75	2 Ki 10:30-11:21; 2 Chr 22:10-23:21	PK 215c-216	The Fall of the House of Ahab
☐ 76	1 Ki 19:19-21	PK 217-221a	The Call of Elisha
☐ 77		PK 221b-224c	The Call of Elisha
☐ 78	2 Ki 2:1-18	PK 224d-228	The Call of Elisha
☐ 79	2 Ki 2:19-22	PK 229-234	The Healing of the Waters
☐ 80	2 Ki 2:23-25; 4:1-37	PK 235-240a	A Prophet of Peace
☐ 81	2 Ki 4:38-44	PK 240b-243	A Prophet of Peace

✓	Day	Bible Reading	SOP Reading	SOP Chapter Title
☐	82	2 Ki 5:1-14	PK 244-249c	Naaman
☐	83	2 Ki 5:15-27	PK 249d-253	Naaman
☐	84	2 Ki 6:8-23; 8:7-15	PK 254-258a	Elisha's Closing Ministry
☐	85	2 Ki 6:24-7:20	PK 258b-260c	Elisha's Closing Ministry
☐	86	2 Ki 6:1-7; 8:1-6; 13	PK 260d-264	Elisha's Closing Ministry
☐	87	Jonah 1-2	PK 265-269b	Ninevah, That Great City
☐	88	Jonah 3-4	PK 269c-273a	Ninevah, That Great City
☐	89		PK 273b-278	Ninevah, That Great City
☐	90	Hosea 5; 7-10	PK 279-280b	The Assyrian Captivity
☐	91	Hosea 4; 6; 12; Amos 5	PK 280c-282c	The Assyrian Captivity
☐	92	Hosea 11; 13; 14	PK 282d-284	The Assyrian Captivity
☐	93	Amos 1-4	PK 285-286b	The Assyrian Captivity
☐	94	Amos 6-9	PK 286c-e	The Assyrian Captivity
☐	95	2 Ki 15:8-31	PK 287a, b	The Assyrian Captivity
☐	96	2 Ki 17; 2 Chr 30:1-12	PK 287c-292	The Assyrian Captivity
☐	97	2 Ki 12; 2 Chr 24		
☐	98	2 Ki 14; 2 Chr 25		
☐	99		PK 293-297	Destroyed for Lack of Knowledge
☐	100	Hosea 1-3	PK 298-300	Destroyed for Lack of Knowledge

✓	Day	Bible Reading	SOP Reading	SOP Chapter Title
☐	101	2 Ki 15:1-7, 32-38; 2 Chr 26-27	PK 303-305a	The Call of Isaiah
☐	102	Isa 1-4	PK 305b-306c	The Call of Isaiah
☐	103	Isa 5-6	PK 306d-310	The Call of Isaiah
☐	104	Isa 8; 10; 13		
☐	105	Isa 14-16		
☐	106	Isa 17-21		
☐	107	Isa 22-24		
☐	108	Isa 25-28		
☐	109	Isa 29-30		
☐	110	Isa 31-35		
☐	111	Isa 40	PK 311-316c	Behold Your God!
☐	112	Isa 12; 41; 44	PK 316d-321	Behold Your God!
☐	113	Isa 43; 46; 48		
☐	114	Isa 50-51; 55		
☐	115	Isa 57-59; 61		
☐	116	Isa 62-65		
☐	117	2 Ki 16:1-4; 2 Chr 28:1-4; Micah 1-3	PK 322-325b	Ahaz
☐	118	Micah 4-6	PK 325c-327c	Ahaz
☐	119	2 Ki 16:5-20; 2 Chr 28:5-27: Isa 7	PK 327d-330	Ahaz

✓	Day	Bible Reading	SOP Reading	SOP Chapter Title
☐	120	2 Ki 18:1-12; 2 Chr 29:1-19	PK 331-333a	Hezekiah
☐	121	2 Chr 29:20-36; Micah 7	PK 333b-335b	Hezekiah
☐	122	2 Chr 30:13-31:21	PK 335c-339	Hezekiah
☐	123	2 Ki 20:1-11; 2 Chr 32:24; Isa 38	PK 340-344a	The Ambassadors From Babylon
☐	124	2 Ki 20:12-19; 2 Chr 32:25-31; Isa 39	PK 344b-348	The Ambassadors From Babylon
☐	125	2 Ki 18:13-17; 2 Chr 32:1-8; Isa 36:1-2	PK 349-352c	Deliverance From Assyria
☐	126	2 Ki 18:18-19:1; 2 Chr 32:9-16; Isa 36:3-37:1	PK 352d-354b	Deliverance From Assyria
☐	127	2 Ki 19:2-13; 2 Chr 32; 17-20; Isa 37:2-13	PK 354c-355b	Deliverance From Assyria
☐	128	2 Ki 19:14-34; Ps 80; Isa 37:14-35	PK 355c-361b	Deliverance From Assyria
☐	129	2 Ki 19:35-37; 20:20-21; 2 Chr 32:21-23, 32-33; Ps 75-76; Isa 37:36-38; Ezek 31:1-9	PK 361c-363c	Deliverance From Assyria
☐	130	Ezek 31:10-18; Nahum 1-3	PK 363d-366	Deliverance From Assyria
☐	131		PK 367-371a	Hope for the Heathen

✓ Day	Bible Reading	SOP Reading	SOP Chapter Title
☐ 132	Isa 9; 52:1-6; 56	PK 371b-373b	Hope for the Heathen
☐ 133	Isa 49; 54; 66	PK 373c-374b	Hope for the Heathen
☐ 134	Isa 45; 52:7-15; 60	PK 374c-376a	Hope for the Heathen
☐ 135	Isa 11; 42	PK 376b-378	Hope for the Heathen
☐ 136	2 Ki 21; 2 Chr 33	PK 381-383	Mannasseh and Josiah
☐ 137	2 Ki 22:1-2; 2 Chr 34:1-2; Hab 1:1-2:4	PK 384-387b	Mannasseh and Josiah
☐ 138	Hab 2:5-3:19	PK 387c-388	Mannasseh and Josiah
☐ 139	Zeph 1-3	PK 389-391	Mannasseh and Josiah
☐ 140	2 Ki 22:3-11; 2 Chr 34:3-19	PK 392-398c	The Book of the Law
☐ 141	2 Ki 22:12-23:1; 2 Chr 34:20-29	PK 398d-400b	The Book of the Law
☐ 142	2 Ki 23:2-27; 2 Chr 34:30-35:19	PK 400c-405b	The Book of the Law
☐ 143	2 Ki 23:28-30; 2 Chr 35:20-27	PK 405c-406	The Book of the Law
☐ 144	Jer 1-2	PK 407-409c	Jeremiah
☐ 145	Jer 3	PK 409d-411a	Jeremiah
☐ 146	Jer 4; 6; 17	PK 411b-412b	Jeremiah
☐ 147	2 Ki 23:31-34; 2 Chr 36:1-4; Jer 7:1-24	PK 412c-414c	Jeremiah
☐ 148	Jer 5; 7:25-34; 15	PK 414d-415b	Jeremiah
☐ 149	Jer 26	PK 415c-419a	Jeremiah

✓ Day	Bible Reading	SOP Reading	SOP Chapter Title
☐ 150	Jer 8-10	PK 419b-420a	Jeremiah
☐ 151	Jer 11-13		
☐ 152	Jer 14; 16; 20	PK 420b-421	Jeremiah
☐ 153	2 Ki 23:35-37; 2 Chr 36:5; Jer 21; 24; 35	PK 422-426a	Approaching Doom
☐ 154	Jer 23	PK 426b-427b	Approaching Doom
☐ 155	Jer 22	PK 427c-430b	Approaching Doom
☐ 156	Jer 19; 25	PK 430c-432b	Approaching Doom
☐ 157	2 Ki 24:1-4; 2 Chr 36:6; Jer 36:1-26	PK 432c-436a	Approaching Doom
☐ 158	2 Ki 24:5-17; 2 Chr 36:7-10; Jer 36:27-32	PK 436b-439	Approaching Doom
☐ 159	2 Ki 24:18; Jer 29; 52:1	PK 440-442c	The Last King of Judah
☐ 160	Jer 27-28	PK 442d-446	The Last King of Judah
☐ 161	2 Ki 24:19-20; 2 Chr 36:11-14; Jer 52:2-3; Ezek 8	PK 447-449	The Last King of Judah
☐ 162	2 Chr 36:15-16; Ezek 12	PK 450-451	The Last King of Judah
☐ 163	Jer 18; 34		
☐ 164	2 Ki 25:1; Jer 37:1-16; Ezek 21	PK 452-454a	Carried Captive Into Babylon

✓ Day	Bible Reading	SOP Reading	SOP Chapter Title
☐ 165	Jer 37:17-21; Ezek 29-30	PK 454b-455c	Carried Captive Into Babylon
☐ 166	Jer 38	PK 455d-458c	Carried Captive Into Babylon
☐ 167	2 Ki 25:2-21; 2 Chr 36:17-21; Jer 39:1-10; 52:4-30	PK 458d-459a	Carried Captive Into Babylon
☐ 168	2 Ki 25:22-30; 2 Chr 36:22-23; Jer 39:11-18; 52:31-34	PK 459b-460b	Carried Captive Into Babylon
☐ 169	Jer 40-43		
☐ 170	Jer 44	PK 460c-461a	Carried Captive Into Babylon
☐ 171	Lam 1-2	PK 461b-463b	Carried Captive Into Babylon
☐ 172	Ps 137; Lam 3-5	PK 463c-e	Carried Captive Into Babylon
☐ 173	Jer 32	PK 464-472c	Light Through Darkness
☐ 174	Jer 30; 33	PK 472d-474d	Light Through Darkness
☐ 175	Jer 31	PK 474e-476	Light Through Darkness
☐ 176	Jer 45-49		
☐ 177	Ezek 1-3		
☐ 178	Ezek 4-7		
☐ 179	Ezek 9-11; 13		
☐ 180	Ezek 14-16		

✓ Day	Bible Reading	SOP Reading	SOP Chapter Title
☐ 181	Ezek 17-19		
☐ 182	Ezek 20; 22		
☐ 183	Ezek 23-24		
☐ 184	Ezek 25-27		
☐ 185	Ezek 28; 32		
☐ 186	Ezek 33-34; Obadiah		
☐ 187	Ezek 35-37		
☐ 188	Ezek 38-40		
☐ 189	Ezek 41-43		
☐ 190	Ezek 44-46		
☐ 191	Ezek 47-48		
☐ 192	Dan 1:1-8	PK 479-483b	In the Court of Babylon
☐ 193	Dan 1:9-20	PK 483c-485b	In the Court of Babylon
☐ 194	Dan 1:21	PK 485c-490	In the Court of Babylon
☐ 195	Dan 2:1-23	PK 491-494b	Nebuchadnezzar's Dream
☐ 196	Dan 2:24-47	PK 494c-499c	Nebuchadnezzar's Dream
☐ 197	Dan 2:48-49	PK 499d-502	Nebuchadnezzar's Dream
☐ 198	Dan 3:1-2	PK 503-506a	The Fiery Furnace
☐ 199	Dan 3:3-25	PK 506b-509b	The Fiery Furnace
☐ 200	Dan 3:26-30	PK 509c-513	The Fiery Furnace
☐ 201	Dan 4:1-18	PK 514-517a	True Greatness

✓ Day	Bible Reading	SOP Reading	SOP Chapter Title
☐ 202	Dan 4:19-37	PK 517b-521	True Greatness
☐ 203	Dan 5:1-9	PK 522-527b	The Unseen Watcher
☐ 204	Dan 5:10-29	PK 527c-530	The Unseen Watcher
☐ 205	Jer 51; Dan 5:30-31	PK 531-532b	The Unseen Watcher
☐ 206	Isa 47; Jer 50	PK 532c-534	The Unseen Watcher
☐ 207		PK 535-538	The Unseen Watcher
☐ 208	Dan 6:1-18	PK 539-544a	The Lions' Den
☐ 209	Dan 6:19-28	PK 544b-548	The Lions' Den
☐ 210	Dan 7	PK 551-554a	The Return of the Exiles
☐ 211	Dan 8	PK 554b	The Return of the Exiles
☐ 212	Dan 9:1-11:2	PK 554c-557b	The Return of the Exiles
☐ 213	Dan 11:3-12:13		
☐ 214	Ezra 1; Ps 126; Isa 44:28-45:13	PK 557c-559c	The Return of the Exiles
☐ 215	Ezra 2; Neh 7		
☐ 216	Ezra 3:1-11	PK 559d-563b	The Return of the Exiles
☐ 217	Ezra 3:12-13; Ps 105	PK 563c-566	The Return of the Exiles
☐ 218	Joel 1-3		
☐ 219	Ezra 4:1-3	PK 567-571a	The Prophets of God Helping Them
☐ 220	Ezra 4:4-24; Haggai 1	PK 571b-575c	The Prophets of God Helping Them

✓ Day	Bible Reading	SOP Reading	SOP Chapter Title
☐ 221	Ezra 5; Haggai 2	PK 575d-578	The Prophets of God Helping Them
☐ 222	Ezra 6:1-12; Zech 1-2	Pk 579a-581	The Prophets of God Helping Them
☐ 223	Zech 3	PK 582-587b	Joshua and the Angel
☐ 224		PK 587c-592	Joshua and the Angel
☐ 225	Ezra 6:13-22; Zech 4	PK 593-597	Not by Might, nor by Power
☐ 226	Zech 5-9		
☐ 227	Zech 10-14		
☐ 228	Esther 1-2	PK 598-600b	In the Days of Queen Esther
☐ 229	Esther 3-4	PK 600c-601	In the Days of Queen Esther
☐ 230	Esther 5-8	PK 602a	In the Days of Queen Esther
☐ 231	Esther 9-10	PK 602b-606	In the Days of Queen Esther
☐ 232	Ezra 7	PK 607-612a	Ezra, the Priest and Scribe
☐ 233	Ezra 8:1-31	PK 612b-617	Ezra, the Priest and Scribe
☐ 234	Ezra 8:32-9:15	PK 618-621	A Spiritual Revival
☐ 235	Ezra 10	PK 622	A Spiritual Revival
☐ 236		PK 623-627	A Spiritual Revival
☐ 237	Neh 1:1-2:9	PK 628-634	A Man of Opportunity
☐ 238	Neh 2:10-18	PK 635-638c	The Builders on the Wall
☐ 239	Neh 2:19-4:3	PK 638d-642a	The Builders on the Wall
☐ 240	Neh 4:4-23	PK 642b-645	The Builders on the Wall

✓ Day	Bible Reading	SOP Reading	SOP Chapter Title
☐ 241	Neh 5:1-11	PK 646-650b	A Rebuke Against Extortion
☐ 242	Neh 5:12-19	PK 650c-652	A Rebuke Against Extortion
☐ 243	Neh 6:1-14	PK 653-656	Heathen Plots
☐ 244	Neh 6:15-19	PK 657-660	Heathen Plots
☐ 245	Neh 8	PK 661-665b	Instructed in the Law of God
☐ 246	Neh 9	PK 665c-666b	Instructed in the Law of God
☐ 247	Neh 10	PK 666c-668	Instructed in the Law of God
☐ 248	Neh 11-12		
☐ 249	Neh 13:1-22	PK 669-673a	Reformation
☐ 250	Neh 13:23-31	PK 673b-678	Reformation
☐ 251		PK 681-688a	The Coming of a Deliverer
☐ 252	Isa 53	PK 688b-692b	The Coming of a Deliverer
☐ 253	Isa 42	PK 692c-697	The Coming of a Deliverer
☐ 254	Dan 9:20-27	PK 698-702	The Coming of a Deliverer
☐ 255	Mal 1-2	PK 703-706b	The House of Israel
☐ 256	Mal 3:7-18	PK 706c-710c	The House of Israel
☐ 257	Mal 3:1-6	PK 710d-715	The House of Israel
☐ 258	Mal 4	PK 716-721	The House of Israel
☐ 259		PK 722-727c	Visions of Future Glory
☐ 260		PK 727d-733	Visions of Future Glory

Section Three

Bible: The birth of Jesus to His return to Heaven
Spirit of Prophecy: *Steps to Christ, The Desire of Ages,*
Thoughts from the Mount of Blessing, and *Christ's Object Lessons*

✓ Day	Bible Reading	SOP Reading	SOP Chapter Title
☐ 1		SC 9-15	God's Love for Man
☐ 2		SC 17-22	The Sinner's Need of Christ
☐ 3		SC 23-30a	Repentance
☐ 4		SC 30b-36	Repentance
☐ 5		SC 37-41	Confession
☐ 6		SC 43-48	Consecration
☐ 7		SC 49-55	Faith and Acceptance
☐ 8		SC 57-65	The Test of Discipleship
☐ 9		SC 67-75	Growing up Into Christ
☐ 10		SC 77-83	The Work and the Life
☐ 11		SC 85-91	A Knowledge of God
☐ 12		SC 93-99b	The Privilege of Prayer
☐ 13		SC 99c-104	The Privilege of Prayer
☐ 14		SC 105-113	What to Do With Doubt
☐ 15		SC 115-121b	Rejoicing in the Lord
☐ 16		SC 121c-126	Rejoicing in the Lord
☐ 17	Matt 1:18-23; Luke 1:26-38	DA 19-22c	God With Us

✓ Day	Bible Reading	SOP Reading	SOP Chapter Title
☐ 18	Luke 1:39-56	DA 22d-26	God With Us
☐ 19	Matt 1:1-17; Luke 3:23-38	DA 27-30	The Chosen People
☐ 20		DA 31-38	The Fullness of the Time
☐ 21	Matt 1:24-25; Luke 2:1-20	DA 43-49	Unto You a Saviour
☐ 22	Luke 2:21-24	DA 50-55a	The Dedication
☐ 23	Luke 2:25-38	DA 55b-58	The Dedication
☐ 24	Matt 2:1-8	DA 59-63a	We Have Seen His Star
☐ 25	Matt 2:9-23	DA 63b-67	We Have Seen His Star
☐ 26	Luke 2:39-40	DA 68-74	As a Child
☐ 27	Luke 2:41-44	DA 75-80	The Passover Visit
☐ 28	Luke 2:45-52	DA 81-83	The Passover Visit
☐ 29		DA 84-88b	Days of Conflict
☐ 30		DA 88c-92	Days of Conflict
☐ 31	Luke 1:1-25, 57-79	DA 97-100b	The Voice in the Wilderness
☐ 32	Matt 3:1-6; Mark 1:1-6; Luke 1:80; 3:1-6	DA 100c-104	The Voice in the Wilderness
☐ 33	Matt 3:7-12; Mark 1:7-8; Luke 3:7-18	DA 105-108	The Voice in the Wilderness
☐ 34	Matt 3:13-17; Mark 1:9-11; Luke 3:21-22	DA 109-113	The Baptism

✓ Day	Bible Reading	SOP Reading	SOP Chapter Title
☐ 35	Matt 4:1-3; Mark 1:12-13; Luke 4:1-3	DA 114-120a	The Temptation
☐ 36	Matt 4:4; Luke 4:4	DA 120b-123	The Temptation
☐ 37	Matt 4:5-11; Luke 4:5-13	DA 124-131	The Victory
☐ 38	John 1:1-34	DA 132-138d	We Have Found the Messias
☐ 39	John 1:35-51	DA 138e-143	We Have Found the Messias
☐ 40	John 2:1-10	DA 144-148c	At the Marriage Feast
☐ 41	John 2:11	DA 148d-153	At the Marriage Feast
☐ 42	John 2:12-17	DA 154-161a	In His Temple
☐ 43	John 2:18-25	DA 161b-166	In His Temple
☐ 44	John 3:1-8	DA 167-173b	Nicodemus
☐ 45	John 3:9-21	DA 173c-177	Nicodemus
☐ 46	John 3:22-4:3	DA 178-182	He Must Increase
☐ 47	John 4:4-26	DA 183-190d	At Jacob's Well
☐ 48	John 4:27-42	DA 190e-195	At Jacob's Well
☐ 49	John 4:43-54	DA 196-200	Except Ye See Signs and Wonders
☐ 50	John 5:1-16	DA 201-204d	Bethesda and the Sanhedrin
☐ 51	John 5:17-21	DA 204e-210a	Bethesda and the Sanhedrin
☐ 52	John 5:22-47	DA 201b-213	Bethesda and the Sanhedrin

✓ Day	Bible Reading	SOP Reading	SOP Chapter Title
☐ 53	Matt 11:1-6; 14:1-5; Mark 6:17-19; Luke 3:19-20; 7:18-23	DA 214-218b	Imprisonment and Death of John
☐ 54	Matt 11:7-24; Luke 7:24-35	DA 218c-220e	Imprisonment and Death of John
☐ 55	Matt 14:6-12; Mark 6:20-29	DA 220f-225	Imprisonment and Death of John
☐ 56	Mark 1:14-15; Luke 4:14-15	DA 231-235	The Kingdom of God Is at Hand
☐ 57	Matt 13:53-56; Mark 6:1-3; Luke 4:16-27	DA 236-240a	Is Not This the Carpenter's Son?
☐ 58	Matt 13:57-58; Mark 6:4-6; Luke 4:28-30	DA 240b-243	Is Not This the Carpenter's Son?
☐ 59	Matt 4:12-25; Mark 1:16-20; Luke 5:1-11	DA 244-251	The Call by the Sea
☐ 60	Mark 1:21-28; Luke 4:31-37	DA 252-256	At Capernaum
☐ 61	Matt 8:14-17; Mark 1:29-39; Luke 4:38-44	DA 257-261	At Capernaum
☐ 62	Matt 8:1-4; 9:32-34; Mark 1:40-45; Luke 5:12-16	DA 262-266	Thou Canst Make Me Clean
☐ 63	Matt 9:1-8; Mark 2:1-12; Luke 5:17-26	DA 267-271	Thou Canst Make Me Clean

✓ Day	Bible Reading	SOP Reading	SOP Chapter Title
☐ 64	Matt 9:9-13; Mark 2:13-17; Luke 5:27-32	DA 272-275e	Levi-Matthew
☐ 65	Matt 9:14-17; Mark 2:18-22; Luke 5:33-39	DA 275f-280	Levi-Matthew
☐ 66	Matt 12:1-8; Mark 2:23-28; Luke 6:1-5	DA 281-286b	The Sabbath
☐ 67	Matt 12:9-21; Mark 3:1-12; Luke 6:6-11	DA 286c-289	The Sabbath
☐ 68	Mark 3:13-18; Luke 6:12-15	DA 290-293b	He Ordained Twelve
☐ 69	Matt 8:18-22; Mark 3:19; Luke 6:16; 9:57-62	DA 293c-297	He Ordained Twelve
☐ 70	Matt 5:1-2; Luke 6:17-19	DA 298-299c; MB vii, viii, 1-5	The Sermon on the Mount/ On the Mountainside
☐ 71	Matt 5:3; Luke 6:20	DA 299d-300b; MB 6-9b	The Sermon on the Mount/ The Beatitudes
☐ 72	Matt 5:4; Luke 6:21b	DA 300c-301c; MB 9c-13b	The Sermon on the Mount/ The Beatitudes
☐ 73	Matt 5:5-6; Luke 6:21a	DA 301d-302b; MB 13c-21c	The Sermon on the Mount/ The Beatitudes
☐ 74	Matt 5:7-8	DA 302c, d; MB 21d-27b	The Sermon on the Mount/ The Beatitudes
☐ 75	Matt 5: 9-10	DA 302e-305b; MB 27c-31a	The Sermon on the Mount/ The Beatitudes

✓ Day	Bible Reading	SOP Reading	SOP Chapter Title
☐ 76	Matt 5:11-13; Luke 6:22-26	DA 305c-306e; MB 31b-38b	The Sermon on the Mount/ The Beatitudes
☐ 77	Matt 5:14-16	DA 306f-307b; MB 38c-44	The Sermon on the Mount/ The Beatitudes
☐ 78	Matt 5:17-18	DA 307c-310a; MB 45-51b	The Sermon on the Mount/ The Spirituality of the Law
☐ 79	Matt 5:19-24	DA 310b-311b; MB 51c-59c	The Sermon on the Mount/ The Spirituality of the Law
☐ 80	Matt 5:25-32; 19:1-12; Mark 10:1-12	MB 59d-65	The Spirituality of the Law
☐ 81	Matt 5:33-42; Luke 6:29-30	MB 66-73a	The Spirituality of the Law
☐ 82	Matt 5:43-48; Luke 6:27-28, 31-36	DA 311c-312a; MB 73b-78	The Sermon on the Mount/ The Spirituality of the Law
☐ 83	Matt 6:1-8	DA 312b,c; MB 79-87a	The Sermon on the Mount/ The True Motive in Service
☐ 84	Matt 6:16-24; Luke 12:32-34	DA 312d-313b; MB 87b-95b	The Sermon on the Mount/ The True Motive in Service
☐ 85	Matt 6:25-34; Luke 12:22-31	DA 313c-e; MB 95c-101	The Sermon on the Mount/ The True Motive in Service
☐ 86	Matt 6:9-10; Luke 11:1-2	MB 102-110a	The Lord's Prayer
☐ 87	Matt 6:11-12; Luke 11:3-4	MB 110b-116b	The Lord's Prayer
☐ 88	Matt 6:13-15	MB 116c-122	The Lord's Prayer
☐ 89	Matt 7:1-5; Luke 6:37, 41-42	DA 314a; MB 123-129a	The Sermon on the Mount/ Not Judging, but Doing

✓ Day	Bible Reading	SOP Reading	SOP Chapter Title
☐ 90	Matt 7:6-11; Luke 6:38-40	MB 129b-134a	Not Judging, but Doing
☐ 91	Matt 7:12-14	MB 134b-141a	Not Judging, but Doing
☐ 92	Matt 7:15-23; Luke 6:43-45; 13:24	DA 314b; MB 141b-147a	The Sermon on the Mount/ Not Judging, but Doing
☐ 93	Matt 7:24-29; Luke 6:46-49	DA 314c,d; MB 147b-152	The Sermon on the Mount/ Not Judging, but Doing
☐ 94	Matt 8:5-13; Luke 7:1-17	DA 315-320	The Centurion
☐ 95		COL 17-27	Teaching in Parables
☐ 96	Matt 13:1-17; Mark 4:1-13; Luke 8:1-11	COL 33-37a	The Sower Went Forth to Sow
☐ 97	Mark 4:14	COL 37b-43b	The Sower Went Forth to Sow
☐ 98	Matt 13:18-21; Mark 4:15-17; Luke 8:12-13	COL 43c-50b	The Sower Went Forth to Sow
☐ 99	Matt 13:22; Mark 4:18-19; Luke 8:14	COL 50c-56a	The Sower Went Forth to Sow
☐ 100	Matt 13:23; Mark 4:20-25; Luke 8:15-18	COL 56b-61	The Sower Went Forth to Sow
☐ 101	Mark 4:26-29	COL 62-69	First the Blade, then the Ear
☐ 102	Matt 13:24-30, 34-43	COL 70-75	Tares

✓ Day	Bible Reading	SOP Reading	SOP Chapter Title
☐ 103	Matt 13:31-32; Mark 4:30-34; Luke 13:18-19	COL 76-79	Like a Grain of Mustard Seed
☐ 104		COL 80-89	Other Lessons from Seed-Sowing
☐ 105	Matt 13:33; Luke 13:20-21	COL 95-102	Like unto Leaven
☐ 106	Matt 13:44	COL 103-108a	Hidden Treasure
☐ 107		COL 108b-114	Hidden Treasure
☐ 108	Matt 13:45-50	COL 115-123	The Pearl/The Net
☐ 109	Matt 13:51-52	COL 124-129c	Things New and Old
☐ 110		COL 129d-134	Things New and Old
☐ 111	Matt 12:22-35; Mark 3:20-27; Luke 11:14-23	DA 321-323a	Who Are My Brethren?
☐ 112	Matt 12:26-50; Mark 3:28-35; Luke 8:19-21; 11:24-36	DA 323b-327	Who Are My Brethren?
☐ 113	Matt 11:25-30	DA 328-332	The Invitation
☐ 114	Matt 8:23-27; Mark 4:35-41; Luke 8:22-25	DA 333-337a	Peace, Be Still
☐ 115	Matt 8:28-34; Mark 5:1-20; Luke 8:26-39	DA 337b-341	Peace, Be Still

✓ Day	Bible Reading	SOP Reading	SOP Chapter Title
☐ 116	Matt 9:18-19, 23-31; Mark 5:21-24, 35-43; Luke 8:40-42, 48-56	DA 342-343d	The Touch of Faith
☐ 117	Matt 9:20-22; Mark 5:25-34; Luke 8:43-47; 17:11-19	DA 343e-348	The Touch of Faith
☐ 118	Matt 10:1-16; Mark 6:7-13; Luke 9:1-6	DA 349-353	The First Evangelists
☐ 119	Matt 10:17-42	DA 354-358	The First Evangelists
☐ 120	Matt 9:35-38; 14:1-2; Mark 6:14-16, 30-32; Luke 9:7-10	DA 359-363	Come Rest Awhile
☐ 121	Matt 14:13-21; Mark 6:33-44; Luke 9:11-17; John 6:1-13	DA 364-366a	Give Ye Them to Eat
☐ 122		DA 366b-371	Give Ye Them to Eat
☐ 123	Matt 14:22-23; Mark 6:45-46; John 6:14-17	DA 377-380a	A Night on the Lake
☐ 124	Matt 14:24-33; Mark 6:47-53; John 6:18-21	DA 380b-382	A Night on the Lake

✓ Day	Bible Reading	SOP Reading	SOP Chapter Title
☐ 125	Matt 14:34-36; Mark 6:54-56; John 6:22-42	DA 383-387d	The Crisis in Galilee
☐ 126	John 6:43-63	DA 387e-391b	The Crisis in Galilee
☐ 127	John 6:64-71	DA 391c-394	The Crisis in Galilee
☐ 128	Matt 15:1-7; Mark 7:1-8; Luke 11:37-38	DA 395-397d	Tradition
☐ 129	Matt 15:8-20; Mark 7:9-23; Luke 11:39-54	DA 397e-398	Tradition
☐ 130	Matt 15:21-28; Mark 7:24-30	DA 399-403	Barriers Broken Down
☐ 131	Matt 15:29-16:4; Mark 7:31-8:13	DA 404-407c	The True Sign
☐ 132	Matt 16:5-12; Mark 8:14-26	DA 407d-409	The True Sign
☐ 133	Matt 16:13-20; Mark 8:27-30; Luke 9:18-21	DA 410-414	The Foreshadowing of the Cross
☐ 134	Matt 16:21-28; Mark 8:31-9:1; Luke 9:22-27	DA 415-418	The Foreshadowing of the Cross
☐ 135	Matt 17:1-13; Mark 9:2-13; Luke 9:28-36	DA 419-425	He Was Transfigured
☐ 136	Matt 17:14-17; Mark 9:14-20; Luke 9:37-41	DA 426-428d	Ministry

✓ Day	Bible Reading	SOP Reading	SOP Chapter Title
☐ 137	Matt 17:18-21; Mark 9:21-29; Luke 9:42-45	DA 428e-431	Ministry
☐ 138	Matt 17:22-27; Mark 9:30-32	DA 432-434e	Who Is the Greatest?
☐ 139	Matt 18:1-5; Mark 9:33-40; Luke 9:46-50	DA 434f-438b	Who Is the Greatest?
☐ 140	Matt 18:6-20; Mark 9:41-50	DA 438c-442	Who Is the Greatest?
☐ 141	Matt 18:21-35	COL 243-251	The Measure of Forgiveness
☐ 142	John 7:1-5	DA 447-450	At the Feast of Tabernacles
☐ 143	John 7:6-15, 37-39	DA 451-454	At the Feast of Tabernacles
☐ 144	John 7:16-36	DA 455-458	Among Snares
☐ 145	John 7:40-8:11	DA 459-462	Among Snares
☐ 146	John 8:12-29	DA 463-465	The Light of Life
☐ 147	John 8:30-59; 10:31-42	DA 466-470c	The Light of Life
☐ 148	John 9:1-25	DA 470d-473d	The Light of Life
☐ 149	John 9:26-41	DA 473e-475	The Light of Life
☐ 150	John 10:1-30	DA 476-478d	The Divine Shepherd
☐ 151		DA 478e-484	The Divine Shepherd
☐ 152	Luke 9:51-56; 10:1-16	DA 485-490a	The Last Journey From Galilee
☐ 153	Luke 10:17-24	DA 490b-496	The Last Journey From Galilee

✓ Day	Bible Reading	SOP Reading	SOP Chapter Title
☐ 154	Luke 10:25-32	COL 376-379c; DA 497-503a	The Good Samaritan/ Who Is My Neighbor?
☐ 155	Luke 10:33-37	COL 379d-382c; DA 503b-505	The Good Samaritan/ Who Is My Neighbor?
☐ 156		COL 382d-389	Who Is My Neighbor?
☐ 157	Luke 11:5-13	COL 139-144b	Asking to Give
☐ 158		COL 144c-149	Asking to Give
☐ 159	Luke 12:1-21	COL 252-259	Gain That Is Loss
☐ 160	Luke 12:49-13:9	COL 212-218	Spare It This Year Also
☐ 161	Luke 13:10-17, 22-35; Luke 14:1-20	COL 219-225b	Go into the Highways and Hedges
☐ 162	Luke 14:21-24	COL 225c-231	Go into the Highways and Hedges
☐ 163		COL 232-237	Go into the Highways and Hedges
☐ 164	Luke 14:25-35; Luke 15:1-7	COL 185-192c	This Man Receiveth Sinners
☐ 165	Luke 15:8-10	COL 192d-197	This Man Receiveth Sinners
☐ 166	Luke 15:11-20	COL 198-203b	Lost and Is Found
☐ 167	Luke 15:21-32	COL 203c-211	Lost and Is Found
☐ 168	Luke 16:1-9	COL 366-371a	Friends by the Mammon of Unrighteousness
☐ 169	Luke 16:10-18	COL 371b-375	Friends by the Mammon of Unrighteousness

√ Day	Bible Reading	SOP Reading	SOP Chapter Title
☐ 170	Luke 16:19-31	COL 260-265d	A Great Gulf Fixed
☐ 171		COL 265e-271	A Great Gulf Fixed
☐ 172	Luke 17:1-10; 17:20-22	DA 506-510	Not With Outward Show
☐ 173	Luke 18:1-8	COL 164-171c	Shall Not God Avenge His Own?
☐ 174		COL 171d-180	Shall Not God Avenge His Own?
☐ 175	Luke 18:9-14	COL 150-156	Two Worshipers
☐ 176		COL 157-163	Two Worshipers
☐ 177	Matt 19:13-15; Mark 10:13-16; Luke 18:15-17	DA 511-517	Blessing the Children
☐ 178	Matt 19:16-22; Mark 10:17-22: Luke 18:18-23	DA 518-523; COL 390-393a	One Thing Thou Lackest/ The Reward of Grace
☐ 179	Matt 19:23-30; Mark 10:23-31; Luke 18:24-30	COL 393b-396a	The Reward of Grace
☐ 180	Matt 20:1-16	COL 396b-404	The Reward of Grace
☐ 181	Luke 10:38-42; John 11:1-16	DA 524-529a	Lazarus, Come Forth
☐ 182	John 11:17-37	DA 529b-534a	Lazarus, Come Forth
☐ 183	John 11:38-44	DA 534b-536	Lazarus, Come Forth
☐ 184	John 11:45-54	DA 537-542	Priestly Plottings

✓ Day	Bible Reading	SOP Reading	SOP Chapter Title
☐ 185	Matt 20:17-28; Mark 10:32-45; Luke 18:31-34	DA 547-551	The Law of the New Kingdom
☐ 186	Matt 20:29-34; Mark 10:46-52; Luke 18:35-43; 19:1-10	DA 552-556	Zacchaeus
☐ 187	Matt 25:14-16; Luke 19: 11-14	COL 325-333a	Talents
☐ 188		COL 333b-339a	Talents
☐ 189		COL 339b-346a	Talents
☐ 190		COL 346b-353a	Talents
☐ 191	Matt 25:17-18	COL 353b-360d	Talents
☐ 192	Matt 25:19-30; Luke 19:15-28	COL 360e-365	Talents
☐ 193	Matt 26:6-9; Mark 14:3-5; Luke 7:36-38; John 11:55-12:6	DA 557-560a	The Feast at Simon's House
☐ 194	Matt 26:10-13; Mark 14:6-11; John 12:7-11	DA 560b-566a	The Feast at Simon's House
☐ 195	Luke 7:39-50	DA 566b-568	The Feast at Simon's House
☐ 196	Matt 21:1-9; Mark 11:1-10; Luke 19:29-40; John 12:12-19	DA 569-575a	Thy King Cometh
☐ 197	Matt 21:10-11; Luke 19:41-44	DA 575b-579	Thy King Cometh

✓ Day	Bible Reading	SOP Reading	SOP Chapter Title
☐ 198	Matt 21:17-20; Mark 11:11-14, 20-21	DA 580-582c	A Doomed People
☐ 199	Matt 21:21-22; Mark 11:22-26	DA 582d-588	A Doomed People
☐ 200	Matt 21:12-16; Mark 11:15-19; Luke 19:45-48	DA 589-593b	The Temple Cleansed Again
☐ 201	Matt 21:23-31; Mark 11:27-33; Luke 20:1-8	COL 272-275b; DA 593c-594d	The Temple Cleansed Again/Saying and Doing
☐ 202	Matt 21:32	COL 275c-278c; DA 594e-596a	The Temple Cleansed Again/Saying and Doing
☐ 203		COL 278d-283	Saying and Doing
☐ 204	Matt 21:33; Mark 12:1; Luke 20:9	COL 284-289b	The Lord's Vineyard
☐ 205	Matt 21:34-36; Mark 12:2-5; Luke 20:10-12	COL 289c-293b	The Lord's Vineyard
☐ 206	Matt 21:37-41; Mark 12:6-9; Luke 20:13-16	COL 293c-295b; DA 596b-597a	The Lord's Vineyard
☐ 207	Matt 21:42-46; Mark 12:10-12; Luke 20:17-19	COL 295c-296b; DA 597b-600	The Lord's Vineyard
☐ 208		COL 296c-301c	The Lord's Vineyard
☐ 209		COL 301d-306	The Lord's Vineyard
☐ 210	Matt 22:1-14	COL 307-312b	Without a Wedding Garment

✓ Day	Bible Reading	SOP Reading	SOP Chapter Title
☐ 211		COL 312c-319	Without a Wedding Garment
☐ 212	Matt 22:15-28; Mark 12:13-23; Luke 20:20-33	DA 601-605a	Controversy
☐ 213	Matt 22:29-46; Mark 12:24-37; Luke 20:34-44	DA 605b-609	Controversy
☐ 214	Matt 23:1-15; Mark 12:38-40; Luke 20:45-47	DA 610-614c	Woes on the Pharisees
☐ 215	Matt 23:16-26; Mark 12:41-44; Luke 21:1-4	DA 614d-617c	Woes on the Pharisees
☐ 216	Matt 23:27-39; Luke 13:34-35	DA 617d-620	Woes on the Pharisees
☐ 217	John 12:20-50	DA 621-626	In the Outer Court
☐ 218	Matt 24:1-20; Mark 13:1-18; Luke 17:31-32; 21:5-24	DA 627-630d	On the Mount of Olives
☐ 219	Matt 24:21-39; Mark 13:19-32; Luke 17:23-30; 21:25-33	DA 630e-634b	On the Mount of Olives
☐ 220	Matt 24:40-51; Mark 13:33-37; Luke 12:35-48; 17:33-37; 21:34-38	DA 634c-636	On the Mount of Olives
☐ 221	Matt 25:1-13	COL 405-414c	To Meet the Bridegroom
☐ 222		COL 414d-421	To Meet the Bridegroom

✓ Day	Bible Reading	SOP Reading	SOP Chapter Title
☐ 223	Matt 25:31-46	DA 637-641	The Least of These My Brethren
☐ 224	Matt 26:1-5, 14-19; Mark 14:1-2, 10-16; Luke 22:1-13, 24; John 13:1-5	DA 642-645b	A Servant of Servants
☐ 225	John 13:6-17	DA 645c-651	A Servant of Servants
☐ 226	Matt 26:20-29; Mark 14:17-25; Luke 22:14-23; John 13:18-30	DA 652-655a	In Remembrance of Me
☐ 227	Luke 22:24-30	DA 655b-661	In Remembrance of Me
☐ 228	John 13:31-14:14	DA 662-668a	Let Not Your Heart Be Troubled
☐ 229	John 14:15-31	DA 668b-672	Let Not Your Heart Be Troubled
☐ 230	Matt 26:30-35; Mark 14:26-31; Luke 22:31-38; John 13:36-38; 15:1-11	DA 673-677b	Let Not Your Heart Be Troubled
☐ 231	John 15:12-17:26	DA 677c-680	Let Not Your Heart Be Troubled
☐ 232	Matt 26:36-41; Mark 14:32-38; Luke 22:39-46	DA 685-689c	Gethsemane
☐ 233	Matt 26:42-46; Mark 14:39-42	DA 689d-694e	Gethsemane

✓ Day	Bible Reading	SOP Reading	SOP Chapter Title
☐ 234	Matt 26:47-56; Mark 14:43-52; Luke 22:47-53; John 18:1-12	DA 694f-697	Gethsemane
☐ 235	Matt 26:57-59; Mark 14:53-56; John 18:13-14, 19-23	DA 698-705c	Before Annas and the Court of Caiaphas
☐ 236	Matt 26:60-68; Mark 14:57-65	DA 705d-710a	Before Annas and the Court of Caiaphas
☐ 237	Matt 26:69-27:1; Mark 14:66-15:1; Luke 22:54-71; John 18:15-18, 24-27	DA 710b-715	Before Annas and the Court of Caiaphas
☐ 238	Matt 27:3-10	DA 716-722	Judas
☐ 239	Matt 27:2,11-14; Mark 15:2-5; Luke 23:1-4; John 18:28-38	DA 723-727e	In Pilate's Judgment Hall
☐ 240	Luke 23:5-12	DA 727f-731e	In Pilate's Judgment Hall
☐ 241	Matt 27:15-23, 27-31; Mark 15:6-13, 16-20; Luke 23:13-22; John 18:39-19:5	DA 731f-736a	In Pilate's Judgment Hall
☐ 242	Matt 27:24-26; Mark 15:14-15; Luke 23:23-25; John 19:6-16	DA 736b-740	In Pilate's Judgment Hall

✓ Day	Bible Reading	SOP Reading	SOP Chapter Title
☐ 243	Matt 27:32-33; Mark 15:21-22; Luke 23:26-31; John 19:17	DA 741-744a	Calvary
☐ 244	Matt 27:34-44; Mark 15:23-32; Luke 23:32-38; John 19:18-24	DA 744b-749c	Calvary
☐ 245	Matt 27:45; Mark 15:33; Luke 23:39-44; John 19:25-27	DA 749d-754c	Calvary
☐ 246	Matt 27:46-53; Mark 15:34-38; Luke 23:45-46; John 19:28-30	DA 754d-757	Calvary
☐ 247		DA 758-764	It Is Finished
☐ 248	Matt 27:54-61; Mark 15:39-47; Luke 23:47-56; John 19:31-42	DA 769-774b	In Joseph's Tomb
☐ 249	Matt 20:17-19; 27:62-66	DA 774c-778	In Joseph's Tomb
☐ 250	Matt 28:2-4, 11-15	DA 779-787	The Lord Is Risen
☐ 251	Matt 28:1, 5-8; Mark 16:1-11; Luke 24:1-12; John 20: 1-18	DA 788-790c	Why Weepest Thou?
☐ 252	Matt 28:9-10	DA 790d-794	Why Weepest Thou?
☐ 253	Mark 16:12-13; Luke 24:13-33	DA 795-801	The Walk to Emmaus

√ Day	Bible Reading	SOP Reading	SOP Chapter Title
☐ 254	Mark 16:14; Luke 24:34-48; John 20:19-21	DA 802-805b	Peace Be Unto You
☐ 255	Luke 24:49; John 20:22-31	DA 805c-808	Peace Be Unto You
☐ 256	John 21:1-14	DA 809-811a	By the Sea Once More
☐ 257	John 21:15-25	DA 811b-817	By the Sea Once More
☐ 258	Matt 28:16-20; Mark 16:15-18	DA 818-822c	Go Teach All Nations
☐ 259		DA 822d-828	Go Teach All Nations
☐ 260	Mark 16:19-20; Luke 24:50-53; Acts 1:1-12	DA 829-835	To My Father, and Your Father

Section Four

Bible: The early Christian church to the earth made new
Spirit of Prophecy: *The Acts of the Apostles*
and *The Great Controversy*

✓ Day	Bible Reading	SOP Reading	SOP Chapter Title
☐ 1		AA 9-16	God's Purpose for His Church
☐ 2		AA 17-24	The Training of the Twelve
☐ 3	Matt 28:19-20; Mark 16:15-18; Acts 1:1-12	AA 25-34	The Great Commission
☐ 4	Acts 1:13-26		
☐ 5	Acts 2:1-13	AA 35-40	Pentecost
☐ 6	Acts 2:14-47	AA 41-46	Pentecost
☐ 7		AA 47-56	The Gift of the Spirit
☐ 8	Acts 3:1-4:4	AA 57-62b	At the Temple Gate
☐ 9	Acts 4:5-31	AA 62c-69	At the Temple Gate
☐ 10	Acts 4:32-5:11	AA 70-76	A Warning Against Hypocrisy
☐ 11	Acts 5:12-32	AA 77-82b	Before the Sanhedrin
☐ 12	Acts 5:33-42	AA 82c-86	Before the Sanhedrin
☐ 13	Acts 6:1-7	AA 87-96	The Seven Deacons
☐ 14	Acts 6:8-7:50	AA 97-100a	The First Christian Martyr
☐ 15	Acts 7:51-60	AA 100b-102	The First Christian Martyr

✓ Day	Bible Reading	SOP Reading	SOP Chapter Title
☐ 16	Acts 8:1-25	AA 103-107b	The Gospel in Samaria
☐ 17	Acts 8:26-40	AA 107c-111	The Gospel in Samaria
☐ 18	Acts 9:1-7	AA 112-117c	From Persecutor to Disciple
☐ 19	Acts 9:8-18	AA 117d-122	From Persecutor to Disciple
☐ 20	Acts 9:19-31; 22:11-21	AA 123-130	Days of Preparation
☐ 21	Acts 9:32-10:16	AA 131-136d	A Seeker for Truth
☐ 22	Acts 10:17-11:18	AA 136e-142	A Seeker for Truth
☐ 23	Acts 12:1-11	AA 143-148b	Delivered From Prison
☐ 24	Acts 12:12-24	AA 148c-154	Delivered From Prison
☐ 25	Acts 11:19-30	AA 155-160a	The Gospel Message in Antioch
☐ 26	Acts 12:25-13:3	AA 160b-165	The Gospel Message in Antioch
☐ 27	Acts 13:4-13	AA 166-170c	Heralds of the Gospel
☐ 28	Acts 13:14-52	AA 170d-176	Heralds of the Gospel
☐ 29	Acts 14:1-18	AA 177-183b	Preaching Among the Heathen
☐ 30	Acts 14:19-26	AA 183c-187	Preaching Among the Heathen
☐ 31	Acts 14:27-15:12	AA 188-194b	Jew and Gentile
☐ 32	Acts 15:13-35; Gal 2:11-21	AA 194c-200	Jew and Gentile
☐ 33	Acts 15:36-16:3	AA 201-205c	Exalting the Cross

✓ Day	Bible Reading	SOP Reading	SOP Chapter Title
☐ 34	Acts 16:4-6	AA 205d-210	Exalting the Cross
☐ 35	Acts 16:7-26	AA 211-215b	In the Regions Beyond
☐ 36	Acts 16:27-40	AA 215c-220	In the Regions Beyond
☐ 37	Acts 17:1-2	AA 221-225a	Thessalonica
☐ 38	Acts 17:3-10	AA 225b-230	Thessalonica
☐ 39	Acts 17:11-21	AA 231-236	Berea and Athens
☐ 40	Acts 17:22-34	AA 237-242	Berea and Athens
☐ 41	Acts 18:1-7	AA 243-249a	Corinth
☐ 42	Acts 18:8-18	AA 249b-254	Corinth
☐ 43	1 Thess 1-2	AA 255-257c	The Thessalonian Letters
☐ 44	1 Thess 4:13-18; 5:1-11	AA 257d-261a	The Thessalonian Letters
☐ 45	1 Thess 3:1-4:12; 5:12-28	AA 261b-264a	The Thessalonian Letters
☐ 46	2 Thess 1-3	AA 264b-268	The Thessalonian Letters
☐ 47	Acts 18:19-28; 1 Cor 2	AA 269-273c	Apollos at Corinth
☐ 48	1 Cor 3	AA 273d-276a	Apollos at Corinth
☐ 49	1 Cor 4	AA 276b-280	Apollos at Corinth
☐ 50	Acts 19:1-7	AA 281-285b	Ephesus
☐ 51	Acts 19:8-20	AA 285c-290	Ephesus
☐ 52	Acts 19:21-20:1	AA 291-297	Days of Toil and Trial
☐ 53	1 Cor 1	AA 298-303b	A Message of Warning and Entreaty

✓ Day	Bible Reading	SOP Reading	SOP Chapter Title
☐ 54	1 Cor 5:1-6:8	AA 303c-306b	A Message of Warning and Entreaty
☐ 55	1 Cor 6:9-8:13	AA 306c-308	A Message of Warning and Entreaty
☐ 56	1 Cor 9	AA 309-315b	Called to Reach a Higher Standard
☐ 57	1 Cor 10-11	AA 315c-317b	Called to Reach a Higher Standard
☐ 58	1 Cor 12-14	AA 317c-319e	Called to Reach a Higher Standard
☐ 59	1 Cor 15-16	AA 319f-322	Called to Reach a Higher Standard
☐ 60	2 Cor 1-2; 7	AA 323-327a	The Message Heeded
☐ 61	2 Cor 3-4	AA 327b-332b	The Message Heeded
☐ 62	2 Cor 5; 9-10; 13	AA 332c-334	The Message Heeded
☐ 63	1 Cor 9:7-14	AA 335-343a	A Liberal Church
☐ 64	2 Cor 8	AA 343b-345	A Liberal Church
☐ 65	2 Cor 11; 2 Thess 3:8-12	AA 346-351c	Laboring Under Difficulties
☐ 66	2 Cor 12	AA 351d-358	Laboring Under Difficulties
☐ 67		AA 359-365b	A Consecrated Ministry
☐ 68	2 Cor 6	AA 365c-371	A Consecrated Ministry
☐ 69	Acts 20:2; Romans 2-3		
☐ 70	Romans 4-5	AA 372-374a	Salvation to the Jews

✓ Day	Bible Reading	SOP Reading	SOP Chapter Title
☐ 71	Romans 6-8		
☐ 72	Romans 9:1-11:15	AA 374b-376b	Salvation to the Jews
☐ 73	Romans 11:16-36	AA 376c-379c	Salvation to the Jews
☐ 74	Romans 1; 12-13	AA 379d-382	Salvation to the Jews
☐ 75	Romans 14-16		
☐ 76	Gal 1; 3:1-5	AA 383-388a	Apostasy in Galatia
☐ 77	Gal 2; 3:6-29	AA 388b	Apostasy in Galatia
☐ 78	Gal 4-6	AA 388c, d	Apostasy in Galatia
☐ 79	Acts 20:3-38	AA 389-396b	Paul's Last Journey to Jerusalem
☐ 80	Acts 21:1-16	AA 396c-398	Paul's Last Journey to Jerusalem
☐ 81	Acts 21:17-19	AA 399-403a	Paul a Prisoner
☐ 82	Acts 21-20-36	AA 403b-408a	Paul a Prisoner
☐ 83	Acts 21:37-23:11	AA 408b-413c	Paul a Prisoner
☐ 84	Acts 23:12-35	AA 413d-418	Paul a Prisoner
☐ 85	Acts 24:1-23	AA 419-422b	The Trial at Cæsarea
☐ 86	Acts 24:24-27	AA 422c-427	The Trial at Cæsarea
☐ 87	Acts 25:1-12	AA 428-432	Paul Appeals to Cæsar
☐ 88	Acts 25:13-27	AA 433-435b	Almost Thou Persuadest Me
☐ 89	Acts 26	AA 435c-438	Almost Thou Persuadest Me
☐ 90	Acts 27:1-20	AA 439-442b	The Voyage and Shipwreck
☐ 91	Acts 27:21-28:10	AA 442c-446	The Voyage and Shipwreck

√ Day	Bible Reading	SOP Reading	SOP Chapter Title
☐ 92	Acts 28:11-22	AA 447-451a	In Rome
☐ 93	Acts 28:23-31	AA 451b-455	In Rome
☐ 94	Philemon	AA 456-460	In Rome
☐ 95		AA 461-468	Cæsar's Household
☐ 96	Eph 1-4	AA 469-470a	Written From Rome
☐ 97	Eph 5-6	AA 470b-471a	Written From Rome
☐ 98	Col 1:1-3:3	AA 471b-476a	Written From Rome
☐ 99	Col 3:4-4:18	AA 476b-478	Written From Rome
☐ 100	Phil 1-2; 4:15-18	AA 479-483b	Written From Rome
☐ 101	Phil 3; 4:1-14, 19-23	AA 483c-484	Written From Rome
☐ 102		AA 485-488	At Liberty
☐ 103	Titus 1-3		
☐ 104	1 Tim 1-4		
☐ 105	1 Tim 5-6	AA 489-491	The Final Arrest
☐ 106		AA 492-497	Paul Before Nero
☐ 107	2 Tim 1-3	AA 498-502c	Paul's Last Letter
☐ 108	2 Tim 4	AA 502d-508	Paul's Last Letter
☐ 109	Heb 1-3	AA 509-513	Condemned to Die
☐ 110	Heb 4-7		
☐ 111	Heb 8-10		
☐ 112	Heb 11-13		

√ Day	Bible Reading	SOP Reading	SOP Chapter Title
☐ 113	James 1-2		
☐ 114	James 3-5		
☐ 115	1 Peter 1:1-12	AA 514-518b	A Faithful Under-Shepherd
☐ 116	1 Peter 1:13-2:10	AA 518c-521	A Faithful Under-Shepherd
☐ 117	1 Peter 2:11-4:19	AA 522-525b	A Faithful Under-Shepherd
☐ 118	1 Peter 5	AA 525c-528	A Faithful Under-Shepherd
☐ 119	2 Peter 1	AA 529-535a	Steadfast Unto the End
☐ 120	2 Peter 2-3	AA 535b-538	Steadfast Unto the End
☐ 121		AA 539-545	John the Beloved
☐ 122	1 John 2:7-4:16	AA 546-550b	A Faithful Witness
☐ 123	1 John 1:1-2:6; 4:17-5:21	AA 550c-554a	A Faithful Witness
☐ 124	2 John; 3 John; Jude	AA 554b-556	A Faithful Witness
☐ 125		AA 557-562a	Transformed by Grace
☐ 126		AA 562b-567	Transformed by Grace
☐ 127		AA 568-577	Patmos
☐ 128	Rev 1	AA 578-585	The Revelation
☐ 129	Rev 2-4	AA 586-589a	The Revelation
☐ 130	Rev 5-11		
☐ 131	Rev 12-15	AA 589b-591c	The Revelation
☐ 132	Rev 16-18		
☐ 133	Rev 19-22	AA 591d-592	The Revelation

✓ Day	Bible Reading	SOP Reading	SOP Chapter Title
☐ 134		AA 593-602	The Church Triumphant
☐ 135		GC v-xii	Introduction
☐ 136		GC 17-24c	The Destruction of Jerusalem
☐ 137		GC 24d-31a	The Destruction of Jerusalem
☐ 138		GC 31b-38	The Destruction of Jerusalem
☐ 139		GC 39-44a	Persecution in the First Centuries
☐ 140		GC 44b-48	Persecution in the First Centuries
☐ 141		GC 49-55a	An Era of Spiritual Darkness
☐ 142		GC 55b-60	An Era of Spiritual Darkness
☐ 143		GC 61-65a	The Waldenses
☐ 144		GC 65b-69c	The Waldenses
☐ 145		GC 69d-73c	The Waldenses
☐ 146		GC 73d-78	The Waldenses
☐ 147		GC 79-83b	John Wycliffe
☐ 148		GC 83c-87c	John Wycliffe
☐ 149		GC 87d-92c	John Wycliffe
☐ 150		GC 92d-96	John Wycliffe
☐ 151		GC 97-103b	Huss and Jerome
☐ 152		GC 103c-110b	Huss and Jerome

√ Day	Bible Reading	SOP Reading	SOP Chapter Title
☐ 153		GC 110c-115c	Huss and Jerome
☐ 154		GC 115d-119	Huss and Jerome
☐ 155		GC 120-125b	Luther's Separation From Rome
☐ 156		GC 125c-131b	Luther's Separation From Rome
☐ 157		GC 131c-134c	Luther's Separation From Rome
☐ 158		GC 134d-139c	Luther's Separation From Rome
☐ 159		GC 139d-144	Luther's Separation From Rome
☐ 160		GC 145-150b	Luther Before the Diet
☐ 161		GC 150c-155a	Luther Before the Diet
☐ 162		GC 155b-160c	Luther Before the Diet
☐ 163		GC 160d-164c	Luther Before the Diet
☐ 164		GC 164d-170	Luther Before the Diet
☐ 165		GC 171-178a	The Swiss Reformer
☐ 166		GC 178b-184	The Swiss Reformer
☐ 167		GC 185-190c	Progress of Reform in Germany
☐ 168		GC 190d-196	Progress of Reform in Germany
☐ 169		GC 197-201c	Protest of the Princes
☐ 170		GC 201d-205d	Protest of the Princes

✓ Day	Bible Reading	SOP Reading	SOP Chapter Title
☐ 171		GC 205e-210	Protest of the Princes
☐ 172		GC 211-215c	The French Reformation
☐ 173		GC 215d-222b	The French Reformation
☐ 174		GC 222c-226b	The French Reformation
☐ 175		GC 226c-230	The French Reformation
☐ 176		GC 231-236	The French Reformation
☐ 177		GC 237-240d	The Netherlands and Scandinavia
☐ 178		GC 240e-244	The Netherlands and Scandinavia
☐ 179		GC 245-249a	Later English Reformers
☐ 180		GC 249b-253a	Later English Reformers
☐ 181		GC 253b-256d	Later English Reformers
☐ 182		GC 256e-260b	Later English Reformers
☐ 183		GC 260c-264	Later English Reformers
☐ 184		GC 265-269a	The Bible and the French Revolution
☐ 185		GC 269b-273a	The Bible and the French Revolution
☐ 186		GC 273b-277a	The Bible and the French Revolution
☐ 187		GC 277b-281a	The Bible and the French Revolution
☐ 188		GC 281b-285b	The Bible and the French Revolution

✓ Day	Bible Reading	SOP Reading	SOP Chapter Title
☐ 189		GC 285c-288	The Bible and the French Revolution
☐ 190		GC 289-293a	The Pilgrim Fathers
☐ 191		GC 293b-298	The Pilgrim Fathers
☐ 192		GC 299-305	Heralds of the Morning
☐ 193		GC 306-311a	Heralds of the Morning
☐ 194		GC 311b-316	Heralds of the Morning
☐ 195		GC 317-324b	An American Reformer
☐ 196		GC 324c-329a	An American Reformer
☐ 197		GC 329b-332	An American Reformer
☐ 198		GC 333-337a	An American Reformer
☐ 199		GC 337b-342	An American Reformer
☐ 200		GC 343-346d	Light Through Darkness
☐ 201		GC 346e-351a	Light Through Darkness
☐ 202		GC 351b-354	Light Through Darkness
☐ 203		GC 355-359a	A Great Religious Awakening
☐ 204		GC 359b-362	A Great Religious Awakening
☐ 205		GC 363-370a	A Great Religious Awakening
☐ 206		GC 370b-374	A Great Religious Awakening
☐ 207		GC 375-379a	A Warning Rejected

✓ Day	Bible Reading	SOP Reading	SOP Chapter Title
☐ 208		GC 379b-382c	A Warning Rejected
☐ 209		GC 382d-386a	A Warning Rejected
☐ 210		GC 386b-390	A Warning Rejected
☐ 211		GC 391-398b	Prophecies Fulfilled
☐ 212		GC 398c-404a	Prophecies Fulfilled
☐ 213		GC 404b-408	Prophecies Fulfilled
☐ 214		GC 409-415b	What Is the Sanctuary?
☐ 215		GC 415c-422	What Is the Sanctuary?
☐ 216		GC 423-428c	In the Holy of Holies
☐ 217		GC 428d-432	In the Holy of Holies
☐ 218		GC 433-437a	God's Law Immutable
☐ 219		GC 437b-441b	God's Law Immutable
☐ 220		GC 441c-446c	God's Law Immutable
☐ 221		GC 446d-450	God's Law Immutable
☐ 222		GC 451-456a	A Work of Reform
☐ 223		GC 456b-460	A Work of Reform
☐ 224		GC 461-467a	Modern Revivals
☐ 225		GC 467b-472b	Modern Revivals
☐ 226		GC 472c-478	Modern Revivals
☐ 227		GC 479-485a	Facing Life's Record
☐ 228		GC 485b-491	Facing Life's Record
☐ 229		GC 492-497a	The Origin of Evil

✓ Day	Bible Reading	SOP Reading	SOP Chapter Title
☐ 230		GC 497b-504	The Origin of Evil
☐ 231		GC 505-510	Enmity Between Man and Satan
☐ 232		GC 511-517	Agency of Evil Spirits
☐ 233		GC 518-524	Snares of Satan
☐ 234		GC 525-530	Snares of Satan
☐ 235		GC 531-537a	The First Great Deception
☐ 236		GC 537b-543b	The First Great Deception
☐ 237		GC 543c-550	The First Great Deception
☐ 238		GC 551-556c	Can Our Dead Speak to Us?
☐ 239		GC 556d-562	Can Our Dead Speak to Us?
☐ 240		GC 563-567c	Liberty of Conscience Threatened
☐ 241		GC 567d-572a	Liberty of Conscience Threatened
☐ 242		GC 572b-577a	Liberty of Conscience Threatened
☐ 243		GC 577b-581	Liberty of Conscience Threatened
☐ 244		GC 582-586b	The Impending Conflict
☐ 245		GC 586c-592	The Impending Conflict
☐ 246		GC 593-598a	The Scriptures a Safeguard
☐ 247		GC 598b-602	The Scriptures a Safeguard
☐ 248		GC 603-607	The Final Warning

✓ Day	Bible Reading	SOP Reading	SOP Chapter Title
☐ 249		GC 608-612	The Final Warning
☐ 250		GC 613-620b	The Time of Trouble
☐ 251		GC 620c-627a	The Time of Trouble
☐ 252		GC 627b-634	The Time of Trouble
☐ 253		GC 635-640b	God's People Delivered
☐ 254		GC 640c-646b	God's People Delivered
☐ 255		GC 646c-652	God's People Delivered
☐ 256		GC 653-656b	Desolation of the Earth
☐ 257		GC 656c-661	Desolation of the Earth
☐ 258		GC 662-667c	The Great Controversy Ended
☐ 259		GC 667d-672b	The Great Controversy Ended
☐ 260		GC 672c-678	The Great Controversy Ended

Appendix B

Online Resources

Online Resources

The following list is not intended to be exhaustive, but rather a sampling or cross-section of the many denominational and supporting ministries that promote the Seventh-day Adventist mission and message. Websites, apps, and resources noted with an asterisk (*) represent those owned, operated, or produced by a supporting ministry of the Seventh-day Adventist Church. Those with no asterisk are owned, operated, or produced by an official denominational entity.

Seventh-Day Adventist Church Governance

Adventist Organizational Directory   www.adventistdirectory.org

Adventist Yearbook   www.adventistyearbook.com

General Conference of Seventh-day Adventists   www.adventist.org

General Conference Office of Archives, Statistics, and Research
                                          www.adventiststatistics.org

Seventh-day Adventist Church Manual (pdf)
                        www.adventist.org/information/church-manual

Publications

Adventist Book Center   www.adventistbookcenter.com

Adventist Review   www.adventistreview.org

Adventist World   www.adventistworld.org

GLOW Tracts   www.glowonline.org

Liberty Magazine   www.libertymagazine.org

Ministry Magazine   www.ministrymagazine.org

Study References

Center for Adventist Research   www.centerforadventistresearch.org

Ellen G. White Estate   www.whiteestate.org

Journal of the Adventist Theological Society (ATS)*   www.atsjats.org

Perspective Digest (Magazine of the Adventist Theological Society)*
     www.perspectivedigest.org

Seventh-day Adventist Biblical Research Institute (BRI)
     www.adventistbiblicalresearch.org

Seventh-day Adventist Geoscience Research Institute   www.grisda.org

Seventh-day Adventist Sabbath School Study Guide (Quarterly)
     www.ssnet.org/study-guides

Spirit Of Prophecy / Ellen G. White

Ellen White Answers*   www.ellenwhiteanswers.org

Ellen G. White Estate   www.whiteestate.org

Ellen G. White Writings   www.text.egwwritings.org

Messenger of the Lord (pdf)   www.whiteestate.org/books/mol/motl.pdf

Media

Adventist News Network   www.news.adventist.org

Amazing Facts*   www.amazingfacts.org

Adventist World Radio   www.awr.org

AudioVerse*   www.audioverse.org

Breath of Life   www.breathoflife.tv

Faith for Today   www.faithfortoday.tv

HOPE Channel   www.hopetv.org

It Is Written   www.itiswritten.com

La Voz de la Esperanza   www.lavoz.org

Life Talk Radio   www.lifetalk.net

Three Angels' Broadcasting Network (3ABN)*	www.3abn.org
Voice of Prophecy	www.vop.com

Other Ministries And Resources

Adventist Development and Relief Agency (ADRA)	www.adra.org
Adventist Education	www.adventisteducation.org
Adventist Frontier Missions*	www.afmonline.org
Adventist Heritage Ministry	www.adventistheritage.org
Adventist Mission	www.adventistmission.org
Adventist-laymen's Services & Industries (ASI)*	www.asiministries.org
Emmanuel Institute of Evangelism	www.emmanuelinstitute.org
International Religious Liberty Association	www.irla.org
Maranatha Volunteers International*	www.maranatha.org
My Bible First!*	www.mybiblefirst.org
North American Division Stewardship	www.igivesda.org
North American Religious Liberty Association	www.religiousliberty.info
Outpost Centers International*	www.outpostcenters.org
Share Him	www.sharehim.org
The Quiet Hour*	www.quiethourministries.net
Training Center Churches	www.trainingcenterchurches.org

Recommended Apps

Adventist News Network	Hope Channel
Adventist World Radio	iGive SDA
Amazing Facts*	It Is Written
ASI Evangelism*	Sabbath School Quarterly
AudioVerse*	SDA Hymnal*
BibleInfo*	Studying Together*
EGW Answers*	The Sabbath App*
EGW Writings	3ABN*